Inside Secret
Societies

Inside Secret Societies

**WHAT THEY DON'T WANT
YOU TO KNOW**

Michael Benson

CITADEL PRESS
Kensington Publishing Corp.
www.kensingtonbooks.com

To David Henry Jacobs

CITADEL PRESS BOOKS are published by

Kensington Publishing Corp.
850 Third Avenue
New York, NY 10022

All Kensington titles, imprints, and distributed lines are available at special quantity discounts for bulk purchases for sales promotions, premiums, fundraising, educational, or institutional use. Special book excerpts or customized printings can also be created to fit specific needs. For details, write or phone the office of the Kensington special sales manager: Kensington Publishing Corp., 850 Third Avenue, New York, NY 10022, attn: Special Sales Department; phone 1-800-221-2647.

CITADEL PRESS and the Citadel logo are Reg. U.S. Pat. & TM Off.

First printing: June 2005

10 9 8 7 6 5 4 3 2 1

Printed in the United States of America

Library of Congress Control Number: 2004099324

ISBN 0-8065-2664-5

Introduction: Alternative Histories of the World—Paranoia or Enlightenment?

THIS BOOK is an encyclopedic listing of secret societies around the world and across history. We will define a secret society as any organization whose membership or activities are routinely kept secret from outsiders. Entries will include the societies themselves and types of groups. Some entries involve key symbols, locations, and myths that form the basis for, and shape the rituals of, secret societies.

These societies come in a wide variety of types. The templates for many are the fraternal or knightly orders, such as the Freemasons and Rosicrucians, as well as their medieval predecessors, the Knights Templar. These brotherhoods involve initiation rituals, and military-type ranks or "degrees." As a member rises through the degrees, he or she gradually is told of the secrets the group keeps, with only those at the very top of the hierarchy in complete knowledge of the group's activities and/or beliefs.

The reasons for secrecy vary depending on the group, but date back to medieval times when any belief system or knowledge that disagreed with the dogma of the Church was punishable by death. Today, groups remain secret in order to effect political or social change, hide subversive beliefs (UFO groups, practitioners of the black arts), or—at the benevolent end—make anonymous charitable contributions. Some groups include only the most wealthy and powerful (the power elite) and exist to further gain power and wealth without regard to public relations. These are the ultimate "good ol' boy" networks that seek to accrue power outside publicly known political, military, and business channels.

Religious beliefs that deviate from the "norm" still account for many secret societies in the world. In addition to the fraternal orders, secret societies also include religious sects, such as OTO, the Church of Satan, and the Temple of Set.

Political parties such as the Nazi party and the Communist party either began as or found their roots in secret societies (see LEAGUE OF THE JUST; VRIL SOCIETY).

Some secret societies are best described as cults, groups that exist as an ego-extension of their founder and leader (see CULTS). Some are terror groups, who secretly plot to inflict terror upon their enemies. (For a listing see TERRORIST GROUPS.)

Some secret societies best fall into the category of law enforcement. These groups form in situations where existing law enforcement is nonexistent or corrupt (see BEATI PAOLI; VIGILANTES OF SAN FRANCISCO).

Other secret societies exist for the commission of organized crime (see ASSASSINS; MAFIA; THUGGEES; TONGS; TRIADS).

History is routinely written by the winners of wars, while the viewpoint of the losers is suppressed and eventually forgotten. Writing history is a matter of connecting the dots—taking known facts and creating a coherent narrative that satisfactorily explains them. Secret societies exist in the spaces between the dots. When a society's secrets are revealed, new dots appear, patterns can be seen where none were previously visible, and out of the chaos "history" is changed.

According to Michael Baigent, Richard Leigh, and Henry Lincoln in their book *Holy Blood, Holy Grail*: "Secret Societies, by virtue of their very secrecy, have often kept historians at bay, and the historians, reluctant to confess their ignorance, prefer to diminish the consequence of their subject. Freemasonry . . . is of vital importance to any social, psychological, cultural, or political history of eighteenth-century Europe, and even to the founding of the United States; but most history books do not even mention it."

When seeking to reshape our narrative of history with our knowledge of secret societies, we must be careful not to be greedy and connect dots that are simply not there. If we occasionally get a glimpse of a large secret society taking part in evil activities, it is tempting to portray the entire group as evil. Avoid the temptations of extrapolation. Just because Freemasons carried out and then covered up a murder in 1826, one cannot assume that Freemasons are murderers, condone murder, or anything of the sort.

Another problem with including information about secret societies in the narrative of history is that so much of that information is unreliable. There are several reasons for this. First and foremost, secret societies are secret. They don't want to be written about. To divert journalists, secret societies frequently deny that they are secret societies, and shape their public image with misinformation. Those who do reveal a secret society's secrets are often disgruntled former members who seem hell-bent on hurting the organization. Corroborated facts are few and far between, so reader beware. Be skeptical of everything you read about secret societies, including the information in this book.

That said, even the most skeptical of readers will agree that the world's secret societies are much more important—as business networks, for example—than just passwords, secret handshakes, and silly ceremonies. But the truth is no doubt more profound. The nature of power indicates that it is best brokered in the dark, around the corner from the public's field of vision.

This is a book about the shadows.

Acknowledgments

THE AUTHOR wishes to thank the following individuals and organizations, without whose help the writing of this book would have been impossible: David Hatcher Childress, Church of Satan, Jake Elwell, Gary Goldstein, Lisa Grasso, Mitch Highfill, David Henry Jacobs, Ontario Consultants on Religious Tolerance, Rosicrucian Order, AMORC.

Inside Secret Societies

A

Aborisha See SANTERIA.

Adepts of Agarthi See GREEN MEN, SOCIETY OF.

The All-Seeing Eye A symbol of God's watchfulness and protection over everyone, the all-seeing eye is usually depicted as a single human eye encircled by radiating beams of light. Sometimes referred to as the "Eye of God," the symbol appears on U.S. money (and has since 1778), as well as the Great Seal of the United States, perched atop an Egyptian-style pyramid.

For the Freemasons, the symbol represents the "Great Architect of the Universe." Many cultures use the symbol, often to ward off "evil eye" curses.

The human eye, Mark Twain pointed out, can see only the outside of things, but the All-Seeing Eye can see through and read the heart and soul.

See also FREEMASONS.

Amaranth, Order of the The Order of the Amaranth is a fraternal society within a fraternal society. To become a member, one must already be a Master Freemason in good standing within the Masonic fraternity. Others who qualify include the adult, immediate female relatives of Master Masons—or of deceased Master Masons who were in good standing with the fraternity at the time of their death.

According to the group's website (www.amaranth.org): "The Order of the Amaranth is a social, fraternal, and charitable organization whose membership is open to both men and women with a Masonic affiliation. The teachings of our ritual impart lessons for

daily living, character building, morality, and ethics. Membership in
the Order of the Amaranth is a privilege; it provides opportunity not
only for service but also for self-improvement and brings a gift of a
special fraternal friendship among its members. The welfare and
support of our members is of vital concern to their fellow members
and it is deemed a privilege to assist another member in need.
Although belief in the existence of a Supreme Being is requisite for
membership, the Organization is not a religious organization and
many faiths are represented among our membership. Since 1972 the
funds raised for our charitable project, The Amaranth Diabetes Foundation Trust, are directed towards research grants that will aid in
finding a cure for diabetes. No expenses are deducted from our donations that are given to the American Diabetes Association."

To become a member, one must complete a petition, have it
signed by two present members of the Order, pay the necessary petition fee, and submit it to the local Court of Amaranth for consider-
ation. After submission, the petition is received by the Court at its
next regular meeting and an Investigating Committee is assigned.
The Investigating Committee checks the character and qualifications
of the applicant for membership.

In practice, the committee is a committee of visitation. It meets
with applicants and gets to know them. It double-checks for Masonic
eligibility and answers questions about the Order. The Investigating
Committee reports its findings to the Court at its second meeting
following the receipt of the petition. The Court votes on the request
for membership. If the applicant is elected, the applicant is informed
by the Court secretary and a date for initiation is scheduled. At the
initiation, the new member receives the degree of the Order of Amaranth and becomes a regular member. There is no hazing. Instead,
the new member is taught lessons concerning the four principal
virtues of the Order: Truth, Faith, Wisdom and Charity.

These lessons are given within the setting of a queenly court
during the period of chivalry. After initiation, the new member
becomes active in the court by participating in its activities and
working with it for the great charitable efforts of the Order.

The official publication of the Supreme Council Order of Amaranth, Inc., is called the *Crown & Sword*. It is published four times

per year in the months of February, May, August, and November. Articles about the Supreme Elected Officers, Supreme Trustees, and the Amaranth Diabetes Board—along with items of interest from Grand Courts and Subordinate Courts under Supreme Council Jurisdiction around the world—are included in each issue. Each Grand Royal Matron or Royal Matron of a Court under Supreme Council Jurisdiction appoints an Honored Lady or Sir Knight from her jurisdiction or court to handle local subscriptions and prepare appropriate news items.

Their mailing address is:

Supreme Council Order of Amaranth, Inc.
P.O. Box 557579
Chicago, IL 60655-7579

See also FREEMASONS.

American Knights of the Ku Klux Klan   See KU KLUX KLAN.

American Nazi Party   Extreme right-wing U.S. anti-Semitic, white supremacist group inspired by the Nazi Party of Germany before and during World War II. According to their own literature, the American Nazi Party is a "legally based political-educational organization dedicated to the preservation of the White Race, the Aryan Republic, and our Western-European cultural heritage. As the world enemy wages war against the White Race and Western Civilization in every corner of the world, we have found that the only way to shock our people awake is through bold action. Too many others would rather try to talk the problem away, while we realize that the time has come to fight! Only the swastika, the age-old symbol of the white man, has the shock-power to shatter the Jewish press blackout and force White America to think about what is going on. Our spiritual leader, George Lincoln Rockwell, has laid down a blueprint for us to follow to success, if we will only have the courage to do so. Some others who thought they knew better have tried a different path, but their failure has only showed us how correct Commander Rockwell was, and is . . . Here at Nazi Headquarters, we are gathering the best and most active of our fighters for the White People, men and women who realize that this is not a game or a club, rather a deadly fight for the struggle of our way of life as a White-European nation." Their slogan—which they refer to as "The Fourteen Words"—is: "We must secure the existence of our people and a future for White children."

George Lincoln Rockwell, the founder of the American Nazi Party, was born on March 9, 1918. His divorced parents were both vaudeville performers, which perhaps explains Rockwell's ease on the stage and speaking ability. He earned a bachelor's degree in sociology and then joined the U.S. Navy. He worked his way up through the ranks until he became Commander of the U.S. Naval Air Base in Iceland. During the 1950s, he formed the American National Nazi party. The party's first order of business was an unsuccessful attempt to get General Douglas MacArthur elected president in 1952, to replace Harry Truman, the man who had fired MacArthur during the Korean War for being too aggressive. Rockwell said that MacArthur would have gotten elected if it weren't for Jewish propaganda. In 1959, Rockwell changed the name of his party to the American Nazi Party. As a candidate with his own party, he made an unsuccessful attempt to be elected governor of Virginia in 1965. His speeches tended to cause riots because they were often attended by those who violently opposed his views.

Rockwell once met with Malcolm X, who was at the time a spokesman for the black separatist group the Nation of Islam. The men agreed on a surprising number of issues, including the idea that the races should not mix. Malcolm X later left the Nation of Islam and changed his separatist views. Both Rockwell and Malcolm died by assassin's gunfire.

Rockwell was murdered on August 25, 1967, in a parking lot in Arlington, Virginia. His killer was a disgruntled ex-party member named John Patler who thought Rockwell was attempting to put Communist material in the party newsletter.

For a monthly fee, members receive an official American Nazi Party membership card and a subscription to *Stormtrooper* magazine.

See also ARYAN BROTHERHOOD; NATION OF ISLAM; SWASTIKA.

Ancient Arabic Order of the Nobles of the Mystic Shrine See SHRINERS.

Ancient Egyptian Arabic Order Nobles of the Mystic Shrine See SHRINERS.

Ancient Order of Hibernians See MOLLY MAGUIRES.

Anunnaki Many secret societies teach myths regarding the origins of the Earth and mankind that differ from the Judeo-Christian version available in the Old Testament of the Bible. One of these myths concerns the Anunnaki, a group that the ancient Sumerians— authors of mankind's first recorded history—believed were astronauts who had come down "from the heavens" to influence and control human affairs.

According to Middle Eastern scholar Zecharia Sitchin, "All the ancient peoples believed in gods who had descended from the heavens and who could at will soar heavenwards. But those tales were never given credibility, having been branded by scholars . . . as myths."

The Old Testament, it is believed, refers to the Anunnaki as Nefilim, which means "Those Who Were Cast Down." Modern Bibles often refer to the Nefilim as "Giants" (Genesis 6:4).

According to translations of the Sumerian texts, Earth was formed four billion years ago when the planet Nibiru, which has an elliptical orbit around our sun like those of comets, passed too close to a large planet called Tiamat. The gravitational stresses caused Tiamat to break apart, forming Earth and the asteroid belt. During the collision one of Nibiru's moons left orbit around that planet and became Earth's moon.

The Sumerians wrote that the Anunnaki arrived on Earth 450,000 years ago, during Earth's second Ice Age. Nibiru, three times bigger than Earth, had an orbit that took it well outside the orbit of the farthest planets, yet once during each of its revolutions around the sun it came very close to Earth, causing great upheavals in weather.

According to the legend, it was while the two planets were in close proximity that the Anunnaki journeyed to Earth in spaceships and set up their headquarters in Mesopotamia. The leader of Nibiru, it was written, was Anu, who stayed on his home planet but who sent to Earth his two sons Enlil and Enki. It was the sons who supervised Earth's colonization. Because of the vast difference in the orbits of our planets, what was several millennia to human beings was only a single year to the Anunnaki. The visitors used rank-and-file Anunnaki labor to mine for gold. (The suggestion that there was mining for gold in prehistoric times is supported by evidence discovered by the Anglo-American Corporation in the 1970s. In South Africa they found evidence of mining that dated to 100,000 years ago.)

According to Dr. David Horn, a former professor of biological anthropology at Colorado State University, in his book *Humanity's Extraterrestrial Origins*, the Anunnaki mined gold on Earth for one hundred thousand years until the rank-and-file Anunnaki mutinied around 300,000 years ago.

Horn writes: "Enlil, their commander-in-chief, wanted to punish them severely and he called an Assembly of the Great Anunnaki, which included his father Anu. Anu was more sympathetic to the plight of the Anunnaki miners. He saw that the work of the mutineers was very hard and that their distress was considerable. He wondered . . . if there wasn't another way to obtain gold. At this point, Enki suggested that a Primitive Worker, an *Adamu*, be created that could take over the difficult work. Enki pointed out that a primitive humanoid—what we call Homo Erectus or a closely related humanoid—was quite prevalent in [Africa] where he worked."

And so the egg from a female humanoid was combined with the sperm of an Anunnaki male and the result was the first human being. The first humans were created and bred as slave labor.

The Sumerians wrote: "When Mankind was first created, they knew not the eating of bread, knew not the dressing with garments, ate plants with their mouth like sheep [and] drank water from a ditch."

At first, because they were a crossbreed, humans could not reproduce. The legend suggests that a male human, Adamu, was cloned in female form, so that human beings could reproduce. This process would have been the basis of the biblical story of Eve being created from Adam's rib.

In the meantime, Anunnaki men continued to cross-breed with human women.

The King James Version of the Holy Bible (Genesis 6:2) reads: "That the sons of God saw the daughters of men that they were fair; and they took them wives of all which they chose."

According to Dr. Horn: "The Anunnaki treated their created slaves poorly, much like we treat domestic animals we are simply exploiting—like cattle. Slavery in human societies was common from the first known civilizations until quite recently. Perhaps it shouldn't surprise us to learn that the Anunnaki were vain, petty, cruel, incestuous, hateful—almost any negative adjective one can think of. The evidence indicates that they worked their slaves very hard and had very little compassion for the plight of humans. Yet, the Anunnaki eventually decided to grant humankind their first civilization, the Sumerian civilization."

Twelve thousand years ago, Nibiru once again passed through our solar system. The Anunnaki who lived on Earth returned to space in their spaceships to avoid the upheavals in climate that the close pass-by of Nibiru would cause. They left the humans on Earth to die. According to the Sumerian history, however, before he returned to his home planet Enki gave the "secrets of the gods" to one of his human assistants, Utnapishtim—and told him to build a boat. These secrets had to do with genetic engineering. So Utnapishtim survived the climatic upheaval and, when the weather became calm, started up human and animal life once again. Obviously, in the Old Testament, Utnapishtim is known as Noah, and the climatic upheaval caused by Nibiru passing close to Earth—the Antarctic ice sheet is said to have slid into the ocean causing sea levels to rise throughout the world—is known as the Great Flood. Before the flood, the humans who were not slave laborers for the Anunnaki were hunter-gatherers. After the flood, humans became farmers. How the secrets of farming were learned is unknown. The Anunnaki returned to Earth following the flood and decided to split up humankind. Humans would be easier to rule that way, it was assumed. A human would be chosen by the Anunnaki to rule each of the three groups. Thus were created the first human kings, who, history tells us, were chosen by the gods. The various groups of humans were given different languages, so it would be difficult for them to unite.

Genesis 11:6–7 reads: "Behold the people is one, and they have all one language. . . . Let us go down, and there confound their language, and they may not understand one another's speech."

Some were sent to lower Mesopotamia, some to the Nile Valley, and some to the Indus Valley. The Anunnaki kept the Sinai peninsula to themselves. The space-flight facilities in Sumer (current-day Iraq) were still underwater following the flood, so new facilities were built on the Sinai peninsula. Since the area was flat and lacked natural landmarks, they built two giant pyramids at Giza, and the control center for their spaceflights was built at Mount Moriah (which means Mount of Directing), at the current site of the city of Jerusalem. Enlil's son Ishku communicated with his chosen people with what would today be called a walkie-talkie device. The device may have been mentioned in the Bible, where it was called the Ark of the Covenant.

The Sumerian civilization and the Anunnaki's reign on Earth, according to the final lines of the Sumerian texts, ended because of internal war and what we might interpret today as the use of nuclear weapons.

The Sumerians wrote: "On the land fell a calamity, one unknown to man; one that had never been seen before, one which could not be withstood. A great storm from heaven . . . a land-annihilating storm . . . a battling storm joined by scorching heat."

In the Bible, this could be the basis for the story of Sodom and Gomorrah, which were destroyed by an explosion that turned Lot's wife into a pillar of salt. The Sumerian text says the people did "vanish" and "turn to vapor." Modern archaeologists have found evidence of Middle Eastern settlements that were abandoned about 2040 B.C.—and there is still a dangerous level of radioactivity in some spring water near the Dead Sea.

According to Jim Marrs in his book *Rule by Secrecy*, "The idea that the origins of man are still largely hidden from us by both time and design is naturally quite disturbing to those who have spent life-long careers presenting mankind's history as one long evolution from savage to civilized man. Yet it is apparent from the available evidence that modern man may just now be regaining knowledge lost millennia ago. It appears that bits and pieces of prehistoric knowledge survived in various esoteric forms through secret societies. . . . These little-understood groups passed along not only religious concepts such as reincarnation or the transmigration of souls, but also real knowledge in architectural design, construction, astronomy, agronomy, and history."

Arogi   See MAU MAU.

Aryan Brotherhood   White supremacist prison gang active in jails and penitentiaries across the United States. The group got its start on the West Coast in the 1960s and exhibits an intense hatred of Blacks and Jews. It reportedly engages in extortion, drug operations, prostitution, and violence in prisons. Members wear a tattoo of a swastika and the Nazi SS lightning bolt.

The group has ties to Aryan Nations, an Idaho-based paramilitary organization that advocates racial violence and white supremacy. Many prisons ban inmates from receiving literature from Aryan Nations and similar groups. Missouri inmates who were members of the Brotherhood were also members of a "Christian Identity" organization, the Church of Jesus Christ Christian. This group believes that Anglo-Saxons and not Jews are the biblical "chosen people," that non-Whites are on the level of animals, and that Jews are the "children of Satan."

See also AMERICAN NAZI PARTY.

Assassins   Formed in the eleventh century, the Assassins were an Islamic secret society of murderers founded by a schoolmate of Persian poet Omar Khayyám named Hasan bin Sabah. Their name is said to be derived from the fact that they smoked hashish before going out to do their killing. Hasan fled Persia into Egypt to avoid punishment for money pilfering. In Egypt he was indoctrinated in the secrets of the Hebrew Cabala and other ancient secrets. He formed the Assassins after studying the structure of a secret society called the Grand Lodge of Cairo, or The Hand of Knowledge. It has been said that the Assassins teamed up at times with the Knights

Templar in military actions, such as the 1129 attack on Damascus led by Jerusalem's King Baldwin.

The Assassins' modus operandi was simple: they killed their enemies and anyone else who stood in their way.

Predictably, their violent nature was also their downfall. Just as modern mobsters sometimes turn upon one another, the Assassin leadership became its own worst enemy. Hasan was killed by his son. The son then plotted to kill his own son, but Hasan's grandson learned of the plot and killed his father before he himself could be killed. Left with a power vacuum at the top, the Assassins were no match for hordes of Mongols who captured the region in 1250.

The legend of the Assassins lives on, however; it is believed that small sects of hashish-smoking murderers claiming to be of the original Assassins still function in the Middle East.

See also GRAND LODGE OF CAIRO; KNIGHTS TEMPLAR.

Aviary   A small group of individuals with extremely high security clearances, who, since sometime in the 1970s, have worked on various aspects of UFO research and policy. According to Dr. Richard J. Boylan, the Aviary consisted of about a dozen individuals who referred to each other by code names, most often the names of birds—thus the name of the organization.

Boylan feels that there is at least some overlap with MJ-12, the supposed U.S. government secret organization in charge of researching and/or covering up UFOs and alien interaction with humans.

According to Boylan, members of the Aviary have included:

- Dr. Christopher Green, the chief of the Biomedical Sciences Department of General Motors, and reportedly former head of the CIA's UFO files at the "Weird Desk." Dr. Green's nickname was "Blue Jay."

- Ron Pandolfi, CIA Deputy Director for the Division of Science and Technology and custodian of UFO files at the "Weird Desk." Nickname: "Pelican."

- Dr. Bruce Maccabee, a well-known UFO expert and research scientist in optical physics and laser weapons applications at the U.S. Naval Surface Weapons Lab, Maryland. Maccabee is a physics/photo-interpretive consultant for the Mutual Unidentified Flying Object Network (MUFON). Nickname: "Sea Gull."

- Hal Puthoff, physicist with the Institute for Advanced Research in Austin, Texas. Nickname: "Owl."

- Lieutenant Colonel John Alexander, Ph.D., U.S. Army Intelligence and Security Command. Col. Alexander is director of the Non-Lethal Weapons Department, Los Alamos National Laboratory. Nickname: "Penguin."

- Commander C.B. Scott Jones, Ph.D., United States Navy (Ret.), former Office of Naval Intelligence officer with thirty years service in U.S. intelligence overseas; involved in the Defense Nuclear Agency, Defense Intelligence Agency, Defense Advanced Research Projects Agency, and other organizations. Nickname: "Chickadee."

- Jacques Vallee, Ph.D., former astrophysicist with GEPAN, the French government's UFO investigative agency. He later worked as principal investigator with the U.S. Defense Department computer network projects. Dr. Vallee has written many books about UFOs. Nickname: "Parrot."

- Dan Smith, civilian UFO researcher who, apparently on a volunteer basis, has served as a liaison between CIA and non-CIA UFO sources. Nickname: "Chicken Little."

- Captain Bob Collins, United States Air Force (Ret.); Special Agent, Air Force Office of Special Investigations. Nickname: "Condor."

- Gordon Novel, CIA employee who was living in New Orleans in 1963 and who was questioned by the FBI on five separate occasions following John F. Kennedy's assassination. While investigating a conspiracy in the J.F.K. assassination in 1967, New Orleans District Attorney Jim Garrison subpoenaed Novel, but Novel fled to Ohio where Garrison failed to obtain his extradition. Today, according to Dr. Boylan, Novel is investigating alleged extra-terrestrial energy technology and titanium aluminide metallurgy for their investment potential. Nickname: "Buzzard."

- Sergeant Richard "Dick" Doty, U.S. Air Force (Ret.); Special Agent, Air Force Office of Special Investigations; reported to have engaged in UFO disinformation projects. Nickname: "Falcon."

- Dale Graff, UFO-related technology specialist and former contracts overseer for the Defense Intelligence Agency (DIA) at Wright-Patterson Air Force Base. Nickname: "Harrier."

- Jack Verona, before he disappeared in the late 1990s, was involved in Project Sleeping Beauty, which researched ways to disable enemy "target" personnel using directed precise-frequency radiated electromagnetic-energy fields. Nickname: "Nightingale."

- Jaime Shandera, Hollywood film producer, discussed in the entry for MJ-12. Nickname: "Woodpecker."

See also MJ-12.

B

Bader-Meinhof Also known as the Red Army Faction, a radical West German group that robbed banks and hid bombs during the 1960s and '70s in an attempt to free their imprisoned leaders, and revolt against the government.

Beati Paoli Possibly fictitious group which may have plotted and fought against Italian tyranny in the late seventeenth and early eighteenth century. The Beati Paoli have appeared, in fictional form, numerous times. According to an article in the electronic version of *Best of Sicily Magazine* by Roberto Savona (www.bestofsicily.com/mag/art13.htm, accessed January 5, 2004), the first references are from Gabriele Quattromani and Vincenzo Linares, writing in the 1830s. Carmelo Piola wrote a book about them in 1848. The group is the subject of the Italian writer Luigi Natoli, writing under the pseudonym William Galt, in a 1909 magazine serial called *I Beati Paoli*. The story appeared in book form in 1921, and was reprinted in 1949. During World War II, the book was banned by the Fascists because it was considered revolutionary. Natoli's book was made into a movie *The Black Masked Knights*, released in 1947.

In Natoli's book, which takes place in the Sicilian capital of Palermo between 1698 and 1719, the secret sect is a cross between the Freemasons and the Ninja. They dressed entirely in black and disguised their identities with black hoods such as those worn by executioners. They came to the defense of ordinary citizens who were being persecuted by the government or the Catholic Church. The government consisted of corrupt local viceroys serving a remote king, and the Church was represented by zealots carrying out the Inquisition.

13

Savona writes: "It is quite possible, as some have suggested, that certain secret fraternities met covertly in the subterranean passages of Palermo—built on the remains of catacombs constructed in the Punic era, and underground channels designed by the Arabs and Normans. They could have used a few segments of these channels to travel secretly around the city. Old Palermo is a vast labyrinth of streets dating from ancient and medieval times, and in Natoli's story the Beati Paoli are strongly identified with the Capo district, where a street and square now bear the sect's name. But did the Beati Paoli plot revolution and social change? We shall never know. Nothing of this kind has been attributed to them by mainstream historians, but their era was characterized by riots whose leaders often went unidentified. This has given rise to the theory that an underground movement plotted some of the revolts. The Beati Paoli would most likely have been nobles and intellectuals unwilling to openly challenge the established order. It is also possible that their 'revolution' amounted to little more than (literally) underground meetings to discuss illegal ideas. That alone could have found them tried as heretics or traitors. But there's a paradox here. Since they were a secret society by definition, the Beati Paoli would not have sought publicity or left documentary proof of their existence. To have done so was to risk death. For their part, the authorities would not know to attribute a particular murder or event to an organization whose very existence was little more than a subdued whisper."

Bilderberg Group   A supranational group of power elite from Europe and North America who may be plotting to take over the world. Like the Knights Templar before them, the group would seem to be striving toward a united Europe. Among the Europe-unifying moves the group has helped bring about include the Treaty of Rome, which gave birth to the European Common Market, and the Euro, a common currency for the continent.

Both membership and the activities of this group are secret. It is a Holland-based pro-EU (European Union) forerunner. The group has no official name. (Having a name, it is thought, would make the group easier to trace.) It is informally called the Bilderberg Group because it was first discovered while meeting at the Bilderberg Hotel in Oosterbeck, Holland, during May 29–31, 1954.

Although meetings of Europe's elite date back to the 1940s, the group didn't formally organize until the early 1950s. The founding father of the Bilderberg Group, it is said, is Dr. Joseph Hieronim Retinger (whose middle name translates as "Member of the Occult"), a Polish socialist. Another charter member was Prince Bernard of the Netherlands. Bernard was a former member of the Nazi *Schutzstaffel* (SS), and through marriage became a major stockholder in Dutch Shell Oil.

The U.S. was initially represented in the group by C.D. Jackson, the CIA-connected publisher of *Life* magazine. Jackson is known for being a special consultant for psychological warfare for President Eisenhower, and as the man who purchased the Zapruder film hours after the assassination of JFK, then protected the official theory of the assassination by preventing that film from being seen by the public.

Among the current members of the Bilderberg is Alan Greenspan, who has been since the Ronald Reagan administration the chairman of the Federal Reserve. Both men and women belong to the group. Some of the members are European royalty. The royal families of the United Kingdom, Sweden, Holland, and Spain have reportedly attended.

The Bilderberg Group is interconnected with other globally influential secret societies. The group's chairman is Lord Peter Carrington of Great Britain, who is also the president of the Royal Institute of International Affairs, which in turn is affiliated with the Council on Foreign Relations (CFR).

According to Dr. John Coleman, Great Britain's MI6 secret service created the Bilderberg Group as a subsidiary of the Royal Institute of International Affairs.

Another familiar name associated with the Bilderbergs is David Rockefeller, whom author Jim Marrs calls "an obvious connecting link between the CFR, Trilateral Commission, and the Bilderbergers."

See also COUNCIL ON FOREIGN RELATIONS; FEDERAL RESERVE; ROYAL INSTITUTE OF INTERNATIONAL AFFAIRS; SS; TRILATERAL COMMISSION.

Black Dragon Society   Pre–World War II Japanese secret society whose systematic assassination of several key pro-peace Japanese ministers paved the way for Tojo's rise to power. According to Violet Sweet Haven in *Gentlemen of Japan: A Study in Rapist Diplomacy*, the decision to go to war with the United States was made during a Black Dragon meeting. Haven wrote: "The signal for war in the Pacific was given on August 26, 1941, at a session of the Black Dragon Society in Tokyo. At this meeting, War Minister Hideki Tojo ordered that preparation be made to wage a total war against the armed forces of the United States, and that Japanese guns be mounted and supplies and munitions concentrated in the Marshalls and Caroline groups of the mandated islands by November, 1941. Approving Tojo's war orders, former Foreign Minister Hirota, head of the Black Dragons, discussed the advantages and consequences of a conflict with the United States. Many of those at the meeting considered December, 1941, or February, 1942, the most suitable time for Japan to attack. 'Tojo,' they said, 'will start the war with America, and after sixty days he will reshuffle the cabinet and become a great dictator.' Both predictions came true, confirming the long-standing deadly antagonism of upper-crust Japanese in the Black Dragon Society toward the United States."

The Black Dragon Society, it was believed, even had members functioning in the United States during the Second World War. According to the March 31, 1942, edition of the *San Francisco News*, "The FBI today was rounding up known and suspected members of the toughest alien Japanese group in San Francisco. The raids were said to have been based on documentary evidence seized in previous raids on Japanese secret societies, that the local group was a 'front' for the ruthless and dread Black Dragon Society, most nationalistic and terroristic of all Japanese secret bodies.

"Nat J.L. Pieper, Northern California FBI chief who directed the roundups, said some of the Japanese already in custody had admitted the secret nature of the local society. Mr. Pieper also declared 'proof of the organization's intense nationalistic program, and direction under the Black Dragon Society, has been found.'"

The group was fictionalized by Hollywood during World War II in the serial *G-Men vs. the Black Dragon*, released in 1943, and directed by William Witney. Made by Republic Studios, the film was later re-edited into a feature and re-named *Black Dragon of Manzanar*.

The Black Hand   Secret society that counted among its members Colonel Dragutin Dimitrijević, the chief of Serbian military intelli-gence who operated under the code name "Apis." Apis conspired to assassinate Archduke Franz Ferdinand in an attempt to liberate Serbs living in southern Austria-Hungary, an act often credited with start-ing World War I. There are several similarities between this assassi-nation and that of President John F. Kennedy in 1963 in Dallas, Texas. Both were shot while riding in an open-topped car just after the car had to slow down to make a sharp, acutely angled curve.

Not to be confused with the extortion method used by the Mafia.

Black Muslims   See NATION OF ISLAM.

B'ne Moshe (Son of Moses)   Jewish group formed in 1889 by Asher Ginzberg, headquartered in Odessa, also home of the Friends of Zion. Originally there were seven members, all known as scholars of Hebrew devoted to Jewish messianic goals. The name of the group was based on the belief by some that there existed, in a secret place, a colony of Jews who were direct descendants of Moses. The group, which slowly grew, worked for Jewish nationalism. Most of the members were eastern Jews, and lodges formed in Galicia, Poland, and Russia. Ginzberg, who believed in the creation of a Jewish state by force if necessary, lost control of the group he founded to Theodor Herzl, a more diplomatic man whose book *Das Judenstat (The Jewish State)* made him wildly popular. Ginzberg regained control in the years before World War I and died in Jewish Palestine in 1927.

Bohemian Grove   Secluded campground in Sonoma County, Cali-fornia where, once a year for two weeks, an all-male group of pow-erful publishers, politicians, and businessmen meet. Those who attend the meetings are sworn to secrecy about what goes on there. All information known about the group comes from reporters who have infiltrated the meetings, sometimes posing as waiters.

Al Neuharth, founder of *USA Today*, attended a meeting but declined to comment about it afterwards. "I went there with the understanding that I would adhere to their privacy rules," he replied. "I think I'd have a little ethical problem giving you the text. . . . I just don't want to do what they would consider unethical."

Because of the publishers in the group, few published pieces describing the group have appeared. During the summer of 1991, Dirk Mathison, San Francisco bureau chief for *People* magazine, infiltrated a meeting but, unfortunately for him, the group included the management of Time-Warner, the owner of *People*, which prevented Mathison from getting a story published. Among the speeches heard by Mathison before he was recognized and expelled were "Smart Weapons" by former Navy Secretary John Lehman, "Major Defense Problems of the 21st Century" by then-Defense Secretary Richard Cheney, "America's Health Revolution—Who Lives, Who Dies, Who Pays?" by former Health, Education, and Welfare Secretary Joseph Califano and "Defining the New World Order" by former Attorney General Elliott Richardson.

The most detailed story about the group was published in the November edition of *Spy* magazine, and was written by Philip Weiss. Members of the group are said to include every Republican president since Calvin Coolidge. George H. W. Bush, Henry Kissinger, James Baker, and David Rockefeller are said to be regular attendees. Members maintain that the meetings are strictly social, but there has allegedly been official business done. The Manhattan Project, the development of atomic weapons during World War II, was reportedly conceived at a Bohemian Group meeting.

Other members of the publishing world who have attended Bohemian Grove meetings include Franklin Murphy, the former CEO of the Times Mirror corporation; William Randolph Hearst, Jr.; Jack Howard and Charles Scripps of the Scripps-Howard newspaper chain; and Tom Johnson, president of CNN and former publisher of the *Los Angeles Times*.

It is said that the group also performs mock-druidic rituals and that the voice of the "Owl of Bohemia" is Walter Cronkite.

Among the more paranoid—or is that enlightened?—researchers into secret societies is Michael A. Hoffman, II, a former reporter for the New York bureau of the Associated Press who believes that secret societies, throughout history, have manipulated world events, and—through the media of the day—the public's perception of those events, to create what he called "psychological warfare," an attempt to control the mood of the people. He says that the ideas spread by the secret societies are designed to convey the sense that it is "useless to resist central, established control. Or it posits a counter-cultural alternative to such control which is actually a counterfeit, covertly emanating from the establishment itself. That the blackening (pollution) of the earth is as unavoidable as entropy. That extinction ('evolution') of the species human being is inevitable. That the reinhabitation of the earth by the 'old gods' (Genesis 6:4), is our stellar scientific destiny."

Bones   See SKULL & BONES.

Brotherhood of Death   See SKULL & BONES.

Brothers of the Hospital   See THE SOVEREIGN ORDER OF SAINT JOHN OF JERUSALEM.

Brothers of the Sword (*Fratres militiae Christi*)   Also known as the Christ Knights or The Militia of Christ of Livonia, this was a Baltic knightly order that joined the Teutonic Order of Prussia in 1237. The group was an imitation of the Knights Templar made up of German warrior monks, and was formed in 1202 by Albert von Bux-hövden, bishop of Riga.

The monks were supposedly vassals to the bishops, but this was generally disregarded by the order. The Brothers of the Sword openly defied Roman church bishops in 1218. The church sought to side with with Danish king Valdemar II. The king, however, joined forces with the Brothers of the Sword instead and together they conquered northern Estonia.

The Brothers of the Sword were headquartered at Viljandi in Estonia in a castle the walls of which still stand. Wenden, Segewold, and Ascheraden were also strongholds of the order. The grand master of the brothers maintained a five-member entourage consisting of the commanders of Viljandi (Fellin), Kuldiga (Goldingen), Aluksne (Marienburg), Tallinn, and the bailiff of Paide (Järva).

In 1236, the year before they joined the Teutonic Order, the Brothers of the Sword fought the Lithuanians at the battle of Siauliai and lost, suffering fifty dead in the process. The Brothers changed some of their rules to agree with those of the Teutonic Order, but they did not completely blend with the Prussians, instead maintaining an independent identity, which allowed them to retain control of lands they had conquered. All of Courland and Livonia were conquered by the Brothers of the Sword between 1288 and 1290. In 1346, the Brothers of the Sword and the Teutonic Order together purchased the unconquered portion of Estonia from the king of Denmark, Valdemar IV Atterdag.

The Teutonic Order lost power during the mid-1500s, so the Brothers of the Sword disenfranchised themselves and once again became a wholly independent group. During the 1550s, the Brothers fought a war against the bishop of Riga, into which the Polish king Sigismund II Augustus intervened. Gotthard Kettler, the last grand master of the Brothers of the Sword, made an agreement with the Polish king that the order would become secular and would convert to the Lutheran church. In the years that followed, the Brothers lost most of the land they had conquered. In southern Estonia, the Polish king created a Duchy of Courland and Semigalia. The rest of the land formerly belonging to the brothers was taken by Denmark and Sweden.

See also TEUTONIC KNIGHTS.

C

Cahaba Boys   See Ku Klux Klan.

Camisards   Also known as the Prophets of Cevennes, this group appeared in London during the first years of the eighteenth century. Among their sympathizers was Sir Isaac Newton, who was alleged to have been a grand master of the Priory of Sion. The Camisards were similar to the Cathars, in that they were Gnostic, believing that religion should be based on knowledge rather than faith. They wore white tunics and questioned the divinity of Jesus.

See also Cathars; Priory of Sion.

Candomble Jege-Nago   See Santeria.

Carbonaria   The name means, literally, "charcoal-burners." The group's flag was designed with horizontal stripes: blue on top, red in the middle, and black at the bottom—the black representing the burning charcoal. This group was a Freemason-like secret society in Italy in the nineteenth century. The group sought to free Italy from foreign domination.

Some say the group's beliefs came to Italy with the invasion of Napoleon's troops. The supporters of Gioacchino Murat—who was Napoleon's brother-in-law and the "King of Naples"—formed secret societies. Various factions of the Carbonari sprung up, including lodges in France and Spain, with limited contact between them. The groups are last heard of around 1840, but during the first quarter of the nineteenth century they were responsible for a series of failed revolutions and riots. Among these were uprisings in July, 1820, in Naples, in March, 1821, in Biella, and in 1828 near Salerno.

The 1820 insurrection is considered their greatest achievement. It was led by General Guglielmo Pepe. Most members were middle-class liberal and intellectual people, who for the most part were not in touch with the masses they sought to represent.

Cathars Peaceful group—their name translates as "Pure Ones"—who lived in the province of Languedoc in southern France during the twelfth and early thirteenth century. The Cathars may have been a derivation of a Bulgarian sect active in the tenth and eleventh centuries called the Bogomils who had migrated into France. Others feel that the Cathars had been in France for centuries and held beliefs contrary to those of the Church that dated back to the dawn of Christianity.

Though Christian, in that they learned the teachings of Jesus, the Cathars were very different from the Roman Church, at a time when it was heretical to disagree with the Church about anything.

The Cathars' priests were called *Perfecti* (Perfect Ones). The Perfecti wore long dark robes and believed in living without material possessions. Technically, all members of the Cathars were considered equal, including women, and equally capable of acting as priest if the need arose. The Cathars believed in living their lives as closely as possible to the way Jesus had lived his—by the principles of love. They believed in reincarnation; and in knowledge rather than faith (the Greek word for knowledge is *gnosis*). The Cathars did not use churches but rather held their religious services outside, so as to be closer to nature. In times of bad weather, any structure could be used to hold the ceremony. They were vegetarians for the most part, but were allowed to eat fish. The group believed in the dualist nature of things, that good and evil are opposite sides of a common cosmic force. They believed that a good god created the heavens whereas an evil god created man and his greed. The Cathars behaved in a manner that twentieth-century people would associate with hippies. A less-threatening group it is hard to imagine—but the Roman Church was threatened.

Perhaps it was because, for reasons that are unclear, the Cathars found the crucifixion of Jesus insignificant. They also did not believe in baptism or communion. The only Cathar sacrament was called *consolamentum*, which was a sacrament of chastity. This did not, however, mean that the Cathars were chaste, as *consolamentum* was only administered upon one's death bed.

Or perhaps it was because the Cathars' popularity was spreading. Cathar groups could be found throughout Germany and the north of France.

One theory as to why the Church reacted so violently against the Cathars has to do with the Knights Templar, who were headquartered nearby in southern France. There was apparently quite a bit of overlap between the Cathars and the Templars. A member of a Cathar family, Bertrand de Blanchefort, became the fourth Grand Master of the Order of the Knights Templar. Blanchefort, who held the position from 1153 to 1170, was considered a significant grand master. It was he who organized the Templars and transformed them into what would today be called an international corporation. It is believed that the Templars had given the Cathars the secrets about Jesus' life that they had learned while digging for treasure at the site of the Temple of Solomon in Jerusalem, and that these secrets involved an alternative biography of Jesus. In this version of Jesus' life, he was married to Mary Magdalene and had children. Following Jesus' death, Mary Magdalene, her brother Lazarus and sister Martha, her maid Marcella, and Jesus' children traveled to Marseilles, France, and that there still exists those who could trace their lineage directly back to Jesus. Since these descendants could claim to be the true rulers of Christianity, they posed an enormous threat to the Church, whose rulers were a direct lineage that could be traced back to Peter, one of Jesus' disciples. (Some corroboration for this version of Jesus' life is offered by the Gospel of Philip, a Gnostic text thought to be written in the late third century.)

According to Michael Baigent, Richard Leigh, and Henry Lincoln, in their book *Holy Blood, Holy Grail*, "Jesus' wife and offspring—and he could have fathered a number of children between the ages of sixteen or seventeen and his supposed death—after fleeing the Holy Land, found refuge in the south of France, and in a Jewish community there preserved their lineage. During the fifth century this lineage appears to have intermarried with the royal line of the Franks, thus engendering the Merovingian dynasty. In 196 A.D.

the Church made a pact with this dynasty, pledging itself in perpe-
tuity of the Merovingian bloodline—presumably in the full knowledge of that bloodline's true identity. When the Church colluded in
the subsequent betrayal of the Merovingian bloodline, it rendered
itself guilty of a crime that could neither be rationalized nor
expunged, it could only be suppressed."

According to author Laurence Gardner in his book *Bloodline of
the Holy Grail*, "The early Christian Church leaders adopted scriptures and teachings that would obscure the truth about the royal
bloodline of Jesus. . . . For centuries after her death, Mary's legacy
remained the greatest of all threats to a fearful church."

Beginning in 1145, the Church plotted to wipe the Cathars out.
For public relations purposes, the Church needed a good excuse to
carry out the genocide. That came on January 14, 1208, when
an assistant to the Pope was murdered by anticlerical rebels near
the Languedoc, and therefore in close proximity to the Cathars.
Although there was no indication that the Cathars had anything to
do with the murder, they were swiftly blamed. In 1209, Pope Innocent III ordered King Philip II of France to proclaim the Cathars
heretics. The crusade against the Cathars, known as the Albigensian
Crusade, was the first by the Vatican to be launched against Christians rather than Muslims. During this fight the Knights Templar
were said to have remained neutral.

One papal legate was asked by a crusade soldier, "How will we
recognize the Cathari?"

The legate replied: "Kill them all. God will know his own."

Those who were not killed were blinded or had their noses
cut off.

The Cathars were eradicated and by 1229 had been all but wiped
out. This has been called the first European genocide. It is estimated
that as many as one hundred thousand Cathars were murdered.
Helping with the eradication of the Cathars was Dominic Guzmán,
a Spanish zealot who later formed the monastic group called the
Dominicans, who in turn carried out the Holy Inquisition.

In 1244, it is said, remaining Cathars escaped from the crusaders, carrying much of the sect's accumulated wealth in gold,
silver, and coins. The treasure was hidden in a cave and then in a

castle at Montségur before disappearing forever. Montségur, it should be noted, is only a half-day's horseback ride from Rennes-le-Château, where the Priory of Sion parchments were discovered. Some Cathars are thought to have survived, hidden among the ranks of the Knights Templar.

The Cathars were a major influence upon the later secret society called Carboneri, who in turn are said to have influenced the Illuminati. They are also said to have been an influence on Martin Luther of Germany and John Calvin of France, whose Reformation ended the domination of the Roman Catholic Church over the Western world.

See also CARBONARIA; ILLUMINATI; PRIORY OF SION.

Chapter 322   See SKULL & BONES.

Chivalric Military Order of the Temple of Jerusalem   Current group in Scotland and continental Europe claiming to be descended from the Knights Templar, but separate from Freemasonry.

See also FREEMASONS; KNIGHTS TEMPLAR.

Christian Unions   Secret societies formed by Johann Valentin Andrea, who—if you believe the documents—was the grand master of the Priory of Sion from 1637 to 1654. The Christian Unions were a series of organizations each led by an anonymous prince and a group of twelve experts in some scientific field. The object was to prevent the loss of scientific knowledge that was considered heretical by the Catholic Church. The societies also gave sanctuary to persons in flight from the Inquisition. Many of the people who sought refuge with the Christian Unions were eventually smuggled into England, where they were absorbed into the Freemasons.

See also FREEMASONS; PRIORY OF SION.

Christ Knights   See BROTHERS OF THE SWORD.

Church of Satan   According to Nigel Cawthorne in his book *Satanic Murder*: "[Founder of the First Church of Satan, Anton Szandor] LaVey claimed that satanic ages last 1,158 years. The last one, where God was on top and Satan was cast down, started in 508 A.D. Consequently, the new satanic age began in 1966 and this time Satan was on top. 1966, LaVey proclaimed, was 'Year one, *Anno Satanas*.'"

This group uses Satan, the Judeo-Christian concept of the devil, as its primary symbol. But the group claims not to be devil-worshippers, per se, but rather uses Satan as a metaphor. According to the church, which was founded by Anton LaVey in San Francisco in 1966, every human is responsible for his or her own destiny. Members are called "Satanists." Although called a "church," the U.S. Government does not recognize Satanism as a religion and has not granted this church tax-exempt status. LaVey remained the "High Priest" of the Church of Satan until his death in 1997. The church is now led by Peter H. Gilmore, and has moved its headquarters to New York City. Members must be eighteen or older, or have permission of their parents. Despite the group's motto, "Do as thou wilt," all members are expected to obey the laws of their country.

See also OTO; THE PROCESS; TEMPLE OF SET.

Committee of 300   According to former MI6 agent Dr. John Coleman, the Committee of 300 is an all-powerful group that knows no national boundaries. Above the laws of all countries, the Committee reportedly controls every aspect of politics, religion, commerce and industry, banking, insurance, mining, the drug trade, and the petroleum industry. It is a group answerable to no one but its members. Coleman says the committee is a "secret, upper-level parallel government that runs Britain and the U.S." This theory dates back at least to 1909, when Walter Ratheneau of General Electric told a German audience that "300 men, all of whom know one another, direct the economic destiny of Europe and choose their successors from among themselves." Coleman says that the committee was often referred to as "The Olympians," and included as a member diamond-tycoon Cecil Rhodes.

In his book, *The Conspirators' Hierarchy: The Committee of 300 (Second Edition)*, Dr. Coleman writes: "The Committee of 300 is the ultimate secret society made up of an untouchable ruling class, which includes the Queen of England, the Queen of the Netherlands, the Queen of Denmark, and the royal families of Europe. These aristocrats decided at the death of Queen Victoria, the matriarch of the Venetian Black Guelphs, that in order to gain world-wide control, it would be necessary for its aristocratic members to 'go into business' with the non-aristocratic but extremely powerful leaders of corporate business on a global scale, and so the doors to ultimate power were opened to what the Queen of England likes to refer to as 'commoners.' From my days in the intelligence business I know that heads of foreign governments refer to this all-powerful body as 'The Magicians.' Stalin coined his own phrase to describe them: 'The Dark Forces.' President Eisenhower . . . referred to it in a colossal understatement as 'the military-industrial complex.'"

Communist Party   See LEAGUE OF THE JUST.

La Cosa Nostra   See MAFIA.

Council on Foreign Relations (CFR)   "A nonprofit and nonpartisan membership organization dedicated to improving the understanding of U.S. foreign policy and international affairs through the exchange of ideas"—or so they say. Many suspect the council is plotting to create a world run by a single government—a one-world community.

Who belongs to the CFR is not a secret, but what they do certainly is. The CFR publishes a list of its membership, but those on the council must take a pledge of silence regarding all CFR activities.

The CFR was born as an outgrowth of meetings conducted during the final months of, and just after, World War I. The nature of the postwar world was the subject of these meetings, which were set up by President Woodrow Wilson's adviser Colonel Edward Mandell House. Out of these meetings came Wilson's "fourteen points." The points called for free and open trade between nations.

When the war ended, Wilson, House, and other influential men, including bankers Bernard Baruch and Paul Warburg, attended the peace conference in Paris. At Paris's Majestic Hotel on May 30, 1919, there was formed the first attempt at a supranational organization, the Institute of International Affairs. Seen as a first step toward one global government, it was divided into two branches: one headquartered in England to be known as the Royal Institute of International Affairs, and one in New York to be called the Council on Foreign Relations.

The CFR took the name of a pre-existing but non-powerful group that had been meeting at a New York dinner club since 1918. The first president was John W. Davis, who was J.P. Morgan's lawyer. This new CFR was incorporated on July 21, 1921. The bylaws of the organization state that any member who discusses the activities of the CFR will immediately be expelled.

From the end of World War II until the present, the CFR has maintained its headquarters in New York City's Harold Pratt House, which was donated to the CFR by the Rockefeller family's Standard Oil (now better known as Exxon). David Rockefeller joined the CFR before World War II and was elected vice president of the council in 1950.

Membership was by invitation only and consisted of what is often referred to as the "northeastern power elite." In the original rules, the CFR was supposed to limit its membership to 1,600 members, but today it is estimated that it has more than twice that many members.

During the 1970s, the CFR stopped being an exclusively white male organization, allowing a smattering of women and African Americans to join. Members of the CFR have included several U.S. Secretaries of State, including Elihu Root, John Foster Dulles, and Christian Herter.

Root (1845–1937), was born in Clinton, New York, son of a professor of mathematics at Hamilton College. Root graduated from the law school of New York University in 1867 and became a prominent lawyer. After years of involvement in local Republican politics, Root was appointed Secretary of War by President William McKinley in 1899. During his years in the president's cabinet, Root reorganized the administrative system of the War Department, established new procedures for promotion, founded the War College, enlarged West Point, opened schools for special branches of the service, created a general staff, and strengthened control over the National Guard. He returned to private practice from 1904 till 1905 when he became President Theodore Roosevelt's Secretary of

State. From 1909 to 1915, Root was a U.S. senator. He dedicated a large portion of his life to the cause of international arbitration. Root was the first president of the Carnegie Endowment for International Peace. He believed that international law presented mankind with its best chance to achieve world peace.

John Foster Dulles (1888–1959) was such a powerful man in the federal government that the Washington, D.C., airport was named after him. His obituary in *The New York Times* read, in part: "For six years John Foster Dulles dominated both the making and the conduct of United States foreign policy. In the realm of foreign affairs he was President Eisenhower's chief adviser, his chief representative on Capitol Hill and his chief agent and negotiator at home and abroad. Mr. Dulles was a highly controversial Secretary of State. Those who followed his career were rarely dispassionate; they divided, usually, between ardent admirers and those who disliked or distrusted him. Certain things, however, were incontestable. First was the extent of his role. He was undoubtedly the strongest personality of the Eisenhower Cabinet, and as such he constantly played a leading role in Washington and often in the councils of the Western alliance. Secondly, whatever his qualities as a policy-maker, he had few peers as an advocate. No one could equal him as a persuader in the White House councils. In facing the Senate Foreign Relations Committee he sometimes encountered criticism and skepticism, but he inevitably had his way. Thirdly, he had extraordinary vitality. He maintained personal contacts and sought to exercise American leadership by constant travel in all parts of the world. As Secretary he flew a total of 479,286 miles outside the United States."

Christian Archibald Herter (1895–1966) was born in France to American parents and had moved to New York City by the time he started school. He graduated from Harvard University in 1915, became attaché to the American Embassy in Berlin in 1916, and in 1919 became a charter member of the CFR. He was governor of Massachusetts before his stint as Secretary of State from 1959 to 1961. Herter was known as an internationalist, interested in improving political and economic relations with Europe. The World Affairs Council of Boston has a Christian A. Herter Award honoring individual contributions to international relations.

Allen Dulles, brother of John Foster, who later served as the Director of Central Intelligence and on the Warren Commission investigating the assassination of President Kennedy, was also a member. Born in 1893, Dulles was the nephew of a secretary of state and the grandson of another. It was hoped by the family that Allen would become the family's third secretary of state, but, despite his many accomplishments, this was never to be. There was a third secretary of state in the family, but it turned out to be Allen's brother, John Foster Dulles. His first government job was at the U.S. Embassy to the Austro-Hungarian Empire, but after the U.S. entered World War I he was moved to Bern, Switzerland. Following the war, he resigned from the state department and went to work on Wall Street. Dulles was a master spy during World War II. He supervised the penetration of the Abwehr (Hitler's military intelligence agency) and the subsequent incorporation of many of its undercover agents into the CIA. Some of those talented and well-connected intelligence people made major contributions to the United States. They had far-reaching contacts of their own that were important for the U.S. to have. Today, some critics of the CIA believe that the agency overlooked the bad side of Nazi intelligence personnel because it needed what the Nazis could deliver. That may be so. Intelligence is not the realm of saints.

In November 1942, Dulles opened the OSS office in Bern, Switzerland. He was designated Agent 110 and referred to in OSS communications as Mr. Bull. After World War II, Dulles practiced law. He first went to work for the CIA in January 1951. Eight months later he was named the Agency's deputy director. As DCI, Dulles ordered his agents to carry out clandestine operations throughout South America and the Middle East. It was during his tenure that the U-2 spy plane was developed and he was responsible for the digging of the Berlin tunnel. He also plotted to kill Fidel Castro, the revolutionary leader of Cuba who had declared his allegiance to the Communists. According to Dulles' Deputy Director of Central Intelligence, Richard Bissell, the CIA-sponsored attempts on the life of Castro were so secret that only Dulles received reports about them. He was fired in 1961 by President John F. Kennedy after the Bay of Pigs fiasco and, ironically, he later became a member of the Warren Commission investigating President Kennedy's assassination. According to the head of General Dwight D. Eisenhower's chief of intelligence during World War II, General Kenneth Strong, "Allen Dulles was undoubtedly the greatest United States professional intelligence officer of his time."

The CFR is so powerful that it often dictates U.S. foreign policy. And, to believe one whistle-blower, the fix is in when it comes to our democratic process.

Says CFR member, Admiral Chester Ward, "CFR, as such, does not write the platforms of both political parties or select their respective presidential candidates, or control U.S. defense and foreign policies. But CFR members, as individuals, acting in concert with other individual CFR members, do."

According to Alvin Moscow in his book *The Rockefeller Inheritance*, "So august has been the membership of the Council that it has been seen in some quarters as the heart of the eastern Establishment. When it comes to foreign affairs, it is the eastern Establishment. In fact, it is difficult to point to a single major policy in U.S. foreign affairs that has been established since [the] Wilson [administration] which was diametrically opposed to then current thinking in the Council on Foreign Relations."

After a round of public criticism from conservative writers, former chairman of the CFR David Rockefeller was instrumental in the formation of a new and similar organization known as the Trilateral Commission.

There is reason to believe that the CFR created the United Nations. Author Ralph Epperson notes that the first U.S. delegation to the United Nations, when it was headquartered in San Francisco, included forty-seven members of the CFR.

Among the members of the CFR is Alan Greenspan, who has been since the Ronald Reagan administration the chairman of the Federal Reserve.

Today's funding for the CFR is said to come from major corporations such as Xerox, Bristol-Meyers Squibb, General Motors, the Ford Foundation, the Andrew W. Mellon Foundation, and the Rockefeller Brothers Fund.

It has been theorized that modern wars are controlled by bankers and businessmen rather than by generals and armies. Members of the CFR first took an interest in Vietnam back in 1951, a full decade before U.S. involvement there. That year the CFR created a study group to analyze the region. The group concluded that British-American domination of the region was recommended. Three years later, one of the founders of the CFR, John Foster Dulles, convened a conference in Manila at which the Southeast Asia Treaty Organization (SEATO) was founded. SEATO committed the British Empire, the United States, France, and the Philippines to defend Indochina, a pact that led to the French and then the U.S. fighting long and bloody wars in the region. According to author Jim Marrs, the CFR roster during the 1960s, which included Robert McNamara, McGeorge Bundy, General Maxwell Taylor, and Henry Cabot Lodge, was a "who's who of the Vietnam era." In 1969, Richard Nixon appointed as his National Security Adviser Henry Kissinger, a member of both the CFR and the Trilateral Commission.

Continuing with the theory that modern wars are run by men wearing white collars, it would therefore please the powers that be to make the wars as long and expensive as possible. With that in mind, recall that General Douglas MacArthur (a Mason), was fired by President Harry Truman when MacArthur sought to quickly and definitively win the Korean War. MacArthur was replaced by General Matthew B. Ridgeway, later a member of the CFR. U.S. military forces in Vietnam were never allowed to use the full brunt of their force against the enemy but were instead handcuffed by "rules of engagement," all but guaranteeing a long and munition-consumptive war without a winner.

According to author G. Edward Griffin, even the Cold War was a machination of secret societies. He wrote: "Communist Russia was financed and controlled from the beginning by the inner circle of America's modern secret societies."

Journalists who are also members of the Council on Foreign Relations include Robert MacNeil, Jim Lehrer, and Dan Rather. All three were in or near Dealey Plaza in Dallas on November 22, 1963, at the time of President Kennedy's assassination.

See also TRILATERAL COMMISSION.

Cult of the Serpent   According to one group of UFO believers, this group is a "secret government" conspiring with alien beings on Earth. In exchange for certain powers over the Earth, the aliens have granted humans advanced alien technology such as Velcro and fiber optics. Even those who find this sort of story ridiculous will be fascinated by its sources, predominantly ex-military intelligence men, whose seemingly organized pattern of disinformation may be evidence, in itself, of a secret society.

Cults   According to cult expert Dee Finney (www.greatdreams.com/ ufos/ufo-cults.htm, accessed March 9, 2004), every cult can be defined as a group having all of the following characteristics: "(1) It uses psychological coercion to recruit, indoctrinate, and retain its members. Special privilege for the leader and members because of their 'chosen' status. (2) It forms an elitist totalitarian society. Exclusive membership and a 'you'll miss out if you don't get involved' mentality. (3) Its founder leader is self-appointed, dogmatic, messianic, not accountable, and has charisma. (4) Divine instruction coming from a deity source, only given to that particular group usually through channeling or 'divine inspiration'. (5) It believes 'the end justifies the means' in order to solicit funds and recruit people. (6) Channeled or divinely inspired messages to save/help mankind. (7) Groups can change/stop future cataclysmic (i.e., floods, earthquakes, etc.) events. (8) Repetitious appeals/prayers/incantations recited daily. (9) Group is usually named such as (i.e., Heaven's Gate, Branch Davidians, The Core Council). (10) Initiates will receive protection from deities/alien races if they maintain membership in the group and do as instructed by the leader. (11) Its wealth does not benefit its members or society."

History's most famous cult was the People's Temple, led by the Reverend Jim Jones. Members were mostly northern California residents who had been moved by their leader to a jungle location in Guyana, which was given the name Jonestown. When a San Francisco congressman named Leo Ryan went to Guyana in November 1978, in response to charges that there were local citizens there being held against their will, he and four others were shot dead at the airport. Soon thereafter, at their leader's instruction, a thousand members of the cult drank poisoned Kool-Aid and died. Jones was found among the dead, having apparently drunk the poison along with his followers. Parents fed the poison to their children before drinking it themselves. There were some isolated incidents of resistance during the mass suicide, but dissenters were shouted down and, for the most part, the cult members were obedient until the end. The bodies were discovered all together, many lying arm in arm. Jones founded the People's Temple during the 1950s in Indiana, preaching integration and racial harmony. He and one hundred followers moved to northern California in 1965. In California, Jones gradually increased the commitment and discipline he demanded from his followers. The "church" was transformed into a "cult." He took from his followers all of their possessions. Members, who referred to Jones as "Father" or "Dad," were forbidden to have contact with outsiders. His sermons began to predict nuclear holocaust. Those who disobeyed his orders were severely punished, often beaten. All of the women were considered to be Jones' "wives." To avoid a scandal involving children Jones had fathered with his female followers, he moved his cult to Guyana in mid-1977.

A tape recorder was rolling during the mass suicide and the tape was later discovered. A portion of the transcript from that tape follows.

JONES: "I've tried my best to give you a good life. In spite of all I've tried, a handful of people, with their lies, have made our life impossible. If we can't live in peace then let's die in peace." (*Applause*) "We have been so terribly betrayed. . . . What's going to happen here in the matter of a few minutes is that one of the people on that plane is going to shoot the pilot—I know that. I didn't plan it, but I know it's going to happen . . . So . . . step over quietly, because we are not committing suicide—it's a revolutionary act. We can't go back."

FIRST WOMAN: "I feel like that as there's life, there's hope."

JONES: "Well, someday everybody dies."

CROWD: "That's right, that's right!"

JONES: "What those people gone and done, and what they get through will make our lives worse than hell. . . . But to me, death is not a fearful thing. It's living that's cursed. . . . Not worth living like this."

FIRST WOMAN: "But I'm afraid to die."

JONES: "I don't think you are. I don't think you are."

FIRST WOMAN: "I think there were too few who left for 1,200 people to give them their lives for those people who left. . . . I look at all the babies and I think they deserve to live."

JONES: "But don't they deserve much more? They deserve peace. The best testimony we can give is to leave this goddamned world." (*Applause*)

FIRST MAN: "It's over, sister. . . . We've made a beautiful day." (*Applause*)

SECOND MAN: "If you tell us we have to give our lives now, we're ready." (*Applause*)

JONES: "Please get some medication. Simple. It's simple. There's no convulsions with it. . . . Don't be afraid to die. You'll see people land out here. They'll torture our people. . . ."

SECOND WOMAN: "There's nothing to worry about. Everybody keep calm and try to keep your children calm. . . . They're not crying from pain; it's just a little bitter tasting."

THIRD WOMAN: "This is nothing to cry about. This is something we could all rejoice about." (*Applause*)

JONES: "Please, for God's sake, let's get on with it. . . . This is a revolutionary suicide. This is not a self-destructive suicide."

THIRD MAN: "Dad has brought us this far. My vote is to go with Dad."

JONES: "We must die with dignity. Hurry, hurry, hurry. We must hurry. . . . Stop this hysterics. Death is a million times more preferable to spending more days in this life. . . . If you knew what was ahead, you'd be glad to be stepping over tonight."

FOURTH WOMAN: "It's been a pleasure walking with all of you in this revolutionary struggle. No other way I would rather go than to give my life for socialism, communism, and I thank Dad very much."

JONES: "Take our life from us. . . . We didn't commit suicide. We committed an act of revolutionary suicide protesting against the conditions of an inhuman world."

Another cult that made the news by committing mass suicide was the Heaven's Gate cult. This was a UFO-believing cult that lived together in a large house in the Rancho Santa Fe suburb of San Diego, California, during the 1990s. The group followed a man named Marshall Applewhite, who taught his followers that a flying saucer was traveling behind the Hale-Bopp comet. This flying saucer was destined to come for them and take them to another level, a level above being human.

Before the mass suicide, this message was posted on Heaven's Gate website. "Hale-Bopp's approach is the 'marker' we've been waiting for—the time for the arrival of the spacecraft from the Level Above Human to take us home to 'Their World'—in the literal Heavens."

We do not know the details of the suicide ritual. Unlike the case with the People's Temple, no tape recorder was rolling. We know only that, on March 26, 1997, the bodies of thirty-nine similarly dressed men and women (all were wearing brand-new athletic shoes made by Nike) were found in the home of the Heaven's Gate cult. All of the victims wore unisex black shirts, and pants, and had purple shrouds placed across their faces. They had ingested applesauce or pudding laced with barbiturates and a shot of vodka, and they had submitted to suffocation from plastic bags placed over their heads. They had taken, it was presumed, their journey to the level above human. Subsequent autopsies showed that many of the men, including the leader, had been chemically castrated, apparently voluntarily. It was believed that the suicides took place over three days, beginning on March 23. Most of the victims were in their forties, but ages ranged from twenty-six to seventy-two.

Marshall Herff Applewhite, known as "Do" (formerly "Bo"), and Bonnie Lu Nettles, known as "Ti" (formerly "Peep"), met in Texas and formed Heaven's Gate in the early 1970s. The cult moved to a secluded location in the Southwest where their numbers grew until there were an estimated one thousand members. Nettles died of cancer in 1985, leaving the leadership of the cult to Applewhite alone. In 1993 the group moved to Rancho Santa Fe.

Another cult that came to a violent end was the Branch Davidians, a group near Waco, Texas, that could trace their origins back to 1942, when they splintered away from the Seventh-Day Adventist Church. They believed that Jesus Christ would soon return to Earth, were strict vegetarians, and celebrated the Sabbath on Saturday.

In 1981, the group was joined by a twenty-two-year-old man named Vernon Howell. He started out as the handyman but quickly moved into a leadership position. Howell changed his name to David Koresh (David after King David of the Israelites, and Koresh after the Babylonian King Cyrus) and it was under his leadership that the sect became a cult. The name Branch Davidians came from sect founder Lois Roden's expression "Get off the dead (Shepherd's) Rod and move onto a living Branch."

The name Branch Davidians was not frequently used by members, who referred to themselves as Students of the Seven Seals, but became the name most commonly used by the public and media.

Koresh, like Jim Jones, dissolved the marriages of his members and proclaimed all of his female followers his own personal "spiritual wives," which granted him full sexual access. Everyone other than Koresh and his wives were forced to remain celibate. Members who had escaped from the cult, and parents seeking release of their children, told authorities that Koresh was physically assaulting children and counted among his wives girls who were in their mid-teens. There were several investigations by Child Protective Services in Waco, but not enough evidence was gathered to file charges. There is a videotape, however, in which Koresh brags of his many children, some of whom have mothers as young as thirteen.

The group turned their Waco headquarters into an armed compound, storing eleven tons of arms including anti-tank rifles. Koresh called the compound Camp Apocalypse, and told his followers that an Earth-ending battle would start there. The actual name of the structure was the Mount Carmel Center.

In February 1993, the Bureau of Alcohol, Tobacco and Firearms attempted to raid the compound but were held off by those inside. A standoff ensued. The compound was surrounded by FBI forces who attempted to get the Branch Davidians to exit the compound using psychological warfare, using loudspeakers twenty-four-hours a day to play loud music and other disturbing noises. The siege lasted for fifty-one days and ended tragically on April 19, 1993. The FBI forced their way inside and filled the building with gas. A rapidly spreading fire ensued. Seventy-four members of the cult and several Federal officers died.

Most cults are not self-destructive, but rather do their best to be self-perpetuating. The largest and most powerful cult in the world today is the Unification Church, comprised of the followers of Sun Myung Moon. This group is commonly referred to as the Moonies. The members do not like to be called Moonies, but they tolerate it because the term is so common. Through the years, using the money and influence of its members, the right-wing cult has gained control of many companies, including the major daily newspaper, the *Washington Times*. Members believe that Moon is the messiah, who has been sent to Earth to complete the work of Jesus Christ. Congress investigated the Moonies in 1978 because of alleged widespread fraud but found no evidence of wrongdoing. Following yet another investigation, Moon was subsequently found guilty of tax fraud and conspiracy to obstruct justice in 1985, and served some jail time. Members are often recruited while in college. It has been claimed that members are prevented from contact with their families, although Moon strongly denies this, and says that members are encouraged to contact their families at least once every ten days. Members marry only other members, often in massive group weddings conducted by Moon himself.

D

The Dark Forces   See COMMITTEE OF 300.

DaVinci, Leonardo   See PRIORY OF SION.

Democratic Clubs   Organized during the 1790s in the United States by Edmond Genet, the French ambassador to the U.S., the Democratic Clubs appeared to be based on the European secret societies that were pushing for revolution in France. President George Washington called for a stop to the clubs' activities before they shook "the government to its foundations." Future president John Quincy Adams said the clubs were indistinguishable from the Jacobin (pre-revolution) clubs of France. Worry about the Democratic Clubs became so strong that in 1798 the U.S. Congress passed the Alien and Sedition Acts. These new laws gave the president the power to imprison or expel from the country any foreigner who attempted to "defame" the U.S. government.

See also JACOBIN CLUBS.

E

Egbo See LEOPARD MEN.

Elks The Order of Elks was formed on February 16, 1868, in the City of New York. Its full corporate name is "Benevolent and Protective Order of Elks of the United States of America." Its declared purposes are to practice its four cardinal virtues: Charity, Justice, Brotherly Love, and Fidelity; to promote the welfare and enhance the happiness of its members; to quicken the spirit of American Patriotism; and to cultivate good fellowship.

The Elk colors are Royal Purple and White, which represent Clergy, Nobility, and "the People."

Among the things that Elks money helps provide are:

- Food to the hungry
- Shelter to the homeless
- Clothing and fuel to the needy
- Milk for undernourished babies
- Medical attention to the sick
- Baskets to the poor at Christmas and Thanksgiving
- Outings for underprivileged children
- Entertainments for shut-ins
- Education for young people
- Artificial limbs for the maimed
- Hospital beds
- Free clinics
- Night schools

- Rehabilitation of crippled children
- Treatment of indigent tubercular patients
- Provision for scholarships for worthy students
- Maintenance of orphans
- Boy's camps
- Training of the blind
- Eyeglasses for needy children
- Cerebral palsy clinics
- Cancer clinics

Essenes   Authors of the Dead Sea Scrolls, the Essenes were a Jewish group that existed from the sixth century B.C. at least until the first century A.D. Many believe that the Essenes were the educators of Jesus, as they had educated the mathematician Pythagoras six hundred years before. Since this group taught modern geometry it has been assumed that they were a precursor to Freemasonry. Although there is no mention of the Essenes in the New Testament, it is believed that they were among the first practitioners of Christianity, a mystic form of the religion based on the "ancient mysteries."

According to an early-twentieth-century writer named Nesta Webster, writing before the discovery of the Dead Sea Scrolls, "The Essenes were . . . not Christians, but a secret society . . . bound by terrible oaths not to divulge the sacred mysteries confided to them. And what were those mysteries but those of the Jewish secret tradition which we now know as the Cabala. . . . The truth is clearly that the Essenes were Cabalists, though doubtless Cabalists of a superior kind. . . . The Essenes are of importance as the first of the secret societies from which a direct line of tradition can be traced up to the present day."

See also GREAT WHITE BROTHERHOOD OF THE THERAPEUTATE.

European Spider's Web   See EUROPEAN UNION.

European Union   Sometimes referred to as the European Spider's Web, or by its initials: EU. Some say that the actual leaders of Europe are actors fronting for the real European power group, those who seek to realize Hitler's vision by creating a unified fascist Europe.

According to the website europa.eu.int (accessed February 26, 2004): EU is a "family of democratic European countries, committed to working together for peace and prosperity. It is not a State intended to replace existing states, but it is more than any other international organization. The EU is, in fact, unique. Its Member States have set up common institutions to which they delegate some of their sovereignty so that decisions on specific matters of joint interest can be made democratically at European level. The historical roots of the European Union lie in the Second World War. The idea of European integration was conceived to prevent such killing and destruction from ever happening again. It was first proposed by the French Foreign Minister Robert Schuman in a speech on 9 May 1950. This date, the 'birthday' of what is now the EU, is celebrated annually as Europe Day. There are five EU institutions, each playing a specific role: European Parliament (elected by the peoples of the Member States); Council of the European Union (representing the governments of the Member States); European Commission (driving force and executive body); Court of Justice (ensuring compliance with the law); Court of Auditors (controlling sound and lawful management of the EU budget). These are flanked by five other important bodies: European Economic and Social Committee (expresses the opinions of organized civil society on economic and social issues); Committee of the Regions (expresses the opinions of regional and local authorities); European Central Bank (responsible for monetary policy and managing the Euro); European Ombudsman (deals with citizens' complaints about maladministration by any EU institution or body); European Investment Bank (helps achieve EU objectives by financing investment projects)."

During the spring of 2004, the European Union expanded eastward. As the *New York Times* put it, the EU ended "the 65-year divide caused by the 20th century's hot and cold wars and shifted the union from a plush club of fifteen like-minded nations into a street bazaar of countries differing in wealth, stature and outlook."

"In historical terms it's an extraordinary moment," Timothy Garton Ash, an Oxford specialist in European studies, said of the expansion. "It's been said that Europe has had a name for 2,500 years but is still in the design stage. France and Germany have led European integration for forty years, and now that's clearly over. We have to wrestle with the question of who is going to set the agenda for this huge, sprawling entity of twenty-five states and 455 million people."

In March 2004, in response to bombings in Madrid that killed 190 victims, leaders of the EU named former Dutch Deputy Interior Minister Gijs de Vries as their antiterrorist "czar." The EU also enacted a raft of measures to improve cooperation between the various countries' police and intelligence services, enact laws on an EU-wide arrest warrant, beef up border controls, and create a European database of terror suspects.

Eye of God   See THE ALL-SEEING EYE.

F

Fabian Society Socialist group formed in 1883, named after Fabius Cunctator, a Roman general who used guerilla warfare tactics to defeat Hannibal. Members included author H. G. Wells and playwright George Bernard Shaw. The Fabian Society was responsible for the formation of the British Labour Party in 1906. The founder of the society was Sidney James Webb, who also founded the London School of Economics. Students at that school included David Rockefeller, Joseph Kennedy, Jr., John F. Kennedy, Senator Daniel Patrick Moynihan, and CBS newscaster Eric Sevareid.

Federal Reserve The Federal Reserve is a privately owned central bank that makes and sells the United States its currency. When the media talk of the United States being trillions of dollars in debt, they mean the nation is in debt to the Federal Reserve. Owned by wealthy families, the Federal Reserve's chairman is Alan Greenspan, who is also a member of the secret society known as the Trilateral Commission.

The law creating the Federal Reserve was passed by Congress due in large part to the efforts of Senator Nelson Aldridge, who was the maternal grandfather of David Rockefeller. The birth of "The Fed," it has been said, ended economic freedom in the United States. The Fed was owned in its entirety by twenty wealthy families. Today nothing has changed. Shares in the Federal Reserve, which makes a profit of approximately 150 billion dollars per year, are owned by the heirs of those same families.

According to the Fed's official website (www.federalreserve.gov, accessed February 26, 2004):

The Federal Reserve, the central bank of the United States, was founded by Congress in 1913 to provide the nation with a safer, more flexible, and more stable monetary and financial system.

Today the Federal Reserve's duties fall into four general areas: (1) conducting the nation's monetary policy; (2) supervising and regulating banking institutions and protecting the credit rights of consumers; (3) maintaining the stability of the financial system; and (4) providing certain financial services to the U.S. government, the public, financial institutions, and foreign official institutions.

The Federal Reserve system, income tax (the Sixteenth Amendment), and America's involvement in the First World War, were all brought about by the same small group of people, whose roster is all but identical to the Jekyll Island group.

The only two United States presidents to issue debt-free currency were Abraham Lincoln and John F. Kennedy. Both were assassinated—Lincoln in 1865 in Washington, D.C., and Kennedy in 1963 in Dallas, Texas.

See also Jekyll Island Group; Trilateral Commission.

Fenian Brotherhood   Founded in the United States by John O'Mahony in 1858 as the American arm of the Irish Republican Army, the Fenian Brotherhood was an Irish-American revolutionary secret society. They were named after Fionn MacCumhail's band of Irish warriors known as the Fianna.

O'Mahony had been part of a group led by William Smith O'Brien that had attempted a failed uprising in Ireland in 1848. In 1852, O'Mahony moved to New York City and, while living there, corresponded with James Stephens, another of O'Brien's men who had fled to Paris. In 1858, Stephens, having returned to Ireland, planned to regroup his revolutionaries and used as his headquarters the Phoenix National and Literary Society in Skibbereen, Ireland. That same year, O'Mahony formed the Fenian Brotherhood, whose members swore allegiance to the Irish Republic and pledged to fight if asked.

The goal of Stephens and O'Mahony was to form a series of groups, in nations all over the world, comprised of Irishmen committed to ending British rule in Ireland. Their model was the Jacobin Club, revolutionary leaders who sought to overthrow the monarchy of King Louis XVI during the late eighteenth century. The French version of the Fenian Brotherhood was disguised under the seemingly innocuous name the Committee of Public Safety. Other branches of the Fenians were formed in Canada, South America, and Australia. Branches sprang up in Great Britain, in Glasgow, Manchester, and London. The Fenians tried but failed to organize Irish farmers and were dealt a further blow when they were denounced by the Catholic Church.

In America, the group gained numbers and power after a convention held at Chicago under O'Mahony's presidency in November, 1863, during the U.S. Civil War. In the meantime, in Dublin, Stephens began publishing a journal called *The Irish People*, which made its away across the Atlantic and urged Irish Americans who had received military training to fight in the Civil War to come to Ireland and fight the British. The magazine was effective and when the American Civil War ended in 1865, battle-experienced Irish Americans returned in droves to their homeland. Unfortunately for the Fenians, the secret operation was infiltrated by informers, and many of the leaders in Ireland were arrested and jailed. Others, including Stephens, managed to escape to France. Because of the arrests, there was dissension in both Ireland and America, where potential recruits balked at crossing the ocean just so they could be incarcerated.

A man named W. R. Roberts became the leader of the Fenians in the United States a few years following the end of the Civil War. Money was raised to support Fenian plots through the sale of bonds printed in the name of the "Irish Republic." The bonds, it was said, would be honored once Ireland gained its independence. Guns were bought and plans were made to invade Canada, where the most convenient British troops could be found. President Andrew Johnson learned of the plans but did nothing to stop the Fenians. The Fenians' Secretary for War was General T. W. Sweeny, and the commander of the raid into Canada was John O'Neill. The Fenian troops, eight hundred strong, launched their attack on June 1, 1866, crossing into Canada over the Niagara River and capturing Fort Erie, in Ontario. The Fenians routed the first two battalions of Canadian volunteers they encountered. Canadian reinforcements were plentiful, however, whereas Fenian reinforcements were non-existent. On June 3, the Fenians fled back across the border and President Johnson finally stepped in, demanding that the Fenians obey U.S. neutrality laws with Canada. The Canadians released their Fenian prisoners and returned Fenian arms that had been seized. It was later learned that the Fenian raids had been harmed because of heavy infiltration by both Canadian and English agents.

Problems with enemy infiltration would harm later Fenian aggression as well. In 1867, in Ireland, the Irish Republic Army attempted the Fenian Rising, which failed miserably. It lacked solid organization or public support. Infiltration was again the problem. One of Stephen's most trusted agents, John Joseph Corydon, was an informant for the British government.

A second invasion of Canada was planned in December 1867 during a convention of the "Brotherhood in America," led by John O'Neill, which was attended by four hundred delegates while an estimated six thousand Fenian soldiers paraded outside. One spy in their midst was Henri Le Caron, who was the "Inspector General of the Irish Republican Army" as well as a secret agent for the English government. When the second invasion finally took place, in April 1870, the Fenians were once again under O'Neill's command. The Fenians crossed into Canada near Franklin, Vermont. They were quickly fired upon by Canadian troops who were waiting for them and ran back across the border. President Ulysses S. Grant promptly had O'Neill arrested.

That was about it for the Fenian Brotherhood, although other organizations in Ireland and elsewhere continued to carry on similar activities. In 1881 a submarine—a submerged boat, that is—called the Fenian Ram was designed by John Philip Holland and launched by the Delamater Iron Company in New York for use by Irish militants against the British, something that was never successfully accomplished. As a military force, the Fenian Brotherhood was a dismal failure, but as a secret society designed to popularize radical Irish nationalist ideas, it was far more successful.

See also JACOBIN CLUB.

Fratres Militiae Christi   See BROTHERS OF THE SWORD.

Freemasons   *Freemasons* are a worldwide secret society (the Free
and Accepted Masons), whose avowed purpose is mutual aid and
fellowship—but the truth may have been, on occasion, a bit more
sinister. Some sources say they may have played a major role in the
Jack the Ripper slayings.

The society is divided into three sections, or lodges. The entry-
level lodge is called the Blue Lodge, which in itself is divided into
three ranks, or degrees—sort of like private, private first class, and
corporal. The middle lodge is known as the York Rite (sometimes
called the Red Lodge), and it is divided into ten degrees. If a Mason
is promoted up the ranks to the top of the York Rite, he may enter
the Scottish Rite, which is divided into thirty two degrees. There is
a thirty-third degree to the Scottish Rite, which can be entered by
invitation only. The degrees are symbolic, and have names such as
the "mark master degree," the "royal arch degree," the "Knights
Templar degree," and the "Prince of Mercy degree." There are thirty-
two vertebrae in the human backbone. The thirty-third degree symbolizes the head sitting atop the spine. (The Stuarts of the British
throne were supporters of Freemasonry and are said to be the originators of Scottish Rite.)

There is still much about Masonic rituals that is unknown to
outsiders. Information comes in snippets, and is almost never reli-
able. We do know that initiates into the royal arch degree are blindfolded (hoodwinked, in the vernacular of the order) and stripped
naked or semi-naked. The initiate is placed under the control of a
member of the degree who is called his conductor or guide. The
guide knocks three times on the door to the room in which the initiation is to be held.

Those inside the room, hearing the knock, reply: "What profane,
or unworthy person or persons are these, coming here to disturb
the peace and harmony of this, our Royal Arch Purple Chapter meeting dedicated by us unto God, and Brother Joshua?"

The door is guarded by a man called a "Tyler," who, often armed
with a sword, functions as the lodge's security officer, to prevent

interlopers. The tradition of the Tyler goes back to the origins of Freemasonry, when initiations were held in caves.

The Tyler says, "They are not profane, nor unworthy at all, but friends with a brother, and a brother with friends, seeking admission into this, your Royal Arch Purple Chapter meeting, dedicated by you unto God and Brother Joshua."

The door is opened and the group's leader asks the initiate a series of questions, which are answered thusly:

"Where are you from?

"The outer Camp of Israel."

"Where are you going?"

"To the inner lines."

"How do you intend to get there?"

"By the benefit of a password."

"Have you that password?"

"I have."

"Will you give it to me?"

"I will, if you begin: Shib-Bo-Leth."

The initiate is then pricked on his bare chest with a sword or other sharp object, sometimes a compass. The questions and answers continue.

"Upon what were you admitted?"

"On the point of a sword pointed to my naked left breast."

"Why to your naked left breast?"

"Because it was nearest my heart."

"Did you feel anything?"

"Three sharp pricks to my naked left breast."

"What did these three sharp pricks to your naked left breast signify?"

"As they were a prick to my flesh in the meantime, so may they be a sting to my conscience hereafter, if ever I should divulge anything I had received or was about to receive."

Then the blindfolded initiate is startled with an unexpected and loud sound. This is created by symbols, a blank gun, or by other means. The leader then asks the initiate:

"What did you hear?"

"A loud report."

"What did this loud report signify?"

"The Lord thundering down his wrath upon the children of Israel for their disobedience unto him."

The initiate then kneels and prays for his own deliverance.

It is said that the true goals and practices of the Masons are known only to those at the very top levels. This is to ensure secrecy. The great majority of Masons cannot reveal the secrets because they are not privy to them. Those who do know are those who have proven the best at keeping secrets. The Masons, it is assumed, not only keep their secrets secret by releasing no information to the public but also by releasing disinformation, false information designed to mislead and confuse the public. Evidence of this is the fact that Masonic lore is filled with absurd historical inaccuracies. Although the Masons claim that it is not their goal to replace religion, it cannot be denied that many Masons use the lodge as a substitute for religion in their lives.

The Masons can trace their roots back as far as the late Middle Ages. The Masons at that time, as their name would imply, worked in stone. Very few buildings were built in stone. Only the castles of kings, and those of a few noblemen, as well as cathedrals, abbeys, and parish churches, were made of stone. Between 1050 and 1350, in France, five hundred churches and eighty cathedrals were built by masons. Some of the cathedrals took more than one hundred years to complete. Two types of masons took on these enormous tasks, the "rough masons" who worked with large blocks of hard stone, and "freemasons" who carved the facades of the structure out of the softer "freestone." Since there weren't always enough masons in an area to build the larger stone structures, the masons moved from place to place, keeping their possessions and eating their meals in places that came to be known as lodges. Generally, masons did not sleep in the lodges, however, preferring accommodations in local inns.

One of the earliest myths regarding masons involved the building of London Bridge. The original bridge, built of wood, "fell down" as the song says, in 1176. It was rebuilt by masons in stone. The "fair lady" mentioned in the song was said to have been a virgin who was walled up alive inside one of the bridge's stone columns to appease God's wrath. That was the reason, it was believed, that the bridge lasted so long. The bridge was not replaced until 1832, at which time it was discovered that there were no virgin's bones inside any of the columns. It was replaced not because it was crumbling, but rather because its columns were too close together and did not allow modern ships to pass underneath.

In the fourteenth century the working hours and wages of masons had been set in England by a Statute of Labourers. The masons were well paid. The Black Death plague had recently killed almost half of the population and those among the living with construction skills were short in supply.

The Middle Ages were a time when the Holy Roman Universal Church, which practiced Catholicism and was led by the Pope, controlled Europe. Those who believed other than what the Church taught were forced underground. The only groups that could move freely from town to town without being under Church sanction were the guilds of stonemasons, necessary because they were the only ones with the skills to build churches and cathedrals.

The Masons held their meetings in their lodges. They claimed that they had the skills to do what they did because they possessed architectural knowledge dating back to ancient Egypt and the building of the Pyramids. (These geometrical secrets are now lost, it is said.) There are several stories as to how the Masons came to possess the secret knowledge in the first place. One story says that Abraham, of the Old Testament of the Bible, possessed the knowledge that existed before Noah's great flood, and taught the secrets to the Egyptians of his time. This knowledge was passed down from generation to generation until it got to the Greek philosopher Euclid, who wrote about it and first called it geometry. Geometry was a science that first came to be known during the Roman empire as architecture.

According to Masonic lore, there were Masons as far back as the building of the Tower of Babel and the Temple of Solomon in Jerusalem. These early Masons claimed to have gotten their knowledge from "gods," and that they were the chosen ones to whom the gods shared their secret knowledge. (See also ANUNNAKI.)

According to Manly P. Hall in his book *What the Ancient Wisdom Expects of its Disciple,* "In the remote past the gods walked with men and they chose from among the sons of men the wisest and the truest. With these specially ordained and illumined sons they left the keys of their great wisdom. They ordained these anointed and appointed ones to be priests or mediators between themselves—the gods—and that humanity which had not yet developed the eyes which permitted them to gaze into the face of Truth and live. . . . These illumined ones founded what we know as the Ancient Mysteries. . . . Freemasonry is therefore more than a mere social organization a few centuries old, and can be regarded as a perpetuation of the philosophical mysteries and initiations of the ancients."

During the Middle Ages, the first group to refer to themselves as Freemasons, which was short for the Order of Free and Accepted Masons, were the architects of Lombardy, in northern Italy. The first known written reference to "Freemasons" is a paper on alchemy from the late fifteenth century. Ignoring Masonic beliefs for a moment, most non-Masonic historians believe that the roots of the secret society lie in the Middle Ages with the Knights Templar, a group founded by Godfrey de Bouillon, who led the First Crusade and conquered Jerusalem. The Knights Templar were forced into exile in the mid-fourteenth century and lasted only a few more generations before becoming extinct. According to German Mason Baron Karl Gottlieb von Hund, his order of Freemasonry, known as the Order of the Strict Observance, was ruled by "unseen superiors" who had supplied him with a list of names, all of whom had served as grand masters of the Knights Templar. His list, it is said, is nearly identical to the one discovered in southern France in the twentieth century by Austrian historian Leo Schidlof. The latter list, though it contains the same names, is supposed to be a list of the "Priory of Sion," a list of those who possessed secret knowledge regarding the offspring of Jesus Christ. (The list has gained fame because of its use in Dan Brown's best-selling novel *The Da Vinci Code*.)

It is said that the secret knowledge possessed by the Freemasons that dated back to before the great flood was lost when England's Henry VIII broke away from Rome and its all-powerful church. He formed his own church, the Church of England, and sought to destroy all reminders of Roman Catholicism in England. In the process, many Masonic records were destroyed. During the purge,

Freemasonry changed. The original knowledge of the actual stonemasons (known as operative Masonry) was lost, but a new knowledge, "speculative" Masonry, replaced it. Bits and pieces of the
stone-building knowledge remained in Masonic rituals and symbols.
But, to take the most obvious inference of the term "speculative,"
we must believe that the new Masons were grand masters of invest-
ing money. Under the new, post-Protestant system, the Masons grew
in influence and spread anew from country to country.

According to William T. Still in his book *New World Order: The
Ancient Plan of Secret Societies*, the founder of modern Freemasonry
in England was Sir Francis Bacon, the same man often suspected of
writing some of the world's greatest plays under the pseudonym
William Shakespeare. According to Jim Marrs, there are two books
that describe Bacon's Masonic beliefs. These were *The New Atlantis*,
a book describing a possible paradise on Earth, and *De Sapientia
Veterum*, which means Ancient Wisdom. The utopia Bacon envi-
sioned was the New World, and as we shall see, there is evidence
that what eventually became the United States of America was
formed under Masonic guidelines.

Bacon was a "Grand Commander" of the Rosicrucians during
the late sixteenth century, which used rituals and traditions that theoretically dated back to the Knights Templar and the times of the
Crusades. Bacon's disciples formed an organization after his death
called the Royal Society of London for the Promotion of Natural
Knowledge, which allegedly functioned as a cover for Masonic activities. The Royal Society held their meetings in a building called
Mason's Hall which was on Mason's Alley in London. According to
Albert Gallatin Mackey in his book *The History of Freemasonry*, this
group took on the name Free and Accepted Masons, which was later
shortened to Freemasons. During the first quarter of the seventeenth
century, Rosicrucianism and Freemasonry were practically one and
the same, although today the Rosicrucians and the Masons are considered separate secret societies.

Perhaps following Bacon's plan, Freemasonry was an important
component of America, dating back to the first Jamestown settlers.
These men, who arrived in North America thirty-six years before the
Pilgrims landed at Plymouth Rock, were disciples of Bacon and

Masonry. The head of this group was Sir Walter Raleigh, who was executed in 1618 allegedly for teaching Masonic beliefs, which were considered treason because of their heresy by King James I. King James was correct in that the Masons of the New World were not going to forever be happy as a colony under British rule. By the first quarter of the eighteenth century, the Masonic lodges in America were already scheming to gain independence, although another sixty years would pass before that revolution would occur.

In the early eighteenth century, Masonic lodges had been established in France, but they functioned under the umbrella of the "United Grand Lodge," which was in England. Despite the purging that came with the reign of Henry VIII, Masons still claimed to have knowledge dating back to ancient times. In 1737, a man named Chevalier Andrew Ramsay, who was the tutor of the children of Great Britain's royal family and a high-ranking Freemason, traveled to Paris to deliver a speech at that city's Grand Lodge. Ramsay told the gathering that Freemasonry could trace its roots back to the Greek goddess Diana and the Egyptian goddess Isis. He said that Freemasonry had been "closely associated" with the Knights Templar of the Crusades. Ramsay. was the mouthpiece for Charles Radclyffe and a brother with Isaac Newton in a society called the Philadelphians. (Both Newton and Radclyffe are said to have been grand masters of the Priory of Sion.)

English Freemasons first announced in 1723 that its members could be of any religion. That rule remains true today. How diverse the men are among the higher degrees, of course, is unknown.

In the 1730s, the Holy Roman Emperor—Francis, duke of Lorraine—became the first European prince to publicly announce that he was a Freemason, telling the world that he had been initiated at the Hague in 1731. Because of the resulting publicity, Freemasonry quickly spread. Francis's Viennese court became a center of Masonic activity. In Francis's castle, known as the Hofburg, he maintained a laboratory for his alchemy experiments. One of the greatest accomplishments of secret societies throughout history was the preservation of scientific thought when such thought was considered heresy and punishable by death due to religious dogma.

Some believe that destroying Christianity is the Freemasons' ultimate goal. The Catholic Church in the early eighteenth century agreed with this point of view. On April 28, 1738, Pope Clement XII issued his bull *In Eminenti*, which threatened Catholics who joined the Freemasons with excommunication. The pope called Freemasonry pagan and unlawful.

Freemasonry was spread to the Caribbean by the slave trade, with the first lodge being opened in that region in 1739 in Jamaica. In 1740 a lodge was built on Barbados, and in 1749 Saint Domingue (later known as Haiti) had a lodge.

During the early eighteenth century, the Freemasons included among their numbers men who were called magi, or magicians. (Magic and science, known as natural philosophy, did not diverge until the mid-eighteenth century.) Most notable of the magi was the Count of Saint-Germain, who spoke all European languages. Addressing a French court during the 1740s, he claimed to be hundreds of years old because he had knowledge of an elixir of youth. He claimed to have known Jesus Christ and Cleopatra. He said that he could, among other magical skills, fix the flaws in diamonds. These skills, he said, came from studying the Pyramids. His claims seem ridiculous now, but less so at the time, and he did exert a practical influence over the world. He arranged for the daughter of a friend to be placed on the Russian throne. History came to know her as Catherine the Great. He counted among his friends Casanova, the lover, and Alessandro Cagliostro, a key participant in the French Revolution.

A contemporary of the Count of Saint-Germain was Hayyim Samuel Jacob Falk, who was nearly burned at the stake in Germany for being a sorcerer, but managed to flee to London in 1742, where it is said he introduced the rituals and concepts of the Cabala into Freemason teachings.

Moving to more practical history, the Masons had a strong hand in the American Revolution of 1776 and in the French Revolution that soon followed. By the third decade of the nineteenth century, there were an estimated fifty thousand Freemasons in the United States, many of whom were those who would today be described as the "best and the brightest."

Masons of the revolutionary period are among the most famous men of the time: including George Washington, Benjamin Franklin, Alexander Hamilton, Thomas Jefferson, James Madison, Patrick Henry, John Hancock, Paul Revere. Take a look at today's U.S. currency and the chances are very good that a picture of a dead Mason will be featured. All but one signer of the Declaration of Independence was allegedly a Freemason, although which one he was has been lost to history. The portraits are not the only Masonic things on U.S. currency. There are also Masonic symbols, including the All-Seeing Eye, and such slogans as *Novus Ordo Seclorum* (New World Order).

Another Freemason slogan is *Ordo ab Chao*, which means Order Out of Chaos. This slogan has been interpreted to mean that Masons find opportunity in chaos because it is easy to exploit humanity's need for order.

A Scottish Mason named Archibald Gracie founded the first savings bank in New York. His East River Mansion is the official residence of the mayor of New York City. Gracie was known for his parties, attended by well-known figures such as Washington Irving, James Fenimore Cooper, and Alexander Hamilton.

According to Arthur Edward Waite in his book *A New Encyclopedia of Freemasonry*, the secrecy of the inner workings of the Masonic lodges helped the colonists plot against the British throne without risk. It is believed that the Boston Tea Party was plotted inside a Masonic Lodge.

That the American Revolution was planned by Masons was a secret not only to the British but also to many of the American soldiers who fought in the war. According to William T. Still, "Most [of the American soldiers] believed they were simply involved in the cause of gaining independence from a tyrant. Masonry was to most of them, as it is to most of the membership today, merely a fraternal organization promoting social skills and providing fellowship to its members."

The Great Seal of the United States contains Masonic symbolism. According to Laurence Gardner in his book *Bloodline of the Holy Grail*, the seal is based on alchemical tradition and an allegory of Egyptian medicine.

Gardner writes, "The eagle, the olive branch, the arrows and the pentagrams," Gardner wrote, "are all occult symbols of opposites: good and evil, male and female, war and peace, darkness and light.

On the reverse—as repeated on the dollar bill—is the truncated pyramid, indicating the loss of the Old Wisdom, severed and forced underground by the Church establishment. But above this are rays of ever-hopeful light, incorporating the 'all-seeing eye,' used as a symbol during the French Revolution."

In 1826, one Mason broke the rules of the society and divulged the secrets. His name was Captain William Morgan of Batavia, New York, who wrote a book called *Illustrations of Masonry by one of the Fraternity Who Has Devoted Thirty Years to the Subject*. The book included the society's secret oaths, purposes, handshakes, and symbols.

Morgan wrote, "The bane of our civil institutions is to be found in Masonry, already powerful and daily becoming more so. I owe my country an exposure of its dangers."

Unfortunately, Morgan did not live to see his book in print. Before his exposé could be published, Morgan and his publisher were kidnapped. The publisher was rescued by concerned friends and neighbors who chased the kidnappers, but those holding Morgan got away and the author vanished forever. A Mason named Henry L. Valance confessed on his deathbed years later that he had been involved in Morgan's kidnapping. According to Valance, Morgan met a watery grave when he was dumped into the rapids of the Niagara River and swept over the falls. Although in the years following Morgan's disappearance his fate was officially unknown, it was generally assumed that nothing good had happened to him.

John Quincy Adams, the sixth president of the United States, wrote about Freemasonry and the murder of William Morgan in a letter to W. L. Stone, which is currently in the Rare Book Archive at the University of Rochester in Rochester, New York.

Adams wrote:

Freemasonry, corporate Freemasonry, is chargeable with the stealing of a free citizen, and the murder of a father and husband. The proof of this subject is perfectly conclusive and is to be found in the reports of the trials of the kidnappers of William Morgan, and in the official accounts given by different Special Attorneys.

It is responsible for having baffled inquiry, for having defeated investigation by the removal of witnesses, and for having produced the acquittal of persons notoriously guilty.

It has been decided by Judge Marcy in New York and by two sets of triers at circuit court held by Judge Gardiner in the same state, and by a court in Rhode Island, that the obligations of Freemasons disqualified a man from being an impartial juror in a case where a brother mason was a party; and such undoubtedly is the law of the land.

The Grand Lodge of New York has given one hundred dollars in charity to one of the most guilty kidnappers of Morgan. The Grand Chapter of the same state has given one thousand dollars to aid and sustain other well-known kidnappers and to enable them to escape from justice, at a time when they had no money to bestow in charity to widows and orphans. This has recently been established in the trial of a libel suit brought by Jacob Gould, which was tried at Albany, New York.

But perhaps the most remarkable evidence of the binding force of Masonic obligations and of the real power of the fraternity, is afforded in the conduct of those who control the newspapers of the country.

When the English forger Stephenson was kidnapped in a distant state and brought forcibly to New York, the whole country rang with the alarm which was sounded by the newspapers and every patriot was called on to resent this invasion of personal liberty.

But when a free citizen of America was dragged from his family, forcibly carried through the country and drowned in the deep waters of the Niagara, a death-like silence pervaded the newspapers; or if they spoke, it was to notice the outrage in terms of irony and as a trifling and unimportant affair.

The papers of every party teemed with the most gross misrepresentations; a simultaneous attack was made on all who were engaged in discovering the offenders; fabricated accounts of Morgan having been at different and distant places were incessantly circulated and every effort was made to delude the public and mislead inquiry.

How tremendously powerful must have been that organization, which could produce that shameful treachery of the press to its public duties!

These facts are as notorious as the sun at noon-day and a stronger proof of their general truth cannot be adduced, than the single circumstance that to this day, thousands and millions of reading citizens of this country are ignorant of Morgan's abduction and murder and are totally uninformed of the abominations of Freemasonry.

The resulting scandal caused many men to quit the Masons. Two thousand lodges closed. In New York State, some estimates say that membership dropped from thirty thousand to three hundred because of Morgan's disappearance. And, despite the kidnapping of the publisher and the author, Morgan's book made it into print anyway, in 1827. Among the secrets Morgan divulged was the oath of secrecy every Mason took upon entering the society's first level, "the First Degree of the Blue Lodge." According to Morgan, the oath said the new member was "binding myself under no less penalty than to have my throat cut across, my tongue torn out by the roots, and my body buried in the rough sands of the sea at low-water mark, where the tide ebbs and flows twice in 24 hours." There was no mention of Niagara Falls.

Because of the publication of Morgan's book, the New York State Senate began investigating Freemasonry and determined that Masons could be found at every level of government—including, we must assume, among their own ranks. The President at the time was Andrew Jackson, who was a Mason, and the scandal caused by Morgan's book and disappearance spawned an anti-Mason Party, the nation's first third party, which eventually evolved into the Whig Party.

There is a theory—stated in Stephen Knight's *Jack the Ripper: the Final Solution* and Alan Moore and Eddie Campbell's *From Hell*—that the Jack the Ripper killings, the nineteenth century murders of a series of prostitutes in London, were Masonic ritual murders directed by the British government to cover up a royal family scandal. Jack, it is written, was actually Sir William Gull, Queen Victoria's physician. According to the theory, he was assisted by actor and painter Walter Sickert, who acted as lookout, and coachman John Netley.

Among the conspirators was Sir Charles Warren, the Commissioner of Police who in 1867, according to Michael A. Hoffman, II, "enacted rituals and engaged in extensive work in the Middle East in connection with the Masonic mission to lay the groundwork for the rebuilding of the Temple of Jerusalem. Warren is credited with the rediscovery of the five-hundred-yard 'Hasmonean Tunnel,' which runs adjacent to the Haram al-Sharif, Islam's third-holiest shrine, and is reputed to be under the former site of the Temple of Herod, destroyed in A.D. 70 by Roman legions."

According to Stephen Knight: "Freemasons applaud violence, terror, and crime providing it is carried out in a crafty manner. One section of the (Masonic) notes says humor is all-important and the most appalling crimes may be committed under its cloak. The one (Jack the Ripper) letter likely to have been genuine suggests that Jack the Ripper was going about his crimes in just this way, committing ghoulish murders with a Puckish sense of fun. If Masonic supremacy appears in jeopardy, it is re-established by a show of strength, by crimes of violence, perpetrated to demonstrate . . . the far-reaching power of Freemasonry to initiates the world over."

During the 1880s, the financial district of London, nicknamed "The City," had the highest concentration of Freemasons in the world. There were so many Masons that each bank in the area, which was about a square mile in size, had its own lodge. Lloyd's Bank had the Black Horse Lodge of Lombard Street. The Bank of England had the appropriately named Bank of England Lodge, which dated back to 1788.

The Jack the Ripper crimes, it is said, were committed to cover up the marriage of a member of the royal family to a Catholic commoner. Prince Eddy—the son of the Prince of Wales, who was also the Grand Master of English Freemasonry—had married Annie Elizabeth Crook. Because Eddy was an heir to the throne, he was forbidden to marry a Catholic. In 1888, Annie Crook was kidnapped and forced into a mental institution. There she was drugged and given a crude lobotomy. Annie's friends who knew of her marriage became the victims of Jack the Ripper.

There are indications that the Jack killings might be Masonic rituals. Four of the victims had their throats cut from left to right. Some of the victims had their intestines removed and flung over their shoulders—a reference, it is said, to "three unworthy assassins" of Masonic lore, Jubela, Jubelo, and Jubelum, who were ritually murdered in such a fashion. The trio, ritual murderers who were ritually murdered, were known as the "Juwes," which is not a reference to the Jewish people. Catherine Eddowes, a Jack victim, was placed at the entrance to Mitre Square, home of the Mitre Tavern, meeting spot of several Masonic lodges. These lodges included those named Hiram, Union, and Joppa. Masonic mythology has it that the Juwes were killed on the coast of Joppa. Catherine Eddowes' blood-soaked apron was found in a hallway of a nearby building. Above the apron, written in chalk on the wall, were the words, "The Juwes are the men that will not be blamed for nothing." Although this message was ordered erased by Sir Charles Warren, it was put into a police report which survived. After the murders, there was an item in a London newspaper stating that Jack the Ripper was a man who was nicknamed "Leather Apron," an apparent reference to the fact that ancient Masons wore leather aprons.

It should be noted that this is just one of many theories regarding the identity and motives of history's first globally notorious serial killer.

By the end of the eighteenth century, there were Masonic Lodges in China, with meetings attended by Chinese Masons. They called the deity the "First Builder." It was during the nineteenth century that the Freemasons most grew in numbers. As the British Empire grew, so did Freemasonry.

During the nineteenth century, and even into the twentieth, many small-town churchyards would refuse to bury actors and other "show business" personnel in consecrated ground. One of the attractions the Masons had for traveling men such as railroaders, show folk, and circus and carnival performers is that they offered a burial service for members, no matter where or how far from home they might expire. Especially back in the early twentieth century, railroaders, show people, and circus folk made up a large proportion of Masonry. In the last few years, the most widely known new Mason is *Seinfeld*'s "Kramer," Michael Richards, who in an interview said that he was inspired to join because his idol, Red Skelton, had been a member.

Secret society theorist Michael A. Hoffman believes that "alchemy," a term used frequently by secret societies, is symbolic

and does not literally mean attempts to transform lead into gold.
The word, he says, refers to a sort of human alchemy, the program-
ming of people through mass mind control, whereby the base elements
of mankind are transformed into something to enhance the
riches of the uppermost class. This is done by frightening those base
elements into inactivity and inaction through "messages of pure
terror," encoded messages (which he called "twilight language") that
are communicated subliminally in the media of the day. People
whose minds are controlled in this fashion display three destructive
symptoms: (1) amnesia; (2) abulia (loss of will); and (3) apathy.

According to Masonic tradition, the secret identity of Satan is
symbolized as coming from the star Sirius personified by the ancient
Egyptian goddess Isis, who was known for her ability to use "words
of power." According to Robert K.G. Temple, in his book *The Sirius
Mystery*: "The heliacal rising (morning rising in the East) of Sirius
was so important to the ancient Egyptians . . . that gigantic temples
were constructed with their main aisles oriented precisely towards
the spot on the horizon where Sirius would appear. . . . The light of
Sirius would be channeled along the corridor (due to the precise
location) to flood the altar in the inner sanctum as if a pin-pointed
spotlight had been switched on. This blast of light focused from a
single star was possible because of the orientation being so incredi-
bly precise and because the temple would be otherwise in total darkness within. In a huge, utterly dark temple, the light of one star
focused solely on the altar must have made quite an impact on those
present." The pentagram is called in Freemasonry the "blazing star,"
and it has been said that the Sirius is the "Great Architect" of
Freemasonry.

Alchemy, says Hoffman, had three goals, all of which were
achieved in the twentieth century. They were:

1. The creation and destruction of primordial matter, which
   was achieved through the explosion of the first atomic bomb
   at the Trinity site near the 33rd parallel in 1945.

2. The Killing of the Divine King, achieved in Dallas, Texas, in
   1963, with the assassination of U.S. President John F.
   Kennedy. (The killing took place near the Trinity River, just
   before the president's limousine went under a Triple Under-

pass, ten miles south of the 33rd parallel. JFK's assassination took place in Dealey Plaza, which was the site of Dallas's first Masonic temple.)

3. The bringing of Prima Materia to Prima Terra, achieved when man walked on the Moon in 1969 and returned moon rocks to Earth. Edwin A. "Buzz" Aldrin, the second man to walk on the moon, carried a flag with symbols of the Knights Templar—a two-headed eagle—with him to the Moon. That flag later was on display at the Masonic grand lodge in Washington, D.C.

Famous Freemasons include U.S. Presidents James Monroe, James K. Polk, James Buchanan, Andrew Jackson, Andrew Johnson, John Garfield, William Howard Taft (whose father was also co-founder of Skull & Bones), Warren G. Harding, Harry S Truman, Gerald R. Ford, Theodore Roosevelt, Franklin D. Roosevelt. Others included Davy Crockett, Jim Bowie, Douglas MacArthur, J. Edgar Hoover, and Hubert Humphrey. In Europe, notable Freemasons included Wolfgang Amadeus Mozart and Johann Wolfgang von Goethe.

Important men of business have been Freemasons. These include financier John Jacob Astor; car manufacturers Henry Ford, Walter P. Chrysler, and Ransom E. Olds; razor-blade mogul King C. Gillette; banker Andrew W. Mellon; and department store founder James C. Penney.

Big names in aviation were Freemasons. These included Charles Lindbergh, the first man to fly solo across the Atlantic Ocean; Edward V. Rickenbacker, the United States' premier flying ace during World War I and Indianapolis 500 race-car driver; John Glenn, the first American to orbit the Earth in outer space and later a U.S. Senator; Mercury astronauts Virgil "Gus" Grissom, and Leroy Gordon Cooper; and the fourth man to walk on the Moon, James B. Irwin.

Gun designers Samuel Colt and Richard J. Gatling were Masons. Franz Anton Mesmer, who introduced hypnotism to the medical world, was an Austrian who moved to the United States and joined a lodge in Philadelphia, Pennsylvania. Dr. Charles H. Mayo, of the Mayo Clinic in Rochester, Minnesota, was a Mason. The man who designed the sleeping car for trains, George M. Pullman, was a member. Hotelier Charles H. Hilton and African American educator Booker T. Washington were members.

Hollywood has always had its share of Masons, dating back to the days of the first silent movies made there. Members included Cecil B. DeMille, MGM's Louis B. Meyer, Florenz Ziegfeld, D. W. Griffith, Twentieth Century-Fox co-founder Darryl F. Zanuck, and Warner Brothers' Jack L. Warner.

Among the actors who were members were Harold Lloyd, W. C. Fields, Douglas Fairbanks, Sr., Al Jolson, Clark Gable, John Wayne, Tom Mix, Oliver Hardy, Ernest Borgnine, Eddie Cantor, Audie Murphy, Arthur Godfrey, Red Skelton, and Roy Rogers.

Composers and musicians who were Masons include Count Basie, Paul Whiteman, Nat King Cole, Duke Ellington, Louis Armstrong, John Philip Sousa, Irving Berlin, and George M. Cohan.

Professional athletes and sports owners who became Masons include Branch Rickey, Rogers Hornsby, Ty Cobb, Sugar Ray Robinson, Jack Johnson, and Jack Dempsey.

Among the circus performers who became members were the two-foot-tall midget Charles S. Stratton, better known as General Tom Thumb, and Robert Pershing, the nine-foot giant.

Famous cowboys who went into show business and became Masons, were "Buffalo Bill" William F. Cody and Kit Carson.

According to Ralph A. Epperson in his book *Masonry: Conspiracy Against Christianity*, the big secret at the top levels of the society is that the Masons worship Lucifer. Another theory is that the Masons are dualists, that they believe in the equal power of good and evil. Some feel that the inner core worships science and believes that a common geometric law rules the universe, from the simplest atom to the universe itself.

Some feel that the reason Freemasonry is so vague about its *raison d'être* is that it wants that very reason for existence to remain flexible. It is a club to join powerful men together so that whatever needs to be accomplished can be accomplished while hidden from the thoroughfares of public knowledge.

Some believe that, because of the importance of the number thirty-three in Freemasonry, that the geographical 33rd parallel of latitude is also of importance. These conspiracy theorists point out that although much of the world's wealth exists above the 33rd parallel, most of the world's population lives below it. It has also been stated that many important murders, including that of President John F. Kennedy in Dallas, took place on or near the 33rd parallel. It has also been noted that the Bermuda Triangle, the Pyramids of Egypt and, in theory, Atlantis, are also on or in close proximity to that supposedly magic line.

According to Day Williams' *Masons and Mystery at the 33rd Parallel* (www.daywilliams.com/masons_mystery_33rd_parallel.html; accessed February 26, 2004): "The number thirty-three is seen in different areas of life: The human foot has thirty-three muscles. The number of turns in a complete sequence of human DNA equals thirty-three. The Holy Bible, New International Version, uses the word 'thirty-three' seven times in seven verses. King David reigned in Jerusalem thirty-three years (2 Samuel 5:5, 1 Kings 2:11, 1 Kings 5:16, 1 Chronicles 3:4, and 1 Chronicles 29:27). Genesis 46:15 states: 'These sons and daughters of his [Israel's or Jacob's] were thirty-three in all'). Leviticus Chapter 12 discusses purification after childbirth. Leviticus 12:4 states that after the boy is circumcised on the eighth day, 'Then the woman must wait thirty-three days to be purified from her bleeding. She must not touch anything sacred or go to the sanctuary until her days of her purification are over.' Jesus Christ, having begun his three-year ministry at about the age of thirty (Luke 3:23), must have died on the cross and risen again at the age of thirty-three. The Catholic Italian poet Dante Alighieri (1265–1321) divided his *Divine Comedy* into one hundred Cantos: one Canto for the introduction, thirty-three Cantos for the *Inferno*, thirty-three Cantos for the *Purgatorio*, and thirty-three Cantos for the *Paradiso*. Masons and their confederates may note that Dante placed the traitors to their guests in a deep pit of Hell in his thirty-third Canto of the Inferno."

During much of the twentieth century, after the invention of the automobile, but before the construction of the interstate highway system, the favorite route linking the Midwest with the West was Route 66. A television show and hit song by that name was made and the road came to symbolize nomadic liberty. Drivers, it was said, "got their kicks on Route 66." The story goes that the road was built along Freemason specifications and was filled with symbolism. The route—from Chicago, Illinois, to Barstow, California—followed a road constructed in 1857 by Lieutenant Edward Beale and the U.S. Camel Corps, which in turn followed an ancient trail known as *Jornada del muerto*, the "Journey of Death."

The Freemasons recently made the news in the New York City area because of a tragic accident inside a Masonic lodge—an incident that inadvertently gave the public some insight into Masonic initiation rituals. On March 8, 2004, forty-seven-year-old William James was shot in the head and killed with a gun that was supposed to be filled with blanks. James was undergoing the rite for the "Fellow Craft Club," a division of the Southside Masonic Lodge Number 493 in Patchogue, Long Island, New York, when the accident occurred in the Oak Street Lodge, a one-story building with the windows bricked over. James was the first of two men who were being initiated that night. After walking across a narrow plank while blindfolded, James stood in the middle of the room facing the ritual leader. In order to frighten the prospective member, a gun loaded with blanks was to be aimed at James and fired from twenty feet away. The shot was to have signified the previously mentioned "Lord thundering down his wrath upon the children of Israel for their disobedience unto him." But the shooter, seventy-six-year-old Albert Eid, a retired oil-burner mechanic, pulled out the wrong weapon, a loaded .32—and killed James with the shot. Police said the lights were on at the time of the accident and James was not wearing a blindfold. The bullet entered James through the nose. When police entered the lodge they also found a nine-foot-tall guillotine and several rat traps. The rat traps were also used to startle initiates. It was unclear what the guillotine was for.

After the shooting, the Masons who were present attempted to render CPR. One ran upstairs to call the police but found that the phone was out of order. Another Mason ran outside and flagged down a police car. Police arrested Eid and charged him with second-degree manslaughter. Eid wore his blue Masonic jacket during his arraignment. He was released on $2,500 bail.

Richard Fletcher of the Masonic Information Center told reporters that there are no official Masonic practices that involve guillotines or guns. Fletcher said, "Sometimes lodges come into habits on their own, and no one knows about them. We were formed in the Middle Ages, before there were guns."

One member of the Patchogue lodge, Michael Paquette, told reporters that when he was initiated into the group in 1999, two mouse traps were placed before him, and he was told that one worked, and one was broken, he said. Another member tested the broken trap, then—as an exercise in trust—told Mr. Paquette to touch the live one. He did, and it was also a dud.

"It was really harmless things," Paquette explained. "It was just for you to be there and realize you were in good hands, and you didn't have to fear anything."

James was buried on March 12, 2004. Although two hundred mourners attended the ceremony, none of them were Masons. Masons were banned by James' widow, Susan James.

About the shooter, Mrs. James said, "The detectives said that he was very distraught and wanted to speak to me, but I can't do that yet. Whatever possessed him to bring a real gun? That's my big question, and I can't get any answers."

A friend of the family likened Masonic rites to college fraternity hazing, saying, "What they did was totally unnecessary. It was something that should have been left behind in college. There's no excuse."

On March 14, Carl Fitje, state grand master of the Free and Accepted Masons, suspended all 170 members of Lodge 493. Fitje appointed a panel of six Masons, all lawyers, to investigate the incident.

"We are deeply anguished and outraged because a fellow Mason has died in an incident that never should have happened," Fitje said. "No Mason can engage in or participate in any ritual that varies from the ritual approved under Grand Lodge Law. Firearms do not, and never have, played any role in any Masonic ritual in the State of New York."

The Patchogue incident was not the worst violence to occur inside a Masonic Temple during March 2004. On March 10, two days after the Long Island shooting, two bombs exploded inside the three-story Masonic Temple in the Kartal district of Istanbul, Turkey. The two blasts took place one right after the other at about 10:30 P.M. Suicide bombers were believed to be behind the blasts, which killed two and injured six. Istanbul Governor Muammer Guler said that two persons came to the Lodge and shot the security guard in his feet. Later the terrorists opened fire on the building from the window and entered the building's restaurant part. One terrorist was killed when he detonated the bomb on himself at the entrance, and one waiter who was near him also died in the explosion. The other terrorist was severely wounded when his explosive ignited. The surviving terrorist told authorities his name was Abdullah Islam. The explosions occurred near the entrance and the wounded were all seated nearby. Apart from broken windows, the building did not suffer much damage. Nobody claimed responsibility for the attack on the Lodge.

The Patchogue Southside Masons once numbered as many as five hundred members but membership there and at other Masonic lodges has fallen over the years. There are now about 150 members. In 2003, the number of Masons in New York State rose to 67,000, the first time that number had not declined in ten years.

The Freemasons' slogan is "Liberty, Equality, and Fraternity."

The most famous Masonic symbol, one that appears on the outside of lodges in full public view, is the letter G inside a square and a compass. It is said that the G stands for Geometry. According to secret-society historian Jim Marrs there are an estimated one hundred thousand lodges and six million Freemasons in the world today.

See also ANUNNAKI; ILLUMINATI; KNIGHTS TEMPLAR; PROPAGANDA DUE; ROSICRUCIANS; ROSSLYN CHAPEL; SHRINERS; SKULL & BONES; V.M.R.D.

G

Gentlemen's Club of Spalding   See PRIORY OF SION.

German Order   See THULE SOCIETY.

Golden Dawn Society   An offshoot of an English Rosicrucian sect, the Golden Dawn Society was born in 1887. A small group, they were said to include some of England's greatest minds. Members practiced ceremonial magic and sought occult powers. One alleged member of the group was occultist Wynn Westcott. The group was in contact with German sects in pre-Nazi Europe that were said to later influence Adolf Hitler, such as Rudolph Steiner's famous anthroposophical movement (awareness of one's humanity). In the twentieth century, the Golden Dawn Society was led by Aleister Crowley, and then by S.L. Mathers. The group claimed to be part of a "wisdom tradition" that dated back to the Knights Templar, and, it was implied, even further into ancient history. When Crowley left the Golden Dawn to join OTO, he published the Golden Dawn's secrets.
See also OTO; ROSICRUCIANS.

Grand Lodge of Cairo   Eleventh-century secret society said to possess ancient knowledge passed down through the generations from the earliest days of the Old Testament. It was after studying the ways of this secret society that Hasan bin Sabah determined the structure for his society of murderers known as the Hashishan, or the Assassins.
See also ASSASSINS.

Grand Orient of Italy See PROPAGANDA DUE.

Great White Brotherhood of the Therapeutate Egyptian group that taught the "mysteries of life." Some have called this group the original Rosicrucians, and it has been said that Jesus himself was initiated into this group and progressed through its degrees until he was a "master."

See also ESSENES.

Green Dragon, Order of the Japanese secret society dedicated to the mastery of the human body—and of the Time Organism, or the Etheric Body. Masters of this secret art, it is said, acquire great power, including the power of prophecy. They are said to be able to control the elements within their bodies. One exercise used to develop the Green Dragon powers is to make a seed germinate through willpower alone. Failure to accomplish a task is met with severe punishments.

It is believed that only three Westerners have ever been accepted as members of the Green Dragon Society. One was Karl Haushofer, a military attaché based in Tokyo before World War I. Haushofer later became a Nazi, a member of the Vril Society, and was a supporter of Hitler's racist policies. According to legend, the Order of the Green Dragon had communicated telepathically with a similar right-wing-oriented group of occultists in Tibet known as the Society of Green Men. In 1944, Haushofer's son was involved in an assassination attempt on Adolf Hitler. At the end of the war, Haushofer killed his wife and then committed suicide.

See also GREEN MEN, SOCIETY OF; VRIL SOCIETY.

Green Men, Society of The Nazi occult group known as the Vril Society traveled to Tibet between 1926 and 1942 trying to contact the Cave Oracles of Tibet. During these expeditions they contacted a group of Tibetan monks known as the Adepts of Agarthi. In 1929, some of the adepts (alchemists) returned to Germany with the Germans and formed a lodge called the Society of Green Men in Berlin. The leader of the Green Men was called the Monk of the Green Gloves/Hands. He was known for his ability to see the future and became a consultant to Adolf Hitler. According to legend, the Green Men had communicated telepathically with the Order of the Green Dragon. Green Dragon and Green Men members met for the first time in Germany during World War II in order to help the Nazi cause. The Green Men, under heavy Nazi security, attempted to will German men to mutate into Aryan supermen. Because the Green Men failed in this task, and were not helping with the war effort, they had fallen out of favor with the Nazis by 1943. The monks were put on concentration camp rations. When the Russians entered Berlin they discovered the bodies of the Tibetan monks, all of whom had committed suicide.

See also GREEN DRAGON, ORDER OF THE; VRIL SOCIETY.

H

Hashishin   See ASSASSINS.

Hells Angels   The Hells Angels Motorcycle Club was formed in 1948 in San Bernardino, California. Since then, chapters of the club have opened across the United States and around the world. While publicly presenting itself as a club of motorcycle enthusiasts who enjoy riding Harley-Davidson motorcycles, frequent arrests have shown that the club is a front for organized crime activities, including the illegal distribution of firearms and the sale of methamphetamine (crank) drugs. Defenders of the organization say that 99 percent of the members are law-abiding.

The most famous member of the group was former Oakland-branch leader Sonny Barger, who arranged for the Hells Angels to supply security at the ill-fated Altamont concert featuring the Rolling Stones in 1969. The Hells Angels (there is no apostrophe in the name of the club) accepted five hundred dollars' worth of beer to police the concert, but one member of the club stabbed a spectator to death in front of the stage after the victim pulled a gun.

Membership is achieved through invitation only. "We don't recruit members, we recognize 'em," is the motto. New members must endure a hazing-type initiation process. Members get to wear denim jackets with the Hells Angels logo (the groups' "colors") sewn onto the back.

In 2002, three people were killed and thirteen more injured in Laughlin, Nevada, during a gunfight between members of the Hells Angels and a rival group known as the Mongols.

Hermetic Brotherhood of Light   See OTO.

Hibernians   See MOLLY MAGUIRES.

Holy Grail   The traditional story of the Holy Grail is this: The gospel says that Joseph of Arimathea acquired the sacred cup that Jesus touched to his lips at the last supper. Following that meal, which Jesus partook of with his disciples, Jesus was tried and then crucified. Joseph of Arimathea received permission from Pontius Pilate to take the body of Christ to his own tomb for burial. At that time, Joseph of Arimathea gathered up Jesus' blood in the chalice. The cup was taken by Joseph of Arimathea to what is now Great Britain and he kept it until he died. After his death, it was handed down to succeeding generations of his family. Its location is unknown, but it was said to have been kept in a castle surrounded by a wasteland and guarded by a custodian called the Fisher King, who suffered from a wound that would not heal.

Some believe the Knights Templar had possession of the Holy Grail. The search for the Holy Grail was the primary quest of the mythological King Arthur and the Knights of the Round Table.

Another story says that the Holy Grail was taken to Nova Scotia in 1398.

An alternative version of the story is that the Holy Grail was not a real cup full of blood at all, but rather a symbol for Mary Magdalene, who carried Jesus' bloodline through his children, a secret that is preserved through the Priory of Sion.

See also KNIGHTS TEMPLAR; PRIORY OF SION.

Hospitallers of Jerusalem   See THE SOVEREIGN ORDER OF SAINT JOHN OF JERUSALEM.

Hospital of St. Mary of the Germans of Jerusalem   See TEUTONIC KNIGHTS.

House of Knowledge   See GRAND LODGE OF CAIRO.

I

Illuminati Founded in Bavaria in 1776 by a law professor named Adam Weishaupt, the Illuminati is made of up individuals claiming to have superhuman knowledge—intelligence granted to them by a mysterious "higher source." Weishaupt taught Canon Law at Ingolstadt University in Bavaria, Germany. Weishaupt had previously studied to become a Jesuit priest and became angry with the Catholic Church after Pope Clement XIV banned the Jesuits from the church in 1773. Because Weishaupt was devoted to the "ancient mysteries," his Illuminati kept time using the Persian calendar.

Weishaupt wrote: "Man is not bad, except as he is made so by arbitrary morality. He is bad because religion, the state, and bad examples pervert him. When at last reason becomes the religion of men, then will the problem be solved."

He also wrote, "The great strength of our Order lies in concealment. Let it never appear in any place in its own name, but always covered by another name, and another occupation. None is fitter than the three lower degrees of Freemasonry; the public is accustomed to it, expect little from it, and therefore takes little notice of it. Next to this, the form of a learned or literary society is best suited to our purpose. . . . By establishing reading societies and subscription libraries . . . we may turn the public mind which way we will. In like manner we must try to obtain an influence in . . . all offices which have any effect, either in forming, or in managing, or even in directing, the mind of man."

He described the Illuminati's pyramid chain of command thusly: "I have two immediately below me into whom I breathe my whole spirit, and each of these two has again two others, and so on. In this way I can set a thousand men in motion and on fire in the simplest manner, and in this way one must impart orders and operate on politics." The structure of the Illuminati was completely secret until Bavarian police raided their lodge and confiscated secret documents.

The Illuminati Order was outlawed in Bavaria in 1783. Because of this, many members left Germany. So the law against the society ended up unintentionally spreading the philosophy as new Illuminati lodges opened across Europe and in America. By the end of that decade, the Illuminati had ceased to function in Germany but had become a global organization.

The Illuminati helped disguise themselves by blending with the higher degrees of Freemasonry. It is suspected that this process began at a Masonic convention of Wilhelmsbad in Hesse in 1782. The convention was attended by Masons from all over Europe and presided over by the Duke of Brunswick. The blended secret societies became known as Illuminized Freemasonry, and their headquarters were established in Frankfurt, Germany, headquarters of German finance. Among the founders of that lodge were representatives of the Rothschild family, the ultra-rich banking family often suspected of plotting to control the world.

Though the Illuminati became all but invisible once merging into Freemasonry, it is suspected that they continue to operate today, turning "the public mind which way we will."

See also ANUNNAKI; FREEMASONS.

Imperial Klans of America   See KU KLUX KLAN.

Institute for Advanced Study (IAS)   Splinter group of the Round Table groups formed in Princeton, New Jersey, following World War I.

See also ROUND TABLE; ROYAL INSTITUTE OF INTERNATIONAL AFFAIRS.

J

Jacobin Club   During the French Revolution (1787–99), revolutionary leaders sought to overthrow the monarchy of King Louis XVI. The revolution, some say, was caused by the workings of a secret society called the Jacobin Club, which was made up of French Masons, most notably the Duke of Orleans, and German Illuminati. According to one version of history, the Duke of Orleans—the grand master of the Grand Orient Lodge of Freemasons—bought up all of France's grain in 1789 and then hid it away, causing a famine. He then blamed the famine on the king. In other words, he created a problem so that he could exploit it.

The Jacobins were named after the seventeenth-century English king James II, whose name in Latin was Jacobus. James was a Catholic Stuart who was evicted from the throne by his Protestant son-in-law, William of Orange. James fled to France where he gathered up Freemason support, and it is said that Freemason rituals in England were altered to support James' agenda. These rituals became known as the "Scottish rite."

It is said that the French ambassador to the United States at the time, Edmond Genet, attempted to cause revolt in America at the same time with a society based on the Jacobins, an attempt which spawned the Alien and Sedition Acts in the U.S.

See also DEMOCRATIC CLUBS; FREEMASONS; ILLUMINATI.

Jekyll Island Group   On November 22, 1910—precisely fifty-three years before the assassination of President Kennedy—a group of seven men, who represented 25 percent of the world's wealth, met on Jekyll Island to plot the formation of a central bank.

The men were Frank A. Vanderlip, later president of the National City Bank in New York, who was there representing the Rockefellers; Abraham Piatt Andrew, then the assistant secretary of the U.S. Treasury; Henry P. Davison, representing J. P. Morgan; Charles D. Norton, president of the First National Bank; Benjamin Strong, another Morgan assistant; Nelson W. Aldrich, chairman of the National Monetary Commission and father-in-law of John D. Rockefeller, Jr.; and Paul Mortiz Warburg, representing the M. M. Warburg banks of Germany and The Netherlands.

Their plot developed into the Federal Reserve Act, which was signed into law by President Woodrow Wilson on December 23, 1913. The Federal Reserve was a centralized bank that was privately owned, from which the United States would borrow money.

It has been said that, with the establishment of the Federal Reserve, a secret government comprised of the world's richest men was legitimized. The Federal Reserve System prints U.S. currency. The only president to seriously suggest changing the Federal Reserve system and to print U.S. money that was not a part of the Federal Reserve system was Kennedy.

According to A. Ralph Epperson in his book *The Unseen Hand: An Introduction to the Conspiratorial View of History*, the billionaire banker Mayer Rothschild once said, "Permit me to control the money of a nation, and I care not who makes its laws."

See also FEDERAL RESERVE.

Jesuits   Formed in 1540 as the Society of Jesus, the Jesuits were a military order formed by the Vatican to battle enemies of the Church and to protect the Church's secrets. Their founder was Ignatius of Loyola, a former soldier who had become a priest. Illuminati founder Adam Weishaupt copied the structure of the Jesuits when forming his own society. Over the next two hundred years, the Jesuits became increasingly independent of the Vatican, until the order was banned in 1773 by Pope Clement XIV. In 1814, Pope Pius VII reinstated the Jesuits.

Johannites   Medieval sect that believed that John the Baptist, and not Jesus, had been the true messiah. They believed that Jesus had been a mortal man and that the story of the Immaculate Conception was fictional, meant to explain Jesus' illegitimacy. The Johannites' beliefs blended with those of the Knights Templar during the first years of the Templars' official existence.

See also KNIGHTS TEMPLAR.

K

Kappa Beta Phi   Wall Street's most secret society. Formed in 1929, this group includes more than 250 of the New York financial district's former chiefs and executives. When forced into public relations, the group portrays itself as a Wall Street version of the Friar's Club, which has campy rites that allow members to poke fun at each other and themselves.

Members are strongly encouraged to keep the rituals of the group secret, although it is unclear if they are forced to take terrible oaths as in other secret societies. One member told a reporter, "It's a secret society. I can't tell you any more, or it wouldn't be a secret."

Publicly at least, the group has no headquarters. Dues are two thousand dollars per year, quite reasonable for a group of the financially elite. The group meets in an annual dinner in January at the St. Regis Hotel. Since membership is for life, members get to join in the fun, even after their careers on Wall Street are through. Such was the case in 2004 when Richard A. Grasso, who had been fired as the chairman and chief executive of the New York Stock Exchange, receiving a 139.5 million–dollar pay package in the process, nonetheless got to attend the dinner where he took a good-natured ribbing.

Another butt of jokes at the 2004 dinner was New York City mayor Michael Bloomberg, a multi-billionaire who is perhaps most famous for being the man who banned smoking in all public places in New York. At the dinner cigars were passed out and many members took great pleasure in breaking municipal law in the mayor's presence—perhaps even in his face.

Both men and women are allowed into the society. One of the new 2004 inductees or "neophytes" as they are called—was Diana

L. Taylor, who was both the New York State banking superintendent
and Mayor Bloomberg's girlfriend. At the dinner, the neophytes performed a song-and-dance routine. Taylor and her fellow neophytes
donned striped prison garb to do a routine about questionable Wall
Street practices. During the show, members threw their dinner rolls
at the performers.

Though none of the performers are told to quit their day jobs in
favor of show business, the performances are taken relatively seriously. Theater coaches are provided and performers are expected to
rehearse.

According to the *New York Times* (February 6, 2004), "The customs of the club are in many ways archaic. The top officers are
referred to as Grand Swipe and Grand Loaf, and its motto is Latin
for 'We Sing and We Drink.' Members are strongly encouraged to
maintain a bond of secrecy with regard to club rituals and the fun is
had at members' expense."

Other members of the society include David H. Komansky,
former chairman and chief executive of Merrill Lynch; Kenneth G.
Langone, who was from 1999 to 2003 the chairman of the New York
Stock Exchange's compensation committee; Martin Lipton, founding
partner of Wachtell Lipton Rosen & Katz; Sanford I. Weill, chairman of Citigroup; James E. Cayne, CEO of Bear Stearns; Laurence
D. Fink, CEO of BlackRock. In 2004, the Grand Swipe was said to
be Ronald E. Blaylock, CEO of Blaylock & Partners and an African
American. Blaylock replaced the 2003 Grand Swipe, Alexandra
Lebenthal, president of the municipal bonds brokerage firm Lebenthal & Company.

Knights Hospitallers   See THE SOVEREIGN ORDER OF SAINT JOHN OF
JERUSALEM.

Knights of Christ   In the early fourteenth century, when the Pope
ordered that the Knights Templar be destroyed throughout Christendom for heresy, the resulting crusade was only really effective in
France. Elsewhere, the Templars were able to go into hiding by joining other secret societies. In Portugal, they managed to avoid persecution simply by changing their name to the Knights of Christ.
Under this new name, the order continued to function for the next

three hundred years. The Knights of Christ were sailors, and formed a world-class navy. Prince Henry the Navigator is said to have been the grand master of the order and Vasco de Gama was also a member. Knights of Christ ships had white sails emblazoned with a red *pattée* cross. This was the same symbol that appeared on the *Nina*, *Pinta*, and *Santa Maria* under the command of Christopher Columbus in 1492. Columbus, it is believed, was married to the daughter of a Knight of Christ, and took advantage of the group's navigating skills.

See also KNIGHTS TEMPLAR.

Knights of Columbus   The Knights of Columbus was founded on October 2, 1881, in the basement of St. Mary's Church on Hillhouse Avenue in New Haven, Connecticut, by Father Michael J. McGivney. The group has grown over the years to become the world's largest Catholic family fraternal service organization.

Incorporated in 1882, the Knights are named after Christopher Columbus, whom they credit with bringing Christianity to the Americas. The group is known for their support of the Roman Catholic Church, programs of evangelization and Catholic education, civic involvement and aid to those in need. There is also a life insurance program to provide for the widows and orphans of deceased members. The governing body of the Knights of Columbus is the Supreme Council.

In 1954, the Knights of Columbus held a successful campaign, in conjunction with other Christian groups, to have the words "under God" added to the Pledge of Allegiance.

Today, there are twelve thousand councils and 1.6 million members throughout the United States, Canada, the Philippines, Mexico, the Dominican Republic, Puerto Rico, Panama, the Bahamas, the Virgin Islands, Guatemala, Guam, and Saipan.

Knights of Cyprus   See THE SOVEREIGN ORDER OF SAINT JOHN OF JERUSALEM.

Knights of Jerusalem   See THE SOVEREIGN ORDER OF SAINT JOHN OF JERUSALEM.

Knights of John See THE SOVEREIGN ORDER OF SAINT JOHN OF
JERUSALEM.

Knights of Malta Group that developed out of the Sovereign
Order of Saint John of Jerusalem (the Hospitallers), after a Turkish
raid forced the Hospitallers to move from Crete to Malta. When
other groups such as the Cathars and the Knights Templar were
being eradicated by the Roman Church, the Knights of Malta
avoided this by aligning themselves with the Church.

As recently as the twentieth century, the Knights of Malta have
been caught attempting coups. In the early 1930s, John J. Raskob,
who was one of the thirteen founding fathers of the American order
of the Knights of Malta, plotted to topple the presidency of President
Franklin D. Roosevelt, but the scheme was foiled when one of his
own ranks blew the whistle. Saving F.D.R. was Knight of Malta
Marine Major General Smedley Butler.

Two Knights of Malta have become the United States Director of
Central Intelligence, John McCone and William Casey.

In the 1980s, an Italian Masonic Lodge infiltrated by Knights of
Malta and run by Licio Gelli became what was called by historian
Jim Marrs a "worldwide fascist conspiracy." Gelli, Marrs says, was in
league with the Mafia, the Vatican Bank, and the CIA, and was conspiring to overthrow the Italian government. The plan, Marrs says,
called for fabricating leftist terrorism in Italy until the people
demanded a fascist takeover. Today, Knights of Malta are thought
to be a principal liaison between the CIA and the Vatican.

The Knights of Malta still exist, headquartered in Rome where,
like the Vatican, they are recognized as a sovereign nation by more
than forty countries.

The Sovereign Order of Saint John of Jerusalem is a Protestant
offshoot of the Knights of Malta, headquartered in London.

According to Albert G. Mackey, M.D., in his 1925 book *Encyclopedia of Freemasonry and Its Kindred Sciences*, "This Order, which at
various times in the progress of its history received the names of
Knights Hospitallers, Knights of St. John of Jerusalem, Knights of
Rhodes, and lastly, Knights of Malta, was one of the most important
of the religious and military orders of knighthood which sprang into

existence during the Crusades which were instituted for the recovery of the Holy Land. It owes its origin to the Hospitallers of Jerusalem, that wholly religious and charitable Order which was established at Jerusalem, in 1048, by pious merchants of Amalfi for the succor of poor and distressed Latin pilgrims. . . . The Organization of the Order in its days of prosperity was very complicated, partaking of both a monarchial and a republican character. Over all presided a Grand Master, who, although invested with extensive powers, was still controlled by the legislative action of the General Chapter. . . . There are now two bodies—one Catholic and the other Protestant, but each repudiates the other. . . . The degree of Knight of Malta is conferred in the United States as 'an appendant Order' in a Commandery of Knights Templar. There is a ritual attached to the degree, but very few are in possession of it, and it is generally communicated after the candidate has been created a Knights Templar. . . ."

According to the website www.cephasministry.com/nwo_christian_ right_cnp_pope_malta.html (accessed February 27, 2004) and a Cold War essay entitled *The Christian Right, the Pope, the Knights of Malta and the CNP*:

> The Knights of Malta are the militia of the Pope, and are sworn to total obedience by a blood oath which is taken extremely seriously and to the death. The Pope as the head of the Vatican is also the head of a foreign national power. This has virtually nothing to do with the Roman Catholic religion, and everything to do with being a participant in one of the four major "player-organizations" for world domination— those players being British Freemasonry, French Freemasonry, International Zionism, and the Vatican. As a member of the Knights of Malta, and by virtue of your blood oath of obedience to the Pope, you are required to support to the death the desires of the head of the Order of the Knights of Malta—in this case, Pope John Paul II—over and above any other allegiance you may feel or pretend to feel toward any other loyalty—such as a loyalty to the Constitution for the United States of America. Those who are presently members of the Knights of Malta must on penalty of death support those policies advocated by the Vatican. It is not hard for them to do

this. They BELIEVE in these policies and principles. The policies which are espoused and proclaimed by Pope John Paul II are as follows:

1. End of sovereignty for the United States and other countries.
2. End of absolute property rights.
3. End of all gun rights.
4. The new International Economic Order (world government).
5. The redistribution of wealth and jobs.
6. Calls for nations to trust the United Nations.
7. Total disarmament.
8. Promote the United Nations as the hope for peace.
9. Promote UNESCO, the deadly educational and cultural arm of the United Nations.
10. Promote interdependence.
11. Support sanctions honoring Father Pierre Teilhard de Chardin—the New Age Humanist Priest.
12. Support the belief that the economic principle of traditional Christian or Catholic social doctrine is the economic principle of communism.
13. Promote the Pope as the acting go-between for the United States and the Soviet Union.

See also THE SOVEREIGN ORDER OF SAINT JOHN OF JERUSALEM; THE VATICAN.

Knights of Rhodes   See THE SOVEREIGN ORDER OF SAINT JOHN OF JERUSALEM.

Knights of Russia   See THE SOVEREIGN ORDER OF SAINT JOHN OF JERUSALEM.

Knights of St. John   See THE SOVEREIGN ORDER OF SAINT JOHN OF JERUSALEM.

Knights of the Golden Circle (KGC)   Organization created by Dr. George W. L. Bickley in 1854 in Cincinnati, Ohio. Many of the charter members were also Cincinnati Freemasons. The Golden Circle was closely affiliated with a French secret group called The Seasons, rumored to be a branch of the Illuminati. Like the Freemasons, the Knights of the Golden Circle had many rituals including secret handshakes and passwords. All members, in order to join, had to take the following oath, while a live snake was held over their head:

> *Whoever dares our cause reveal,*
> *Shall test the strength of Knightly steel;*
> *And when the torture proves too dull,*
> *We'll scrape the brains from out his skulls*
> *And place a lamp within the shell*
> *To light his soul from here to hell.*

Bickley's master plan for his Golden Circle was to create a new nation that would include the southeastern United States, Cuba and the West Indies, Mexico, and Central America. In this new nation slavery would be legal. Because of this free labor, while slavery was being outlawed elsewhere, the new nation would dominate the global market in coffee, tobacco, rice, and sugar.

Like many secret societies, the KGC was concerned with ethnic purity. They believed that their new nation should be led only by men of pure Anglo-Saxon blood, and that Mexicans should be removed. This ethnic cleansing would be called "Texasizing."

In 1860, an army of KGC members, fifty thousand strong, was headquartered in San Antonio, Texas, and mobilized not only to kill Mexicans within Texas, but to attack the Mexican border. Two brief and unenthusiastic attacks were actually carried out, but Mexico adequately defended its border. It was the year before the Civil War and the KGC determined it was the powerful men of the North who were the real enemies, not the Mexicans. New slogans involved "killing Wall Street" and "attacking Washington."

Like the Freemasons, the KGC was divided by degrees. There were three main sections of the group: the Foreign and Home Guard Militia (the army), the Foreign and Home Guard Corps (civilians), and the American Legion (the governing body). By the beginning of the Civil War in 1861, there were sixty five thousand KGC members

in the South and another twenty thousand in the North. These northern members were plotting to create a "Northern Confederacy."
Thirteen thousand of these men had to be imprisoned during the war,
charged with disloyalty, after a huge conspiracy was uncovered in
which the northern members of the KGC planned to seize Union arse-
nals. Many Northerners criticized the mass imprisonment, saying that
only a small percentage of the imprisoned were actually KGC members, and that Lincoln was using the threat presented by the KGC as
an excuse to imprison anyone who criticized his administration.

According to an 1861 KGC publication, the soon-to-be-realized
Civil War between the Union and the Confederacy was the result of
a plot by the northeastern and European secret societies, using
money supplied by the Rothschild family.

The KGC had two spin-offs during the war. These were the
Order of American Knights and the Sons of Liberty. Following the
war, the KGC went underground and evolved into the Ku Klux Klan.

Two of the most notorious members of the KGC were John
Wilkes Booth, the man who assassinated Abraham Lincoln, and
outlaw Jesse James. Booth was part of a complex plot to overthrow
the U.S. government involving KGC agents, of which Lincoln's assassination was originally only a small part.

See also KU KLUX KLAN.

Knights of the White Kamelia   See KU KLUX KLAN.

Knights Templar   During the Dark Ages, the Roman Church controlled the Western world. During the centuries leading up to the
Renaissance, the Church repeatedly sent armies of its best young
men into the Middle East in attempts to conquer the Holy Land
from the Muslims who possessed it. These were called the Crusades,
which means Wars of the Cross. There were eight major crusades.
According to most history books, these were: the first, 1095–1101;
the second, headed by Louis VII of France, 1145–47; the third, conducted by Philip Augustus of France and Richard the Lion-Hearted,
1188–92; the fourth, during which Constantinople was taken, 1204;
the fifth, which featured the conquest of Damietta, 1217; the sixth,
in which Holy Roman Emperor Frederick II took part (1228–29);

the seventh, led by Saint Louis (Louis IX), 1249–52; the eighth, also under that king, 1270. There were many smaller crusades as well, such as the eradication of the Albigensian heresy (see CATHARS) which began in 1209. These crusades continued until the late 1600s; for example, the crusade of Lepanto in 1571, of Hungary in 1664, and the crusade of the Duke of Burgundy to Candia, in 1669.

There existed in southern France Christians who believed in a very different version of the Christ story than that taught by the Roman church. They believed that Jesus Christ had not been celibate but had been married to Mary Magdalene. The couple had had children who had traveled to southern France following Christ's death. There the descendants of Christ still lived. They believed that the Roman Church had purposely covered up the importance of Mary Magdalene in Christ's life, and had mistranslated the gospels to imply that she was a prostitute. They believed that the church did this to prevent women from having a meaningful role in the church and to make sure that the leader of the church, the Pope, was always picked by a group traceable back to Christ's disciples and not through Christ's bloodline. It is believed that, while in the Holy Land, those who believed the alternative version of Christ's life searched for proof of their beliefs, and that the proof may have been found and carried back to Europe. This group of crusaders became known as the Knights Templar.

What was the proof of Christ's bloodline? It is believed that in 1118 nine French Crusaders, said to be related to Flemish royalty, who had traveled to Jerusalem, contacted King Baldwin II of that city and asked to be allowed to act as road guard to protect pilgrims traveling to and from the Holy Land. (The city of Jerusalem had been in the possession of the Crusaders since 1099, when it was captured by the knights of the First Crusade led by Geoffrey de Bouillon. Despite this, the roads to and from the Holy Land remained dangerous because of the remaining Muslims in the area.) In return, the French Crusaders—among them Hugues de Payen; Bisol de St. Omer; Hugues, Comte de Champagne; André de Montbard (the uncle of Saint Bernard); and Archambaud de Saint-Aignan—wanted permission to live in the King's palace, adjacent to the Al-Aqsa Mosque, which had been built above the ruins of Solomon's Temple.

They became known as the Order of the Poor Knights of Christ and of the Temple of Solomon. This was eventually shortened to the Knights of the Temple, and finally to Knights Templar.

Whether the Knights Templar actually protected any pilgrims from roadside attacks is a matter of debate. It is believed that this task actually was handled by another group known as the Sovereign Order of Saint John of Jerusalem (a.k.a. the Hospitallers).

The Knights Templar did, however, spend much time excavating the Temple of Solomon. The temple had been built and destroyed many times, dating back at least to the sixth century B.C. Before it had been converted into a Muslim mosque it had been the temple of Herod the Great, destroyed by the Jews in 70 A.D. only four years after its completion. It had existed before, during, and after the time of Christ. So there was plenty to excavate. It is said that they found "scrolls of knowledge" that dealt with the life of Jesus and predated the Gospels. This was a knowledge that, for some reason, gave them power over the Roman Church.

The first written account of the Knights Templar comes from Frankish historian Guillaume de Tyre, who wrote of them from 1175 to 1185. There is quite a gap, then, more than a lifetime, between the Templars' origins and the first written account of them. Guillaume's writings have been described as "vague" and "sketchy"—so this version of the group's origin should not be considered conclusive history. It is simply the only story we have. There are elements of the story at which skeptics raise an eyebrow. For example, the original nine knights allowed no new candidates into their order for nine years and were so poor that two had to ride on the same horse. (A Templar emblem showing two knights upon one horse, presumably because of poverty, lasted into the thirteenth century—by which time the Templars were wealthy.) Some feel that, if the origins of the Templars are indeed as written by Guillaume, there would be corroboration. The French king had an official historian named Fulk de Chartres whose writings of the period still exist, yet they contain no mention of the Templars. This is odd, since they would have been noted if they had actually been employed to protect pilgrims on the highways as they traveled to and from the Holy Land.

According to Manly P. Hall, "The knowledge of the Templars

concerning the early history of Christianity was undoubtedly one of the main reasons for their persecution and final annihilation."

The Knights Templar were officially recognized by the church in 1128 after Templar grand masters traveled to Troyes, seventy-five miles southeast of Paris. There they met with Catholic leaders, including the man who would later be canonized as Saint Bernard. The church recognized the knights as an official military and religious order. The church also gave the knights an "Order"—a set of rules—which meant that all knights had to take a vow of chastity and poverty, that in times of war they were not allowed to retreat except under particularly dire circumstances, and that they were allowed to collect contributions. Hugues de Payen was given the title of grand master. They had to cut their hair but were forbidden to cut their beards. They were made at that time to wear white cloaks, garb for which they are still known. (In 1146, the splayed red cross was added to their cloaks.) It was determined that new admissions to the order would have to sign over all of their possessions.

Following the church's sanctioning of the Templars, they immediately began to acquire grand wealth, predominantly by assuming the estates of the more wealthy new members. Within a year, the Templars owned land and castles from Scotland to the Holy Land. As their numbers grew, they developed into the strongest military force in the world. The order had its own doctors, and medical knowledge among the Templars was ahead of its time. The importance of hygiene, for example, was understood by the knights, who lived in a world in which cleanliness was considered unhealthy. Epilepsy, common at the time, was considered demonic possession by the most of the world, but the Templars understood it to be a disease that was controllable.

It has been said that the Knights Templar teamed up at times with the Islamic sect known as the Assassins in military actions, such as the 1129 attack on Damascus led by Jerusalem's King Baldwin. Other sources refer to the Templars and the Assassins as "mortal enemies." Of course, both could be true.

The Knights Templar took on a structure that provided a template for future secret societies, including Freemasonry. They divided themselves by rank and ritually kept secrets—not just from the public but from each other as well. New members were recruited until membership was estimated to be as large as twenty thousand.

The inner core of the Knights Templar became enormously wealthy. In 1139, Pope Innocent II said that the Knights Templar needn't answer to any authority but the Church. They acquired land, and changed money for a fee. In fact, the Templars, it is believed, invented the concept of credit. They issued the first credit cards. In England, one of the services they performed for the King was tax collecting, a chore they did for a percentage of the take.

According to Jim Marrs, "Along with banking practices, the Templars brought to Europe their acquired knowledge of architecture, astronomy, mathematics, medicine, and medical techniques. In less than one hundred years after formation of the order, the Knights Templar had evolved into the medieval equivalent of today's multi-national corporation."

The Templars began to form a powerful empire that spread from Germany across Europe to Constantinople. With the exception of the Church itself, the Knights Templar were the most powerful organization in the Western world by 1150.

Bertrand de Blanchefort was the fourth Grand Master of the Order of the Knights Templar. He held the position from 1153 to 1170, and was considered a significant grand master. It was he who organized the Templars and transformed them into what would today be called an international corporation.

By 1200, the Templars owned approximately nine thousand castles across Europe. Many of these structures they had built themselves. They built churches and military fortresses as well. The forts were often built on peninsulas or on mountaintops, to make an attack more difficult.

Sometime between 1195 and 1220, Wolfram von Eschenbach wrote the epic romantic poem *Parzival*. In it, the Templars' power is explained by the fact that it is they who guard the Holy Grail, the Grail family, and the Grail castle.

The Templars had their own powerful army and navy. The Templar ships flew a flag with a skull and crossbones on it, a symbol that would later become associated with piracy. It is suspected that the skull and crossbones may have had something to do with the secret the Templars held, the key to their power. The Templars were state-of-the-art navigators at sea and were among the first to use the magnetic compass, which allowed navigation on nights when the stars were not visible.

An explanation of the origin of the Templars' skull and cross-bones symbol is offered by J.S.M. Ward in his book *Freemasonry and the Ancient Gods*. Ward writes: "A great lady of Maraclea was loved by a Templar, a Lord of Sidon; but she died in her youth, and on the night of her burial, this wicked lover crept to the grave, dug up her body and violated it. Then a voice from the void bade him return in nine months time for he would find a son. He obeyed the injunction and at the appointed time opened the grave again and found a head on the leg bones of the skeleton (skull and crossbones). The same voice bade him, 'guard it well, for it would be the giver of all good things,' and so he carried it away with him. It became his protecting genius, and he was able to defeat his enemies by merely showing them the magic head. In due course, it passed into possession of the Order."

In the early thirteenth century, during the Albigensian Crusade to eradicate the Cathars sect of southern France, in which an estimated two hundred thousand were murdered, the only Cathars to survive were hidden among the ranks of the Templars. Bertrand de Blanchefort had been a member of a Cathar family.

A famous structure built by the Templars that still stands and remains a tourist attraction is the Chartres Cathedral on the Eure River southwest of Paris. Construction on the cathedral began in 1145. A fire in 1194 required twenty-six years of reconstruction. The cathedral is located at 48"26'51" North, 1"29'14" East. It is thought to be the first structure to be built in the Gothic style. Buildings at the time were as a rule short and block-shaped, whereas this structure had impressively high ceilings and used the previously unheard-of flying buttresses as an architectural technique.

According to John Julius Norwich in *The World Atlas of Architecture*: "In 1194, the master-builder of Chartres outlined new principles which would inspire all the great architects of the thirteenth century. The elevation was in three tiers as it had no gallery (the relationship between the three levels should be noted), and the vaulting was quadripartite, which eliminated the need for alternating supports. Externally, an important change was introduced by abandoning the five towers initially planned over the transepts."

There is a carving of the Ark of the Covenant being carried in a wagon on the north door of the Chartres Cathedral. This carving had often been interpreted as evidence that the Knights Templar found the Ark and took it with them back to Europe.

Interestingly, none of the cathedrals built by the Templars depict Christ's crucifixion.

By the middle of the thirteenth century, the Templars had become one of the most powerful military forces in the world. They had both a land army and a naval fleet, which was based in the Atlantic at the French port of La Rochelle. The Templars, because of their power, were no longer willing to be dictated to by any other world power—neither the Church, nor the English. According to Jim Marrs, a Templar leader threatened King Henry III of England in 1252, saying, "So long as thou dost exercise justice, thou wilt reign. But if thou infringe it, thou wilt cease to be king."

In 1291, the Muslims took back the Holy Land from the Christians. The Templars were among those who fought in vain to maintain control. It is said, in fact, that they fought heroically, and that the grand master continued to fight to his death despite horrendous wounds.

The reason for the formation of the Templars was now gone. Templars stationed in the Middle East were forced to move to Crete, which the Templars had earlier purchased from Richard the Lion-Hearted. The group known as the Sovereign Order of Saint John of Jerusalem (Hospitallers) also moved to Crete.

Although the Knights Templar had been officially sanctioned by the Church and had fought in the Church's crusades, the order had spread so far and had become so powerful that it had become, to use a modern term, multicultural. It was not uncommon for Knights to employ Muslims as clerks and servants. Many Knights spoke Arabic. The Templars had a close rapport with many Jewish communities. They had members who had previously belonged to the Cathar sect, and many Knights openly spoke of their belief in Gnostic dualism. None of this was approved of by the Church.

In the early 1300s the power of the Templars peaked. It was around that time that they incurred the wrath of the French king Philip IV, who found them drunken and arrogant. In 1305 the French king went to Rome and met with Pope Clement V. He was fairly certain that Clement would give him an audience, as the pope at that time was a puppet of Philip. (Philip had plotted to assassinate Pope Boniface VII and his replacement Benedict XI had also died mysteriously. Pope Clement had been the archbishop of Bordeaux and was subservient to Philip.)

Philip told Pope Clement that the Templars were plotting to topple the Church. Just as had been the case with the Cathars, the Church ordered a crusade to destroy the Templar menace. Before a physical attack on the Templars, there was an apparent propaganda attack. Nasty rumors spread about the knights. People began to say that the Templars were homosexuals, that they were cannibals who killed babies, and that they worshipped a devil named Baphomet. It was said that they held rituals that denied Christ's divinity, that they spit and trampled upon the cross. (Although we can be fairly certain that the Templars did not stick 100 percent to the orthodoxy of the Church, their actual beliefs remain a mystery.)

There is evidence that several knights in their writings did refer to "Baphomet" but no hint is given as to what Baphomet is. It is clear that Baphomet is regarded with reverence and it is associated with demonlike sculptures. The word was also displayed in association with a bearded head, leading some to believe that it is a reference to the Shroud of Turin, which was believed to have been in the possession of the Templars from 1204 until 1307.

Reports of bizarre rituals involving Templars and Baphomet persist. According to Peter Tompkins in his book *The Magic of Obelisks*, "Public indignation was aroused by . . . charges of . . . worshipping the devil in the form of an idol called Baphomet." Baphomet was "the Templar symbol of Gnostic rites based on phallic worship and the power of directed will. The androgynous figure with a goat's beard and cloven hooves is linked to the horned god of antiquity, the goat of Mendes."

John J. Robinson wrote in his 1991 book *Dungeon, Fire and Sword*: "Some confessed that they had also worshipped an idol in the form of a cat, which was red, or gray, or black, or mottled. Sometimes the idol worship required kissing the cat below the tail. Sometimes the cat was greased with the fat from roasted babies. The Templars were forced to eat food that contained the ashes of dead Templars, a form of witchcraft that passed on the courage of the fallen knights."

Author Ian Wilson states in *The Shroud of Turin—The Burial Cloth of Jesus Christ?*: "In the Inquisition evidence there are several references to members of the order receiving on initiation a little cord that had been in contact with the 'head'."

Philip the Fair described the idol as: ". . . a man's head with a large beard, which head they kiss and worship at all their provincial chapters, but this not all the brothers know, save only the Grand Master and the old ones."

A Templar named Brother Jean Taillefer of Genay gave evidence against the order during the Templars' trial in 1307. He said he "was received into the order at Mormant, one of the three perceptories under the jurisdiction of the Grand Priory of Champagne at Voulaine. He said at his initiation 'an idol representing a human face' was placed on the altar before him. Hughes de Bure, another Burgundian from a daughter house of Voulaine, described how the 'head' was taken out of a cupboard, or aumbry, in the chapel, and that it seemed to him to be of gold or silver, and to represent the head of a man with a long beard. Brother Pierre d'Arbley suspected that the 'idol' had two faces, and his kinsman Guillaume d'Arbley made the point that the 'idol' itself, as distinct from copies, was exhibited at general chapters, implying that it was only shown to senior members of the order on special occasions."

According to Peter Partner in *The Murdered Magicians*, ". . . They bestowed worship in their chapter on a heathen idol, variously described as to its physical characteristics, but known as a 'Baphomet', which etymologically was the same word [in Old French] as 'Mohammed'. [Once or twice the form Mahomet is actually used by witnesses in the trial.] Like so many persecuted heretical groups of the past, they were said to hold their chapters only secretly and at night. . . . It was impossible for the Templars to have 'picked up in the East' the practice of worshipping an idol bearing

the name of the Prophet Mohammed, since no such idol existed any-
where in the Levant, even among breakaway sects such as the
Ismailis or the Druse. The idea that Muslims were idolaters was
itself a part of another system of 'smears,' the pejorative representation of the oriental world by western Christians."

The attack on the Templars began on Friday, October 13, 1307—
which was the original Friday the 13th, mighty bad luck indeed if
you were a Templar. Knights were rounded up, tortured, and burned
to death. Though much effort had been put into keeping secret the
attacks on the Templars, some Knights were forewarned and managed to move and hide Templar treasures. The treasure that had
been stored in the Templars' Paris temple disappeared. The Templars' naval fleet also went missing. Although Church orders were
for Templars to be killed throughout the Christian world, the crusade lacked enthusiasm everywhere except in France. Philip's son-in-
law was Edward II of England, and even Edward did not want to go
to war against the Templars—although he begrudgingly (and half-
heartedly) complied. England was at war with Scotland, and a new
battle against the Templars was an unwanted distraction. Because of
the war between the English and the Scottish, the papal command
to dissolve the order of the Knights Templar never reached Scotland, and Scotland became the only land in Christendom where the
Templars still officially existed.

The Inquisition drew up a list of charges against the Templars
on August 12, 1308. The charges read, in part: "Item, that in each
province the order had idols, namely heads, of which some had
three races and some one, and others had a human skull. Item, that
they adored these idols or that idol, and especially in their great
chapters and assemblies. Item, that they venerated (them). Item, that
(they venerated them) as God. Item, that (they venerated them) as
their Savior. . . . Item, that they said that the head could save them.
Item, that [it could] make riches. Item, that it made the trees flower.
Item, that [it made] the land germinate. Item, that they surrounded
or touched each head of the aforesaid idols with small cords, which
they wore around themselves next to the shirt or the flesh. Item,
that in his reception, the aforesaid small cords or some lengths of
them were given to each of the brethren. Item, that they did this in

veneration of an idol. Item, that they (the receptors) enjoined them (the postulants) on oath not to reveal the aforesaid to anyone."

Templars in Germany continued to function, hiding out inside other secret societies such as the Hospitallers of Saint John and the Teutonic Knights. The same thing happened in Spain, where persecuted Templars wore the cloaks of other orders and continued to function. In Portugal, the Templars didn't join another society, but merely changed their name to Knights of Christ.

In 1314, the Templar's last official grand master, Jacques Molay, was captured and burned at the stake. Molay had been a Templar since 1265, and had become grand master in 1298. Molay's contribution to the Templars' beliefs had been the addition of the heresy of a group called the Johannites—that John the Baptist, not Jesus, had been the true messiah.

It became part of the Templars' legend that Molay, as he burned at the stake, put a curse on his persecutors. He said that within a year, Pope Clement and King Philip would join him before the "court of God." In less than a month the pope died of dysentery. And Philip died before the year was out as well, with the cause of death unknown.

There is a theory that some Templars traveled across the Atlantic and ended up in the New World, almost two hundred years before Columbus. According to Christopher Knight, and Robert Lomas in their book *The Hiram Key: Pharaohs, Freemasons and the Discovery of the Secret Scrolls of Jesus*, the Templar fleet stopped in Portugal for supplies and then headed west for a land they called "La Merica." They arrived at what is today Westford, Massachusetts, in 1308. There is evidence that this theory is true. In Westford there is an engraving of a Templar with a shield. On the shield is a ship and a single star. In Newport, Rhode Island, there is a tower so old that the date it was built is unknown. Its architecture indicates that it could have been built by the Templars. Another indication that Templar ships went to the New World—and returned—is Rosslyn Chapel, completed in 1486. On the ceilings are illustrations of cactus and corn, North American plants theoretically unknown at the time in Europe.

Not everyone went along with the Pope's orders to wipe out the

Templars. In England, captured Templars were given light sentences and released. Some Templars stayed in Portugal and, for safety, changed the name of their group to the Knights of Christ, and explored the sea. Columbus allegedly married the daughter of a Knight of Christ and had access to his father-in-law's charts. Others moved to Scotland where they merged with the Hospitallers.

Is there physical proof, above and beyond the documentation already noted, that the Knights Templar actually existed? Yes. A group of British engineers mapping vaults under Mount Moriah in 1894 found artifacts such as a Templar cross, and part of a sword and a lance in passageways with keystone arches. These are believed to be proof and now comprise museum exhibits in Scotland.

Today, in the twenty-first century, there are at least three, and probably more, secret societies that use the name Templar, and claim to be able to trace their roots back to the Middle Ages. There are also certain Masonic lodges that include Templar as one of their grades.

See also ASSASSINS; CATHARS; CHIVALRIC MILITARY ORDER OF THE TEMPLE OF JERUSALEM; FREEMASONS; KNIGHTS OF CHRIST; ORDER OF THE NEW TEMPLARS; ROSSLYN CHAPEL; SOVEREIGN ORDER OF SAINT JOHN OF JERUSALEM.

Kreisau Circle   Anti-Nazi group formed in Germany in 1933. Group consisted of professionals and career military officers, led by Helmut James Graft von Moltke. Meetings were held at von Moltke's estate. The Kreisau Circle plotted to kill Hitler, but their attempts failed. One member, Count Claus von Stauffenberg, planted a bomb near Hitler during the summer of 1944. Following this failed assassination attempt many members of the group were captured and executed. The remaining members sent letters to members of British and American intelligence to make sure that the Allies recognized them as anti-Nazi after the war ended.

Ku Klux Klan (KKK)   After the American Civil War, a group of disgruntled Confederate soldiers calling themselves the Ku Klux Klan banded together to threaten, torment, and kill perceived enemies of the "white race"—African Americans and Jews. They are best known for their white hoods, their burning of crosses, and thousands of lynchings.

The secret society was formed to combat the Freeman's Bureau, which was established by the U.S. Congress on March 3, 1865, to protect the interests of former slaves by helping them find jobs and get an education. Money was also set aside to make sure that the former slaves had food and shelter. An attempt by the Freeman's Bureau in 1866 to extend their powers was vetoed by President Andrew Johnson. That same year, the president also vetoed a Civil Rights Bill, which would have protected freed slaves from Southern Black Codes. Those codes denied the freed slaves the right to vote, limited their ability to testify in court against white men, and prevented them from sitting on juries. The former slaves were also prohibited from working in certain types of jobs and from carrying weapons in public.

In 1867, Congress passed the first Reconstruction Act, which divided the South into five military districts. Elections were scheduled with freed male slaves allowed to vote. The act also said that the Southern states would be readmitted to the Union as soon as they ratified the Fourteenth Amendment, which guaranteed voting rights to all adult males, regardless of color. President Johnson vetoed the act but Congress swiftly overrode his veto. In reaction to these moves within the U.S. government, the first branch of the KKK was formed in Pulaski, Tennessee. By 1867, many local branches of the KKK had formed, with many of the leaders being former members of the Confederate Army. The first grand wizard was former Confederate general Nathan Forrest. All-out war was declared right from the start. The early KKK members wore masks, white cardboard hats, and robes made out of white sheets as they murdered blacks and sympathetic whites. The first order of business was to prevent black men from voting.

The KKK then focused its attacks on successful black businessmen, and members and leaders of black trade unions. In 1870, President Ulysses S. Grant called for an investigation into the KKK. The resulting grand jury reported: "There has existed since 1868 . . . an organization known as the Ku Klux Klan, or Invisible Empire of the South, which embraces in its membership a large proportion of the white population of every profession and class. The Klan has a constitution and bylaws, which provides, among other things, that each member shall furnish himself with a pistol, a Ku Klux gown and a signal instrument. The operations of the Klan are executed in the night and are invariably directed against members of the Republican Party. The Klan is inflicting summary vengeance on the colored citizens by breaking into their houses at the dead of night, dragging them from their beds, torturing them in the most inhuman manner, and in many instances murdering."

On April 20, 1871, Congress passed the Ku Klux Act, which strengthened the president's power to combat Klan activities. The KKK all but disappeared as a result.

The Klan reformed in 1915 with a preacher named William J. Simmons as the leader. He had been inspired by the D.W. Griffith film *Birth of a Nation* and by the 1905 book by Thomas Dixon called *The Ku Klux Klan*. The new Klan's primary enemy was the National Association for the Advancement of Colored People (NAACP). Following the first World War, the KKK added to their list of enemies Jews, Catholics, liberals, and immigrants.

In 1922, Hiram W. Evans became the KKK's new Imperial Wizard. Membership grew. Under his command KKK members were elected to political office. By 1925, it was estimated that there were four million Klansmen. By the end of that decade, however, the KKK was once again coming apart at the seams. Scandals involving the governor of Indiana and the mayor of Indianapolis caused membership to dwindle. A murder conviction of Klan leader David C. Stephenson also caused dissension within the ranks. The KKK was disbanded for a second time during World War II.

Smaller groups using the KKK name appeared during the 1950s, again attacking blacks who wanted to vote and activists in the newborn civil rights movement. One of the largest of these groups was led by Robert Shelton and called the White Knights of the Ku Klux Klan. The new groups were effective. In Mississippi in 1960, 42 percent of the population was black, but blacks accounted for only 2 percent of the registered voters.

A leaflet circulated by the Ku Klux Klan in Mississippi in 1964 read:

Here are Twenty Reasons WHY you should, if qualified, join, aid and support the White Knights of the KU KLUX KLAN of Mississippi: (1) Because it is a Christian, fraternal and benevolent organization. (2) Because it is a democratic organization, governed by its members. (3) Because it is a democratic and just organization. (4) Because it is a working organization which not only talks but ACTS. (5) Because it is a very secret organization and no one will know that you are a member. (6) Because it is a legal organization and no one can be prosecuted for being a member. (7) Because it is a politically independent organization, and is not pledged to any political party. (8) Because it is a Pro-American organization that opposes any thing, person or organization that is Un-American. (9) Because it is an organization that is sworn to uphold the lawful Constitution of the United States of America. (10) Because it is composed of native-born, white, gentile and protestant American citizens who are sound of mind and of good moral character. (11) Because the goals of the KKK are the total segregation of the races and the total destruction of communism in all its forms. (12) Because the KKK has twice saved this nation from destruction as history clearly records. [Note: We're not sure to which occasions this refers—MB] (13) Because there comes a time in the life of every man when he has to choose between the right or wrong side of life. (14) Because there are today many alien forces entering the United States of America bent upon its destruction. (15) Because it informs its members, and an informed citizen is a good citizen. (16) Because a Christian-like brotherhood among men must be revived in America. (17) Because one of the goals of the KKK is States' Rights and complete State Sovereignty. (18) Because neither the Conservatives nor the Liberals will save our nation, for patriots always save a nation. (19) Because it is clear now that if communism is to be defeated in America, it will be done in the South and primarily in Mississippi. (20) Because the KKK needs you today to help fight America's battles.

One of the most heinous crimes ever committed by the group took place on September 15, 1963, with the bombing of the Sixteenth Street Baptist Church in Birmingham, Alabama. Four girls, aged eleven through fourteen, who had been attending Sunday School were killed. On May 17, 2000, the FBI announced that the Sixteenth Street Baptist Church bombing had been carried out by the Ku Klux Klan splinter group, the Cahaba Boys. It was claimed that four men, Robert Chambliss, Herman Cash, Thomas Blanton, and Bobby Cherry, had been responsible for the crime. Cash was dead but Blanton and Cherry were arrested. In May 2002, the seventy-one-year-old Bobby Cherry was convicted of the murder of Denise McNair, Addie Mae Collins, Carole Robertson, and Cynthia Wesley and was sentenced to life in prison.

Over the last forty years, the KKK has protested events which offend its sensibilities. They can be found counter-protesting during civil-rights marches—and have been known to protest courthouses where trials are being held for black men accused of killing white men. As one KKK leader once said, "If a black man can get away with killing a white man, we ought to be able to get away with killing a black man."

In 1981, a black man, Michael Donald, was lynched in Mobile, Alabama, by KKK members. A resulting civil suit resulted in a judge awarding the victim's family seven million dollars. As a result, the Klan had to hand over all of its assets including its Tuscaloosa head-quarters. On the criminal side of the case, the accused, Henry Hayes, was executed on June 6, 1997. It was the first time a white man had been executed in the United States for a crime against an African American since 1913.

See also KNIGHTS OF THE GOLDEN CIRCLE.

L

League of the Just   Secret society composed mainly of emigrant German handicraftsmen who met in London in June, 1847, to formulate a political program. Among those persuaded to join was Karl Marx, who changed the name of the group to the Communist League. Marx then wrote the group's constitution: "Manifesto of the Communist Party."

Leopard Men   West Africa secret society, also known as Egbo. The Egbo were responsible for capturing slaves and delivering them to Europeans for transport to the New World. The Egbo maintained discipline through fear, often induced through psychoactive drugs. A favorite drug was the Calabar bean (*Physostigma venenosum*). Until the beginning of the twentieth century, the bean was used for some medicinal purposes. It can be used for eye diseases and as a stimulant to the muscles of the intestines in chronic constipation. The drug slows the pulse and raises blood pressure. It also depresses the central nervous system.

Even after the time of slavery, the Leopard Men thrived as a well-paid source of intimidation. The African public was convinced that Leopard Men could gain the strength of leopards by wearing leopard-skin garb. The Leopard Men were most numerous in the areas now known as Sierra Leone and Nigeria, and most powerful in the 1930s. The Leopard Men believed in shape-shifting, the physical and mental transformation of a human into an animal. A person who can accomplish shape-shifting is called a theriomorph.

Theriomorphs, it is said, can exist as men, animals, or as combinations of the two. They can accomplish these transformations both on Earth and/or on the astral plane. It is suspected that belief in shape-shifting spawned belief in lycanthropy (werewolves) and vampirism.

Since there is no evidence that shape-shifting is actually possible, the Leopard Men live in a world of "spiritual theriomorphs," or those who find aspects of their own behavior or appearance in animals.

Shape-shifters gather in "sacred circles" and partake in ritual dances in which they contort and move in the fashion of the animal, under the theory that the animal's spirit will be more apt to enter the person if the body is moving in a fashion with which the animal is comfortable. During these rituals, the men also make sounds that resemble those of the chosen animal. Leopard Men have reported that their senses are altered by these rituals, with their senses of smell and sight becoming heightened. They feel increased dexterity in their arms and legs and experience a feeling of savage power.

As a secret society, the Leopard Men, it is suspected, used the rumors that they could shape-shift as propaganda, so they would be feared as a group. Travelers in the jungle in areas where the Leopard Men functioned were sometimes found clawed to death. Although civilization has just about wiped out the Leopard Men, it is suspected that remnants of the society still exist in the most remote parts of the West African jungle.

Lions Club   The International Association of Lions Clubs was founded during the summer of 1917 by Chicago insurance man Melvin Jones, who sought to bring together a group of successful businessmen who could use their power to make their communities and the world a better place. Jones was tired of business groups that helped only other businesses, and not the world at large.

The first national convention of the Lions Club was held in Dallas, Texas, in the autumn. At the convention, Dr. William P. Woods of Indiana was elected the first Lions Club president. Jones became the club's secretary, a position he held until his death in 1961.

Although only two months old, there were already more than twenty Lions Club chapters in nine different states. Members of the club practice what is called "lionism," which is selfless charity.

The club's motto is: "We serve." The slogan is: "(L)iberty,

(I)ntelligence, (O)ur (N)ations (S)afety." Members, of course, are encouraged to be charitable but it is against the by-laws of the club to take credit for that charity or to otherwise use charitable contributions for personal gain. That's the secret part.

In 1920, the Lions Club became international when the first chapter in Canada was founded. Before the end of that decade, chapters had formed in China, Mexico, and Cuba as well.

By the end of the 1920s there were an estimated sixty thousand members and more than one thousand chapters worldwide. The first Central American Lions Club was opened in Panama in 1935. The first South American chapter opened in 1936 in Colombia. The first Lions Clubs in Europe opened in 1948 in France, Sweden, and Switzerland. Japan's first branch opened in 1952.

Today, more than 160 countries are represented. Members of the Lions Club can recognize each other by the emblems they wear on their lapels. The emblem is a gold "L" against a purple background. On either side of the letter are two outward-facing lion profiles, also in gold. (Gold and purple are the club's official colors.) The lions are facing in opposite directions because, symbolically, one is supposed to be facing the past while other faces the future. At the top of the emblem is the word "Lions." At the bottom it reads "International."

Lukumi   See SANTERIA.

Luminous Lodge   See VRIL SOCIETY.

M

Macumba   See SANTERIA.

Mafia   Sicily is a tough island, with poor soil and a harsh climate. Throughout its history, it has frequently been overrun by the conquering armies of other nations, and the natives, almost universally poor, tended to over time acquire a feeling of helplessness. Out of this atmosphere was born the Mafia, a secret society, which offered a structure of power and protection for the natives outside the usually corrupt government. Thus, the name "La Cosa Nostra," which means "Our Thing."

Also known as the Mob, the name Mafia has become a somewhat generic term for ethnic organized crime. Today we refer to the "Irish Mafia," or the "Russian Mafia," but the Mafia we will discuss here first came to the United States during the massive influx into the United States of immigrants from Italy and Sicily between 1880 and 1914.

These immigrants were poor people who lived almost exclusively in large cities. Jobs were hard to come by. Many of the immigrants—due both to the facts at hand and their experiences in their homeland—thought the federal, state, and local governments of the United States were corrupt and weren't giving them a fair shake. (Sicily had spent so many years under foreign rule—Greeks, Romans, Byzantines, Muslims, Normans, French, Spanish, and Austrians had all conquered the island—it became an unwritten rule in Sicilian families to leave the authorities out of private affairs.) A small percentage of these immigrants turned to crime, and organized themselves along the lines of the Sicilian Mafia. In some cases, crime bosses left Sicily and resumed their rackets in America.

Mafia members live by the code of *omerta*, which goes something like this: "Those who call the police are fools or cowards. Those who need police protection are both. If you are attacked, do not give the name of your attacker. Once you recover, you will want to avenge the attack yourself. A wounded man shall say to his assailant: 'If I live, I will kill you. If I die you are forgiven.'"

In the early days of the American Mafia, the top money-maker was extortion, a technique called "The Black Hand." In exchange for money, a person's business would be "protected." If the money wasn't paid, something bad would happen. A fire might break out in the store in the middle of the night, or, less subtly, it would be destroyed by a bomb.

Another early Mafia business venture was counterfeiting. In 1909, Ignazio Lupo was tried and convicted of counterfeiting in New York City. He was sentenced to thirty years in prison. However, Lupo—an underling of crime boss Peter "The Clutch Hand" Morello, of what would one day be known as the Genovese family—served only twelve years because President Warren G. Harding commuted his sentence.

Prostitution has also been a big Mafia business throughout its existence. The mobsters did not actually run the brothels, however, since this was considered demeaning. Instead, they took a cut of the profits in exchange for protection.

While today legal casinos exist in many parts of the United States, legalized gambling was unknown during the early years of the twentieth century. In those days, the only casinos were illegal and operated by organized crime. These casinos were not huge operations such as the ones today in Las Vegas, Atlantic City, or on various Native American reservations. They were "back room" affairs and functioned behind social clubs, barber shops, and stores. Available were all sorts of card games and slot machines.

Another popular form of organized crime gambling was the "numbers" game, which was much like today's legalized Lotto.

With the Great Depression and Prohibition of the 1920s and '30s, the Mafia grew. The Mafia groups of criminals organized into "families," which were sometimes real families, but were called families even if their membership did not follow strict bloodlines. Sometimes the family in question was merely the family of the boss, whose sons were, like princes, expected to take over the family business.

During Prohibition, when the U.S. government banned the sale and use of alcoholic beverages, the Mafia went into "bootlegging," and the party continued. Speakeasies—illegal taverns—operated in big cities across the country. Liquor was either made illegally in bathtubs by mobsters or was smuggled from countries where its production was still legal.

Not all mobsters got along with one another. Both inter- and intra-family battles took place. Some families often competed with other families over "turf," while other families had internal battles over matters of leadership. The Mafia became known as a very violent organization, but an organization that killed each other more often than outsiders.

Perhaps the most famous example of Mafia violence came on Valentine's Day in 1929, when mobsters working for Al Capone machine-gunned to death seven members of the rival Bugs Moran gang in a garage in Chicago, Illinois.

During World War II, the U.S. government first worked side by side with the Mafia as the organized crime group helped provide intelligence regarding the Nazis and fascists who were then in control of Italy and Sicily. Later, the U.S. intelligence services called upon U.S. mobsters who had casinos in Cuba, seeking their aid in kicking Fidel Castro out of Cuba.

After World War II, the Mafia became more aggressive. They sought to take over labor unions. They fixed elections to put their friends in political offices. As illegal drugs became big business in the U.S.—the new prohibition—the Mafia quickly took over drug smuggling and sales operations.

At one time there were twenty-six families operating in the United States, which amounted to approximately one per major city. The families were connected via a "commission," which included the various bosses. In general, the families of New York City and its surroundings were in charge.

For decades, there were many people who denied the Mafia's existence, including FBI head J. Edgar Hoover. That is, until 1957, when a meeting of the "committee"—with representatives from many of the major families throughout the United States—was raided in the small town of Apalachin, New York.

During the early 1960s, President John F. Kennedy's brother, Attorney General Robert Kennedy, made the Mafia a prime target of Justice Department resources. After the president was assassinated in Dallas, Mafia leaders behaved suspiciously, sometimes bragging about complicity in the crime.

One of the mob leaders most frequently mentioned as a suspect in the presidential assassination is Carlos Marcello. Marcello was born Calogero Minacero and became the boss of America's oldest Mafia family, based in New Orleans, Louisiana. He was a crime boss during the 1950s, '60s, and '70s. During that time, Marcello's power spread from New Orleans westward and, by the time of the assassination, encompassed Dallas. Marcello was furious with the Kennedys after Attorney General Robert Kennedy had him deported in April 1961. Marcello was "kidnapped" (his word) and flown to Guatemala without being allowed even to make a phone call. While in Latin America, Marcello had a hellish experience, wandering several days in the jungle with a broken rib. He was flown back to the United States four months later, according to the U.S. Border Patrol, by CIA pilot (and assassination suspect) David Ferrie.

After his return, Marcello reportedly said of the Kennedys, "Take the stone out of my shoe."

On November 22, 1963, the day Kennedy was killed in Dallas, Ferrie was working for Marcello's lawyer G. Wray Gill on Marcello's defense against immigration fraud charges. (Marcello was acquitted of these charges on the day of the assassination.) FBI reports indicate that Ferrie flew to Guatemala aboard Delta Airlines twice during the fall of 1963, evidence that Ferrie's detective work for G. Wray Gill was directly related to his defense of Carlos Marcello's immigration-fraud charges.

Ferrie and Marcello saw each other frequently in the days leading up to the assassination, since Marcello's trial was taking place and Ferrie was doing investigative work for Marcello's lawyer. Marcello and Ferrie were together on the weekends of November 9–10 and November 16–17 at Churchill Farms, Marcello's six thousand-acre estate. As part of an FBI sting called BRILAB, the FBI made

1,350 tapes of Marcello's conversations between February 1979 and February 1980. Agents Mike Wacks, Larry Montague, and Joseph Hauser made the tapes. The tapes were sealed by Judge Morey Sear at the start of Marcello's bribery and conspiracy trial in 1981. The judge ordered them permanently sealed, ruling that they would prejudice the jury against Marcello.

According to former Chief Counsel of the House Select Committee on Assassinations, G. Robert Blakey, Marcello "implicated himself in the assassination on three of those tapes. . . . On one tape, Marcello asked the other person to leave the room and resume the conversation in the secrecy of his car when the assassination came up. Marcello said something like, 'We don't talk about that in here.'"

Assassination researcher John Davis, who believes that organized crime was behind President Kennedy's death, writes that the tapes amount to a veiled "admission of complicity" by Marcello and his brother Joe. Though Davis filed a 1988 Freedom of Information Act suit for the release of the tapes, the tapes remain sealed.

Las Vegas private investigator Ed Becker says Marcello told him in September 1962 about a plan to assassinate President Kennedy that included the using of a "nut" to deflect blame from the mob. Becker says he told the FBI about the plot a year before the assassination. In 1978, Becker repeated the story to the House Select Committee, who found him credible. Some feel the assassination, as executed, was beyond the scope of mobsters. According to Harrison Edward Livingstone, "There is no way Carlos Marcello [and other mobsters] . . . could have done all this alone or covered any of it up."

Frank Ragano was, for twenty-seven years, the lawyer for Florida mob boss Santos Trafficante. For fifteen of those years he also represented Teamster president Jimmy Hoffa. In 1992, Ragano revealed knowledge of a plot involving Hoffa, Trafficante, and Marcello to assassinate the president. All three men are dead now, but at the time of Ragano's statement Marcello was still alive, in jail, where he reportedly was suffering from Alzheimer's disease. Ragano said he became an "unwitting intermediary" to the plot when he met with Hoffa at Teamsters headquarters in Washington in January or February 1963. Ragano, who was about to fly to New Orleans for a meeting with Trafficante and Marcello, says Hoffa told him, "Tell Marcello and Trafficante they have to kill the president."

Ragano continued, "Hoffa said to me, 'This has to be done.' Jimmy was ranting and raving for a long time. I didn't take it seriously because I knew Jimmy was a hothead with a short attention span. Marcello and Trafficante never met Hoffa. I had lawyer-client privilege with Hoffa and Trafficante, so I was designated intermediary. Marcello and Trafficante were extremely cautious. They always wanted to be able to truthfully tell a grand jury they never met Hoffa."

A few days later Ragano claims he met with Trafficante and Marcello at the Royal Orleans Hotel.

Ragano continued, "I told them, 'You won't believe what Hoffa wants me to tell you. Jimmy wants you to kill the president.' They didn't laugh. . . . Their looks scared me. It made me think they already had such a thought in mind."

Ragano says he returned to Washington, told Hoffa he had delivered the message and Hoffa reportedly replied, "It is going to be done."

On November 22, 1963, Hoffa called Ragano three or four minutes after the first news bulletins.

"Have you heard the good news?" Hoffa asked. "They killed the S.O.B. This means Bobby is out as Attorney General."

Marcello gave immunized testimony to the House Select Committee on Assassinations on January 11, 1978. At that time Marcello expressed "a deep dislike" for Robert Kennedy. Marcello stated that he had been "illegally kidnapped" by Government agents during his deportation. He admitted that David Ferrie worked for his lawyer G. Wray Gill. Marcello denied, however, that Ferrie worked directly for him—or that he had a close relationship with Ferrie.

The House Select Committee concluded that "Marcello had the motive, means, and opportunity to have President John F. Kennedy assassinated, though [the Committee] was unable to establish direct evidence of Marcello's complicity. . . . In its investigation of Marcello, the committee identified the presence of one critical evidentiary element that was lacking with the other organized crime figures examined by the committee: credible associations relating both Lee

Harvey Oswald and Jack Ruby to figures having a relationship, albeit tenuous, with Marcello's crime family or organization."

Lee Harvey Oswald, the accused assassin of President Kennedy, had an uncle named Dutz Murret who worked for Marcello. Oswald's mother had dated men who worked for Marcello. Two days after the assassination Oswald himself was murdered by Jack Ruby, a Dallas strip-club owner with a background in organized crime.

The House Committee also established "associations between Jack Ruby and several individuals affiliated with the underworld activities of Carlos Marcello. Ruby was a personal acquaintance of Joseph Civello, the Marcello associate who allegedly headed organized crime activities in Dallas . . . [and] a New Orleans nightclub figure, Harold Tanenbaum, with whom Ruby was considering going into partnership in the fall of 1963."

During the late 1960s, New Orleans District Attorney Jim Garrison conducted his own investigation into the assassination of President Kennedy. Garrison's assassination investigation has been criticized because it didn't include the possibility of Marcello's involvement. Garrison, when questioned about this, always said that he had seen no evidence that Marcello was a member of organized crime.

Garrison's blind spot toward Marcello may have been explained by a *Life* magazine (September 8, 1967) article which noted that Garrison knew Marcello aide Mario Marino and that Marino "picked up a couple of hotel bills" for Garrison on visits to Las Vegas.

FBI agent Joseph Hauser went undercover in 1979 to investigate Marcello's crime organization. According to Hauser, Marcello admitted to knowing Oswald and his uncle, Charles "Dutz" Murret, and that Oswald worked for him in 1963 as a runner for his betting operation. This is corroborated by an independent report from an FBI informant that Oswald received money from Carlos Marcello's crime lieutenant Joe Poretto in the New Orleans Town and Country Restaurant managed by Marcello's brother Anthony.

In 1980, Hauser talked to Carlos' brother, Joseph, about the way the Kennedys had hassled him and his brother during the early 1960s. Joseph Marcello reportedly replied, "Don't worry, we took care of them, didn't we?"

According to an FBI teletype dated March 3, 1989, Marcello—who had been in prison in Minneapolis, Minnesota, since 1983 for conspiracy to bribe a judge—mistook his prison guards for personal bodyguards while apparently suffering from dementia. Marcello told the men that he had just driven back to New Orleans from New York City where he had had a meeting with Tony Provenzano, a captain in the Genovese crime family and a Teamsters International vice-president. He and Provenzano, Marcello said, had decided to "get Kennedy in Dallas."

Another suspect in President Kennedy's death was Florida Mafia boss Santos Trafficante, who was based in Tampa and controlled mob operations in Cuba before Castro's revolution. Trafficante maintained close ties to the paramilitary Cuban exiles after Castro took over.

The House Select Committee on Assassinations reported that: "Trafficante, like Marcello, had the motive, means and opportunity to assassinate President Kennedy. . . . Trafficante was a key subject of the Justice Department crackdown on organized crime during the Kennedy administration, with his name being added to a list of the top ten syndicate leaders targeted for investigation. [U.S. Attorney General Robert Kennedy's] strong interest in having Trafficante prosecuted occurred during the same period in which CIA officials, unbeknown to the Attorney General, were using Trafficante's services in assassination plots against . . . Fidel Castro. The committee found that . . . Trafficante's stature in the national syndicate of organized crime, notably the violent narcotics trade, and his role as the mob's chief liaison to criminal figures within the Cuban exile community, provided him with the capability of formulating an assassination conspiracy against President Kennedy. Trafficante had recruited Cuban nationals to help plan and execute the CIA's assignment to assassinate Castro. (The CIA gave the assignment to former FBI agent Robert Maheu, who passed the contract along to Mafia figures Sam Giancana and John Roselli. They, in turn, enlisted Trafficante to have the intended assassination carried out.)"

Trafficante admitted to his role in the plot to kill Castro during his House Select Committee on Assassinations testimony, but "categorically denied ever having discussed any plans to assassinate President Kennedy."

Regarding Trafficante's association with Ruby, the House Select Committee reported, "Ruby may have met with Trafficante at Trescornia prison in Cuba during one of his visits to Havana in 1959, as the CIA had learned but had discounted in 1964. While the committee was not able to determine the purpose of the meeting, there was considerable evidence that it did take place."

The CIA sent a copy of a memo to a Lyndon Johnson aide, McGeorge Bundy, on November 28, 1963, stating that, in 1959, Trafficante had been visited by Ruby in jail in Cuba.

A July 21, 1961, Treasury Department memo made public in 1976 stated that there were "unconfirmed rumors in the Cuban refugee population in Miami that when Fidel Castro ran the American racketeers out of Cuba and seized the casinos, he kept . . . Trafficante . . . in jail to make it appear he had a personal dislike for Trafficante, when in fact Trafficante is an agent of Castro. Trafficante is allegedly Castro's outlet for illegal contraband in this country."

Anthony Summers wrote that Ruby arrived in Havana on August 8, 1959, having told his doctor that he was going to make some money gambling at the (Havana) Tropicana, where he was subsequently seen by many witnesses in the company of Lewis McWillie, who was managing the Tropicana for Trafficante.

Trafficante died following triple-bypass surgery in 1987 in Houston, Texas. On his deathbed, he told his lawyer, Frank Ragano, "Carlos [Marcello] fucked up. We should not have killed Giovanni [John]. We should have killed Bobby."

According to an FBI wiretap, following Johnny Roselli's death in August 1976, Trafficante said, "Now only two people are alive who know who killed Kennedy and they're not talking."

The third most frequently discussed Mafia suspect in the presidential assassination was Chicago mob boss Sam Giancana. In the early 1960s, Giancana helped the CIA (with money and personnel) in covert operations within Cuba to rid that country of Castro. For a time, Giancana and JFK shared a mistress, Judith Exner.

In 1988, Exner told *People* magazine, "I lied when I said that President Kennedy was unaware of my friendship with mobsters. He knew everything about my dealings with Sam Giancana and Johnny Roselli because I was seeing them for him."

According to Anthony Summers, "For eighteen months in 1960 and 1961, Exner said, she repeatedly carried envelopes from the President to Giancana and Roselli. There were, she calculated, some ten meetings between the President and [Giancana], one of them in the White House."

Exner offered her opinion on why these meetings were held: "I was probably helping Jack orchestrate the attempted assassination of Fidel Castro with the help of the Mafia."

Exner died on September 24, 1999, of breast cancer at age 65 in Duarte, California.

Giancana wasn't known for his ability to keep a secret. When the CIA/Mafia teams were planning to assassinate Castro in 1960, J. Edgar Hoover got wind of the plan because Giancana "told several friends."

According to Giancana's half-brother Charles (Chuck) and his nephew Sam in their book *Double Cross*, President Kennedy was murdered by a team of Chicago hitmen sent to Dallas by Giancana. The fatal shot, they claim, was fired by Giancana lieutenant Richard Cain, from the Texas School Book Depository's sixth floor. Cain himself was murdered in 1973, "gangland style." The book states that the assassination was orchestrated by Lyndon Johnson, Richard Nixon, and others, and funded by Texas oil money. The book also claims that Giancana ordered the murder of his mistress Marilyn Monroe, who was killed by Giancana henchmen with a poison suppository. Giancana had been talking to a Senate Intelligence Committee when he died on June 19, 1975, at age 67 while under police protection, shot with a .22 pistol once in the back of his head and six times around his mouth—Mafia symbolism for "talks too much." The murder weapon was later found on the bank of the Des Plaines River. It was a silenced Suramatic semi-automatic .22 pistol.

In the late 1960s, after recommendations by a presidential commission, Congress passed the Omnibus Crime Control Act and the Organized Crime Control Act, which gave law enforcement greater power to combat the Mafia. During the last two decades of the twentieth century, the FBI spearheaded a massive assault on the Mafia that crippled the organization. Many Mafia heads were convicted of racketeering or murder and put in prison. Today, Mafia families continue to operate in New York and Chicago, and smaller less-powerful groups remain in other cities.

The Mafia has regularly been glamorized by Hollywood through such vehicles as the *Godfather* movies and *The Sopranos* television show.

The Magicians   See COMMITTEE OF 300.

Majestic-12   See MJ-12.

Mau Mau   During the 1950s, the Mau Maus were a Kenyan secret society that responded to oppression by transforming into an underground military force. The great majority of their members belonged to the Gikuyu people. The Mau Maus fought the Europeans who had moved into their country and were attempting to take over.

Before the arrival of the Europeans, the Kenyans lived in a society of privately owned land, with no monetary system. The Europeans swept in, issued money with which the Kenyans were to buy things, collected money back in the form of taxes (another concept with which the Kenyans were unfamiliar), and then, under the mistaken impression that the Kenyan government had owned all of the land, declared that—since they were the government now—they owned the land.

All the private landowners believed, and rightfully so, that the colonialists were stealing their land away from them. Thus, insurrection ensued.

Thousands of people who had previously been self-employed now found themselves employees of the Europeans—and in some cases they were farming the same land they had farmed before the Europeans' arrival, land they considered to be their own.

To further aggravate matters, the Europeans paid the natives only one-fifth of what was paid white settlers for the same work.

The people of Kenya, using secret societies, began to plot against the white interlopers. The Mau Mau was an outgrowth of an already-existing secret society known as Arogi. The Gikuyu were the most populous tribe in Kenya, and were the first to complete Western educations. The first Mau Maus preached to the people the benefits of autonomy, and were quickly declared illegal by the white settlers. The Mau Maus took all of the possessions of its members and put them toward the cause.

Many Kenyan people agreed to help the Mau Maus, so they were well-supplied. What they didn't get through donations, they stole. The Western world was told at the time that the Mau Maus were being financed by Communists, but there doesn't appear to be any evidence of this.

On March 26, 1953, following a massacre of Kenyans by colonialists at Lari, in which the Lukas Kahangara family was wiped out—ninety-seven people died, most of them women and children—the Mau Maus lost much of their popular support. The Mau Mau insurrection spawned a mass hysteria and a bloody purging that has been compared to the Salem witch hunts and the Red Scare of the 1950s.

By the following year, the infrastructure of the Mau Maus was in disarray. According to British sources, 10,527 Mau Mau fighters were slaughtered and 2,633 captured by the British forces between 1952 and 1956 when the insurgence against colonialism peaked. Within the life of the Mau Mau, only sixty-three Europeans and three Asian soldiers were killed.

Merovingian Kings The Merovingian kings were the first line of kings in the land now called France. Their name comes from Merovius, a man who could, it is said, trace his lineage to Jesus. It is believed descendants of Jesus and Mary Magdalene settled in southern France, and bred with a large Jewish community of the region. In the fifth century, the descendants of Jesus interbred with Frankish royalty and thus started the Merovingian lineage.

The Vatican, which based its power on a lineage tracing back to Jesus' disciples, under the theory that Jesus was celibate and had no offspring, did everything they could to suppress knowledge of the Merovingian bloodline.

The Merovingian bloodline was still altering world events even in the twentieth century. According to one story, the Thule Society was determined to return the Merovingians to the thrones of Europe.

Adolf Hitler and his Nazi party, the story goes, stepped in and prevented this from happening.

Not all theories regarding the origin of the Merovingian bloodline say that it traces back to Jesus of Nazareth and Mary Magdalene. According to one French author, Gerard de Sede, the Merovingians were the descendants of extraterrestrials who interbred with ancient Israelites. Another tale of the origin of the Merovingians states that the founder of the royal line was said to be Merovech, a man with two fathers, one human and one mythological. His mother, the story goes, was already pregnant by King Chlodio when she was seduced while swimming in the ocean by a mythical creature called a Quinotaur. The Merovingian monarchs were sacred rather than ruling kings. The actual governing was done by chancellors called Mayors of the Palace.

The Merovingian kings never cut their hair and bore a distinctive birthmark, a red cross on their backs. They wore robes fringed with tassels that were supposed to have healing powers. Found in one Merovingian tomb was a golden bull's head, a crystal ball, and several golden miniature bees. One legend has it that the Merovingians were descended from the Trojans. Homer wrote that Troy was founded by a colony of Arcadians. According to the documents of the Priory of Sion (see PRIORY OF SION) the Arcadians were descended from Benjamites driven out of Palestine by their fellow Israelites for idolatry.

A Merovingian king named Clovis made a deal with the Roman church. He would subdue the church's enemies—the Arian Visigoths and the pagan Lombard—in return for recognition of his right to rule a new Roman empire as "Novus Constantinus." This arrangement continued until his descendant, Dagobert II, was murdered and the church reneged on its pact with Clovis by endorsing the assassination. The church recognized the murderer's family as legitimate and eventually Charlemagne was crowned as Holy Roman Emperor. The church believed that the Merovingian bloodline had been extinguished, but it has been written that Dagobert's son, Siegebert IV, survived. A Merovingian principality is said to have continued in Septimania by Guillem de Gellone, an ancestor of Godfroi de Bouillon.

See also CATHARS; KNIGHTS TEMPLAR; PRIORY OF SION; THULE SOCIETY.

The Militia of Christ of Livonia   See BROTHERS OF THE SWORD.

MJ-12   Jaime Shandera, a UFO researcher, is the first known source of documents purporting to acknowledge the existence of a secret U.S. Government panel to investigate UFOs called MJ-12. In December of 1984, Shandera received a package with an Albuquerque postmark and no return address. Inside the package was a roll of film that when developed showed an eight-page document that appeared to be a briefing paper dated November 18, 1952, to President-elect Dwight D. Eisenhower from Vice Admiral Roscoe Hillenkoetter regarding the recovery of two crashed UFOs. The document goes on to say that, at the site of the first UFO crash, in July 1947, the dead bodies of four humanoids, apparently from outer space, were recovered. Attached to this memo was another document. This appeared to be a presidential order written by Truman, creating a super-secret investigation unit to study the crashed airships and the humanoid remains. The document says the group was to be called "Majestic-12."

Shandera later visited the National Archives in Washington, D.C., with his associate William Moore, and there the two men discovered a memo dated sometime in July 1954, from the president's assistant General Robert Cutler to President Eisenhower, stating that a meeting of "MJ-12" was scheduled for the White House on July 16, 1954. Shandera and Moore did not make the MJ-12 memo public until 1987, when they learned that British UFO researcher Timothy Good had acquired a copy of the memo and was going to publish it. Not wanting to be scooped, Shandera went public.

John Lear is a former CIA pilot who flew missions over Vietnam, and the son of William P. Lear, the developer of the Lear jet. In 1988, Lear, a resident of Nevada, released a nine-page letter to the UFO research community saying that "we must face the shocking facts . . . the 'horrible truth' the government has been hiding from us over forty years. Unfortunately, the 'horrible truth' is far more horrible than the government ever imagined. . . . In its effort to protect democracy, our government sold us to the aliens. And here is how it happened. But before I begin, I'd like to offer a word in the defense of those who bargained us away. They had the best of intentions. . . .

Germany may have recovered a flying saucer as early as 1939. General James H. Doolittle went to Sweden in 1946 to inspect a flying saucer that had crashed there in Spitzbergen. . . . The 'horrible truth' was known by only a very few persons: They were indeed ugly little creatures, shaped like praying mantises and who were more advanced than us by perhaps a billion years. Of the original group that were the first to learn the 'horrible truth,' several committed suicide, the most prominent of which was General James V. Forrestal. . . . General Forrestal's medical records are sealed to this day. . . . President Truman quickly put a lid on the secret and turned the screws so tight that the general public still thinks that flying saucers are a joke. Have I ever got a surprise for them. . . . In 1947, President Truman established a group of twelve of the top military scientific personnel of their time. They were known as MJ-12. Although the group still exists today, none of the original members are still alive."

The letter goes on to say that our scientists and the aliens cut a deal: In exchange for some of the aliens' advanced technology, the scientists agreed to ignore their abduction of humans and their mutilation of cattle.

Lear wrote, "The EBEs assured MJ-12 that the abductions . . . were merely the ongoing monitoring of developing civilizations."

The letter then said that the EBEs had deceived MJ-12 and that their plans actually included "parasitical consumption of human biological matter," the killing of humans who got in their way, and the cross-breeding of humans and aliens.

Forrestal, who was the first United States Secretary of Defense (previously the position had been known as the Secretary of War), told a friend fifteen months before the beginning of the Korean War that American soldiers would soon be fighting in Korea. He had apparently been troubled by the fact that, during the first years following World War II, top officials in the U.S. government were making concession after concession to the Soviet Union. President Harry Truman asked for Forrestal's resignation on March 2, 1949. In May 1949, Forrestal was taken to Bethesda Naval Hospital for what was called a routine examination. Days later, Forrestal's body was found in a room. A noose was around its neck. His death was called a suicide. Forrestal's diary was held for more than a year before an edited version was released to the public.

The existence of MJ-12 is seemingly corroborated by Robert I. Sarbacher, a scientist, and a consultant for the U.S. Department of Defense Research and Development Board. An expert of instrumental physics and communications engineering, Sarbacher researched guided missiles for the Pentagon. He was also a high-ranking official at the Washington Institute of Technology. Sarbacher says that MJ-12 possessed the bodies of dead aliens. Though he never saw the dead aliens, he had seen lightweight but strong metallic material from a crashed craft, presumably material confiscated from Mac Brazel in Roswell, New Mexico, in 1947.

Sarbacher said, "[The] instruments or people operating these machines were also of very light weight, sufficient to withstand the tremendous deceleration and acceleration associated with the machinery. I remember in talking with some of the people at the office that I got the impression these 'aliens' were constructed like certain insects we have observed on earth, wherein because of the low mass the inertial forces involved in operation of these instruments would be quite low."

Writing on November 29, 1983, Dr. Sarbacher said, "I still do not know why the high order of classification has been given and why the denial of the existence of these devices."

According to Sarbacher's documents, members of MJ-12 included:

- Scientist Vannevar Bush, who was then head of the U.S. Department of Defense Research and Development Board.

- Secretary of Defense James V. Forrestal, who served as a member until his death on May 22, 1949.

- General Walter B. Smith, who replaced Forrestal starting on August 1, 1950. Smith, born in 1895, served as chief of staff to General of the Army Dwight D. Eisenhower, the Supreme Allied Commander in Europe, during World War II. He was called by Eisenhower "the general manager of the war." Following high school, Smith joined the Indiana National Guard. During the First World War, he served as an infantry soldier with the 4th Division in France. He was commissioned in 1917 and served as an intelligence officer. Following World War II, Smith was named by President Truman to be the U.S. ambassador to the Soviet Union. In 1949, he became the Commanding General of the First Army and was stationed in New York City. He was named the Director of Central Intelligence by Truman in October 1950, following U.S. intelligence's failure to foresee the invasion of South Korea by North Korea that summer. Does the CIA have its own "X-Files"? Maybe. Smith thought that UFOs could have national security implications and ordered a study to be done. The results remain classified. Smith left the CIA and retired from active duty in the army in 1953. He became the Under-Secretary of State for a year before retiring to a writing career during which he published books such as *Eisenhower's Six Great Decisions* (1956) and *My Three Years in Moscow* (1949). Smith died in 1961.

- Gordon Gray (1909–1982), a lawyer who from 1937 to 1947 was a newspaper publisher (the *Winston-Salem Journal* and the *Twin City Sentinel*). He was chairman of the board of the Piedmont Publishing Company. Gray was appointed in 1950 as special assistant to President Truman on National Security Affairs. He became national security director of the CIA's Psychological Strategy Board in 1951.

- Top American scientist J. Robert Oppenheimer (1904–1967). Famous physicist known as the father of the atomic bomb, Oppenheimer attended Harvard, Cambridge and Gottingen University. He received his doctorate in 1927. Oppenheimer taught advanced physics at Berkeley and Cal Tech for fifteen years. During World War II, Oppenheimer was appointed by President Franklin Roosevelt as head of the Manhattan Project, the research and development program that produced the atom bomb. Oppenheimer worked out of Los Alamos. After the bomb was developed, Oppenheimer advised against using it against the Japanese. After the war, he supported international efforts to control atomic energy. In 1953, President Eisenhower removed Oppenheimer's security clearance because of alleged left-wing leanings. Oppenheimer continued his work at Princeton's Institute for Advanced Study and was honored with the Enrico Fermi Award in 1963.

- Thornton Page, former professor of astronomy at the University of Chicago; Deputy Director of the Johns Hopkins Operations Research Office.

- H.P. Robertson, CIA physicist and Director of the Weapons Systems Evaluation Group in the Office of the Secretary of Defense. During January 1953, worried that the Soviet Union might attempt to destabilize the United States with tales of a UFO invasion, Robertson suggested to a CIA panel investigating UFOs that the United States Air Force start a "debunking" campaign using celebrities saying that they didn't believe in UFOs and we shouldn't either. He also suggested that "police" keep a close eye on UFO research organizations, since such groups could easily be used for "subversive purposes."

- Sidney W. Souers. Souers was appointed by President Truman as the first Director of Central Intelligence on January 23, 1946, one day after he signed the presidential directive that gave birth to the Central Intelligence Group. Souers, born in 1892, was a 1914 graduate of Miami University in Ohio. He was a businessman who had great success with his investments. Souers was appointed a lieutenant commander—an intelligence officer—in the Naval Reserve, in April 1929, and, as far as we know, was not called into active duty until 1940. During the first years of World War II, Souers worked in district intelligence offices in Great Lakes, Illinois; Charleston, South Carolina; and San Juan, Puerto Rico. He must have done some good things because he received a major promotion in July 1944 when he was named assistant chief of naval intelligence in charge of plans and the deputy chief of naval intelligence in Washington, D.C. That is a considerable jump in rank and duties. He was promoted to rear admiral in 1945 and served on a committee representing the Secretary of the Navy, determining the feasibility of forming a central intelligence organization. President Truman liked Souers' proposal so much that he put him in charge of the Central Intelligence Group's formation, and named him its first director. Considering that Truman excelled at picking good people for important jobs, we can assume that Souers had the credentials to achieve what the President wanted done and the perseverance to get it done. After getting the CIG up and running, Souers retired briefly to private life before returning to government work at the request of the Atomic Energy Commission, for whom he conducted a study to determine the security requirements of preserving the secret of the Bomb. In September 1947, Truman appointed Souers the first executive secretary of the National Security Council, and Souers remained in that position until 1950. He retired from the Naval Reserve in 1953 and spent much of the 1950s speaking out against McCarthyism and its indiscriminate anti-Communism, a symptom of paranoia, he felt, more destructive than Communism itself.

- Dr. Detlev Wulf Bronk, a biophysicist whose specialty was the human nervous system. Bronk was, according to some reports, the leader of an autopsy team for aliens supposedly found near a UFO crash near Roswell, New Mexico, in July 1947.

- John Von Neumann, top American scientist during the 1940s and '50s.

Does MJ-12 still exist? Dr. Steven Greer, director of the Center for the Study of Extraterrestrial Intelligence (CSETI), has reported that the MJ-12 Group is now designated PI-40.

Molly Maguires The Molly Maguires were a union of Pennsylvania coal miners that formed around the time of the Civil War. The members of the union, which was officially called Workingmen's Benevolent Association, were predominantly Irish, and most of them were also members of the secret society known as the Ancient Order of Hibernians, which began in Ireland and spread to the United States. The group earned the nickname Molly Maguires after a group of Irish peasants who dressed up as women to antagonize their corrupt landlords. Dressed in drag as a disguise, the original Molly Maguires became known as murderers. Therefore, when the U.S. press labeled the Pennsylvania miners as Molly Maguires, it wasn't exactly a compliment. As a result, many miners who might have wanted to participate in union activities decided not to because they did not want to be called a "Molly."

The group had good reason to form a union. Not only were the miners underpaid, but their working conditions were hideously dangerous. Mines were never inspected for safety. Collapses were frequent. There was no ventilation. Lung problems were common. Things improved slightly in 1870 when a law was passed stating that all coal mines needed two entrances so that there would be an escape route in case of a collapse or fire. This legislation, which was local-only and poorly enforced, did not come as a result of union activities, but rather because of the "Avondale Fire" in 1869 that killed 179 men.

Other grievances the men had included the "bob-tailed check," which meant that the men were not paid in cash at the end of the week but instead in overpriced goods and groceries from the company-owned store. Strikes in 1868 and 1875 were unsuccessful.

The Mollies, working in secret, became a militant and violent group. In response, owners intimidated miners into submission by maiming and murdering those suspected of union activism. Over the long haul, many more miners were killed in the struggle than corporate employees. The Catholic Church came out on the side of management and threatened to excommunicate Mollies.

Men who were arrested as Mollies were quickly tried and hanged, despite sometimes-flimsy evidence against them. In 1877, nineteen men were tried for Molly crimes and all were executed.

The Molly Maguires of Pennsylvania represented the first large movement solely by workers.

The Cleveland, Ohio, baseball franchise of the American League, now called the Indians, was known as the Molly Maguires during the years 1912–14.

N

National Restoration Organization   How large and how organized this Vietnamese secret society is remains unknown, but they have managed to create a stir in that country since 2001, largely through a letter-writing campaign. Thousands of letters from the group to major media outlets throughout the country call for a removal of the Communist Party from power. Specifically, the letters denounce the Fourth Amendment of the Vietnamese constitution, which says that the Vietnamese Communist Party represents the hope and dreams of the Vietnamese people and it is committed to Marxist-Leninist ideology and the socialist ideals of Ho Chi Minh.

One letter said, "But the communist party is an unworkable party. It is full of infighting and factionalism. . . . It manages to have complete power over the people of Vietnam because of the 4th Amendment and it continues to oppress religious groups and all social activities that it deems threatening to its survival."

National Security Council   The National Security Council (NSC) was created on July 26, 1947, by the National Security Act. That Act also provided for a Secretary of Defense, a National Military Establishment, Central Intelligence Agency, National Security Agency, and National Security Resources Board. Since the NSC's birth, council members have also been, more often than not, members of the Council on Foreign Relations and/or the Trilateral Commission.

The NSC advises the U.S. president on issues of foreign and defense policy. The council coordinates foreign and defense policy, and reconciles diplomatic and military commitments and requirements. According to the law, the NSC consists of the President, the Vice President, the Secretary of State, and the Secretary of Defense, with the Joint Chiefs of Staff, the Director of the CIA, and the Assistant to the President for National Security Affairs—otherwise known as the "National Security Adviser." (The position of National Security Adviser was created by President Dwight D. Eisenhower on March 23, 1953, in response to a report on NSC organization by Robert Cutler. By design, the National Security Adviser has the President's ear when it comes to all matters of National Security. Just how much he or she dominates the President's ear, or shares it with other members of the NSC, depends on the president.)

The President can also request that other officials take part. The National Security Council is at the center of the United States' foreign policy coordination system. It has changed many times since its birth in 1947, and usually reflects the attitudes, needs, and inclinations of the President, who changes the personnel on the council in an attempt to avoid the problems and deficiencies of his predecessor's council.

Chaired by the President of the United States, the council was created to coordinate political and military questions, but in practice it serves only the President, who uses it as a means of controlling and managing competing departments.

The Chairman of the Joint Chiefs of Staff is the statutory military adviser to the Council, and the Director of Central Intelligence is the intelligence adviser. The Chief of Staff to the President, Counsel to the President, and the Assistant to the President for Economic Policy are invited to attend any NSC meeting.

The Attorney General and the Director of the Office of Management and Budget are invited to attend meetings pertaining to their responsibilities. The heads of other executive departments and agencies, as well as other senior officials, are invited to attend meetings of the NSC when appropriate.

One can always tell a lot about the personality of a president by who dominates his NSC. Truman's NSC was pretty much run by the Secretary of State. Eisenhower (being a retired general) had an NSC dominated by the military. Kennedy's easy style tended to blur the line between policy-making and operations.

Johnson distrusted the NSC structure and tended to rely more on the advice of trusted friends. Under Nixon and Ford, Secretary of

State Henry Kissinger dominated the NSC, which concentrated on acquiring analytical information. Carter allowed his National Security Adviser to become a principal source of foreign affairs ideas.

Under Reagan, the National Security Adviser was downgraded, and the Chief of Staff to the President exercised a coordinating role in the White House. The first President Bush—who was the Director of Central Intelligence himself during 1976–77—brought his own considerable foreign policy experience to his leadership of the National Security Council, and reorganized the NSC organization to include a Principals Committee, Deputies Committee, and eight Policy Coordinating Committees.

Under Clinton, the NSC membership was expanded to include the Secretary of the Treasury, the U.S. Representative to the United Nations, the newly created Assistant to the President for Economic Policy (who was also head of a newly created National Economic Council or NEC, parallel to the NSC), the President's Chief of Staff, and the President's National Security Adviser.

The NSC played an effective role during such major developments as the collapse of the Soviet Union, the unification of Germany, and the deployment of American troops in Iraq and Panama.

Nation of Islam   The religious sect known as the Nation of Islam was made popular by Elijah Muhammad, who was born Elijah Poole around October 7, 1897, in a rural part of Georgia known as Sandersville. The exact date of his birth is uncertain because of poor record-keeping in the area at that time. Elijah was one of twelve children of William and Marie Poole. His father was a minister. In 1919, Elijah married a woman named Clara Evans. The couple eventually had eight children. At the time of his marriage, Elijah worked for both the railroad and a brick company. But in April 1923, he took his family north to Detroit, Michigan, where he got a job working on an automobile assembly line.

In 1930, Elijah met the founder of the Nation of Islam (then known as the Temple of Islam), Wallace D. Ford, who preached that it was time for black people to return to Islam, the religion of their ancestors. When Elijah met him, Ford was selling silk products door-to-door, but he said he was a prophet who came from Africa to help blacks understand their heritage. The black race, according to Ford, was the superior "original race," and black Americans were Islam's lost sheep and he wanted to bring them back home.

According to Elijah's later teachings, he learned from Ford that in the early days of the world, black men were in charge. Black scientists, Ford claimed, created the seas and the mountains. They were in contact with nine-foot-tall men from Mars who caused the moon to blast into orbit around the Earth from its previous place beneath the Pacific Ocean.

Elijah became Ford's chief aide and devoted disciple. Ford gave Elijah his Muslim name, Muhammad. In 1934, Elijah was arrested for encouraging Black Muslim parents to send their children to Muslim schools, which were not considered legitimate schools by the Michigan State Board of Education. Elijah did not serve jail time, but his schools were closed down.

In response, Elijah, along with Ford, moved to Chicago. Ford disappeared on February 26, 1934, and to this day no one knows what happened to him. After his disappearance, Elijah took control of the Nation of Islam.

The next year, Elijah moved to Washington, D.C., after hearing rumors of death threats against him. In 1942, during World War II, Elijah was arrested, along with many other Black Muslims, for draft evasion. Elijah was imprisoned, even though he was forty-five years old—too old to be drafted. He was not released from prison until World War II ended in 1945.

In the years following the war, the Nation of Islam went on a membership drive, preaching the message of black power to people in ghettos and prisons.

During the 1950s, one of the men recruited by the Nation of Islam while serving a prison term was Malcolm Little, the man who would become famous to the world as Malcolm X. During the 1960s, the most famous recruit of the Nation of Islam was the World Heavyweight Boxing Champion Cassius Clay, who changed his name to Muhammad Ali.

Malcolm X left the Nation of Islam in 1964 after he learned that Elijah Muhammad had been unfaithful to his wife and had fathered children out of wedlock. Malcolm became a member of the Islamic religion, which is not associated with the Nation of Islam. The Nation of Islam immediately declared that Malcolm was their enemy.

In 1965, Malcolm X was assassinated by members of the Nation of Islam while delivering a speech at the Audubon Ballroom in New York City. By the time of Malcolm's death, the Nation of Islam had spread to more than sixty cities in the United States and to Ghana, Mexico, and Caribbean countries.

In 1972, Elijah appointed Louis Farrakhan as the Nation's new spokesman. Farrakhan was born Louis Eugene Walcott on May 11, 1933, in Roxbury, Massachusetts, and was raised by his mother, a native of St. Kitts, an island in the Caribbean Sea. His mother taught him about the African American struggle for equality, freedom, and justice. Recognizing Louis's musical talent, his mother gave him a violin for his sixth birthday. A child prodigy, by age thirteen he had played with the Boston College Orchestra and the Boston Civic Symphony. The following year, he became nationally famous when he won a talent contest on the *Ted Mack Amateur Hour*, a popular TV show at the time.

As an entertainer, he became known as "The Charmer." Louis graduated from high school at age sixteen. Because he had also been a track-and-field star, he earned a scholarship to Winston-Salem Teacher's College in North Carolina, where he excelled in English. Louis married his childhood sweetheart in September 1953, during his senior year. Needing money to support his new family, he quit college and became a professional performing artist—singing, dancing, and playing the violin.

In February 1955, while appearing on a show called Calypso Follies, Louis was invited by Malcolm X to visit the Nation of Islam's Temple Number Two. Soon afterward, Louis joined the organization and became known as Louis X. He gave up show business and became a minister for the Nation of Islam's Boston temple in 1956.

At first, Louis was a devoted follower of Malcolm, even patterning his speaking style after him. But when Malcolm split from the Nation of Islam, Louis turned on him, calling him a traitor. (Today, Malcolm's family says that Louis turned on Malcolm earlier than he admits.)

After Malcolm X was assassinated, Louis became head of the Nation's Harlem mosque. He quickly became the Nation's number-one spokesman, and continued to promote Elijah Muhammad's teachings even after Elijah died in 1975. Farrakhan has been the spokeman for the Nation of Islam for thirty-five years. Under his leadership, the "Black Muslims" have thrived.

In 1995, Farrakhan organized the successful Million Man March in Washington, D.C. Hundreds of thousands of black men attended the march and vowed to renew their commitment to family, community, and personal responsibility.

While the Nation of Islam works to create healthier black individuals and communities, it has been heavily criticized for its hateful teachings about white people, especially Jewish people. Many black leaders have condemned Farrakhan's anti-Semitic remarks. The Nation still talks of Martians being involved in the creation of the world.

In 1995, Farrakhan told a gathering that he had had a vision of a UFO. He said that Martians had abducted him and taken him to the mother ship, where he met Elijah Muhammad, who gave Louis the idea for the Million Man March. Unlike Malcolm X, who never had any money of his own, Louis Farrakhan lives in luxury in a mansion in Michigan. He is the father of nine children and has many grandchildren and great grandchildren.

New Templars, Order of the   SEE ORDER OF THR NEW TEMPLARS.

Ninja   The Japanese word *ninjutsu* means "the art of stealing in," something we would refer to today as "espionage." These highly secretive black-clad warriors originated as mystics who developed secret techniques to protect themselves from outsiders, inventing new bombs, masks, poisons, and martial arts techniques.

The history of ninja has been passed down from generation to generation. According to entertheninja.com (accessed March 2, 2004): "*Nonuse* ('the art of stealth') was first introduced to Japan in 522 A.D. as a religion practiced by priests. These priests were not violent people, they were 'mystics' who gathered and shared information for the ruling classes. The ninja as we know them were not introduced until later. It wasn't until 645 A.D. that the priests perfected their fighting skills and made use of their knowledge of *nonuse*. This was because they found themselves being harassed by the central government and found it necessary to protect themselves. In A.D. 794–1192 the new civilization flourished and with it, a new class of wealthy, privileged families. These families fought with one another in attempts to make or destroy emperors. The need for spies, informants, and now assassins grew as these families dueled for power. They were suspicious and jealous of one another and would resort to any means necessary to eliminate any possible threats. Therefore, the practitioners of *nonuse* were in great demand. With this, the ninja was born. As the ninja gained popularity, so did the stories of their superhuman abilities. This reputation was often encouraged by the ninja themselves. Because they were a relatively weaker people then their counterparts, the samurai, and were vulnerable to attack by the many warring families around them, it was to their advantage to have others believe they had such powers. Powers like having the strength of ten men, ability to turn into animals, fly, and become invisible at will. The ninja movies also added to the abilities by having the ninja jump over buildings in a single jump, catch bullets in their teeth and see into the future."

The Japanese outlawed *ninjutsu* in the 1600s, but the shadowy agents simply moved their operations further underground.

Nobles of the Mystic Shrine   See SHRINERS.

O

ODESSA/Die Spinne   Two well-financed pro-Nazi organizations that formed after World War II out of the chaos of war-torn Europe, reportedly under the auspices of the Vatican. Odessa/Die Spinne helped as many as 30,000 Nazis escape Europe, often moving them to South America. Other criminals were moved to the Middle East and the United States.

The Vatican aided these groups to "provide spiritual and material assistance to the impoverished" and has always claimed that they did not know the identity and background of those who were helped. However, it has been alleged that high-ranking priests did know that there were war criminals among those in Odessa.

The finger of guilt is most frequently pointed at a Roman Catholic Bishop named Alois Hudal, Rector of the Pontificio Santa Maria dell'Anima. During World War II, Bishop Hudal had spoken publicly about the unity between the Catholic Church and the Nazi government. Bishop Hudal is one of the things that Odessa and Die Spinne had in common.

ODESSA stood for the *Organisation Der Ehemaligen SS-Angehörigen* ("Organization of Former SS Members"). It was formed in 1947 by Luftwaffe ace Hans-Ulrich Rudel and Otto Skorzeny. The escape routes were called "rat lines."

According to Gitta Sereny's book *Into That Darkness*, Bishop Hudal provided sleeping quarters and transportation for the postwar Nazis, and "seemed to have plenty of money for extra payoffs, bribes, and emergencies that may arise."

Odessa supposedly ceased to exist around 1952, replaced by *Kameradenwerke* ("Comrade Workshop"). This new organization was dedicated to helping former Nazis evade capture or exposure in their host countries by developing new identities and cover stories.

The organization gained notoriety in 1972 with the publication of the suspense thriller *The Odessa File* by Frederick Forsyth.

Odd Fellows   An international organization dedicated to helping one another in time of misfortune. It has its own complex system of rites and passwords. The Independent Order of Odd Fellows was organized on April 26, 1819, in Baltimore, Maryland, by Thomas Wildey and four other Odd Fellows from England.

The group claims to be the world's largest united international fraternal order, having 22,000 lodges and a membership numbering in the millions. Lodges are in Norway, Sweden, Iceland, Holland, Belgium, Cuba, Denmark, Germany, Australia, Switzerland, Mexico, Hawaii, South America, Finland, Panama Canal Zone, France, Canada, and the United States.

The commands of Odd Fellowship are to:

1. Visit the Sick,
2. Relieve the Distressed,
3. Bury the Dead, and
4. Educate the Orphan.

The three principles of the Order are Friendship, Love, and Truth. It seeks to "make good men better citizens, better fathers, better sons, husbands, and Brothers." The Odd Fellows' slogan is "We seek to elevate and improve the character of man." Sixty Odd Fellows Homes for children and the aged are operated in the United States and Canada.

The Odd Fellows were the first fraternal order to recognize a ladies' auxillary, the Rebekahs. According to their website: "Our Sisters of the Rebekah Degree are a vital and integral part of Odd Fellowship; working hand in hand with the Brothers in promoting the principles, and practicing the commands of our Order."

There are also Junior Odd Fellow Lodges for boys and Theta Rho Clubs for girls, ages twelve to twenty-one years.

Famous Odd Fellows include Franklin D. Roosevelt; Chief Justice Earl Warren; William Jennings Bryan; Governor Goodwin J. Knight; President Warren G. Harding; and Vice President Schuyler Colfax.

Contact info:

The Sovereign Grand Lodge
Independent Order of Odd Fellows
422 N. Trade Street
Winston-Salem, NC 27101
(919) 725-5955

Olympians   See COMMITTEE OF 300.

Opus Dei   Opus Dei, founded in Spain in 1928 by Josemaría Escrivá de Balaguer, says that its intended purpose is to "spread throughout society a profound awareness of the universal call to holiness and apostolate through one's professional work carried out with freedom and personal responsibility." The founder of the group died in 1975. In a controversial move, the Pope beatified him in 1992 and canonized him on October 6, 2002.

Both Catholic priests and Catholic lay people can be members. There are an estimated eighty thousand members worldwide. Most Opus Dei groups are urban, and many exist near major universities. College students, as a group, are the most heavily recruited. Members may be employed in the secular world, but their spiritual lives are strictly guided by Opus Dei. Members follow what is called "The Plan of Life." This consists of a series of spiritual practices including daily Mass, rosary, and spiritual reading.

There are different classes of membership. The strictest class is the Numerary Class. Members belonging to this class have committed their lives to Opus Dei. They live in Opus Dei houses and practice celibacy. All of their money goes to Opus Dei. They are not allowed to have their own bank accounts. They are given small weekly allowances with which to live their lives. Their incoming and outgoing mail is screened by their Opus Dei directors. Also screened and/or controlled by the directors are the members' reading material, radio listening, and television viewing.

There is a list almost three hundred pages long of books that are forbidden by Opus Dei. Forbidden books include Protestant Bibles and anything mentioning the theory of evolution.

All personal movements outside the residence must be approved by the director. Members believe that pain is good and cleanses the spirit. They inflict pain upon themselves both as penance for sins and to stifle sexual urges. These self-inflicted punishments are called corporal mortification. They wear a spiked chain around their thigh called a *cilice* and whip their own backs with a knotted whip. The cilice is worn two hours each day, except Sundays. The whip is used on the back or buttocks once a week. If members choose to use the whip on themselves more often, they must ask permission. Members are instructed to take cold rather than hot showers.

According to one former member: "The cilice and disciplines are so foreign to the experience of most people, that they just conclude that Opus Dei is very odd for mandating them. That is true as far as it goes, but there is a more important point to be made. Because of the dangers of masochism, the traditional Catholic teaching on this sort of mortification is that it be done under obedience to a spiritual director. Such supervision in fact exists in Opus Dei, although often authority is entrusted to people who lack requisite maturity and prudence. The real point is that even if the cilice and the discipline are acceptable forms of penance, their use shows that Opus Dei members are not ordinary people, are not free agents."

Members are often required to sleep on the floor. Some members of this class join as lay members and are then chosen for the Opus Dei priesthood, for which they are subsequently trained. Each Opus Dei house has its own priest who says mass and takes confessions. Members are discouraged from confessing to non-member priests.

Numerary assistants are women who are the housekeepers at Opus Dei residences.

The next class of Opus Dei is the Supernumerary Class. Members belonging to this class are allowed to marry and have families. They also follow the practices of the "Plan of Life," but are generally kept uninformed regarding the extreme practices of their Numerary Class counterparts. They live in their own homes, yet still contribute a majority of their income to Opus Dei. All of the leaders of Opus Dei are Numerary priests. It has been claimed that Opus Dei has infiltrated the Vatican and that many high-ranking officials serving the Pope are Opus Dei Numerary priests.

Then there is the Associate Class, made up of members who live in their own homes but pledge celibacy. Finally there are the "Cooperators" who are not considered official members of the group but who supply financial assistance. Cooperators do not necessarily have to be Catholic.

Like many cults, Opus Dei discourages their members from contact with their families. They are told that it would be a waste of time discussing Opus Dei with their families because they "would not understand." Many members are instructed to keep their families ignorant of the fact that they have joined the group.

Members form teams who formulate aggressive recruiting strategies. The interests and hobbies of potential recruits are analyzed and like-minded members are assigned to use the common interest to make contact. Opus Dei meetings always include a rundown of potential recruits and how things are going regarding them. All members are encouraged to have ten to twenty "friends" who might eventually join the group. Members use friendship as bait and end friendships with people who are unlikely to join the group. Potential recruits are unaware that their recruitment is being formally plotted. At some colleges and universities, Opus Dei recruits through "front organizations." Clubs are formed that are completely run by Opus Dei, but under another name. These include Right to Life and prayer groups. Those who join the club are then aggressively recruited for Opus Dei. Recruiting is also done within Roman Catholic parishes.

Because of a ruling in the early 1980s by the Vatican that Opus Dei is a "personal Prelature" within the Church, local dioceses have no control over the activities of Opus Dei residences that may be functioning in their neighborhoods. It is impossible for outsiders to determine the extent of Opus Dei infiltration within a parish because Opus Dei activities are kept secret. Pressure to join is frequently put upon people whose lives are in crisis, when the potential recruit is emotionally vulnerable.

Since 1991, a group called the Opus Dei Awareness Network (ODAN) has existed to educate the world about what they refer to as the "questionable practices" of Opus Dei. ODAN is comprised of former members of Opus Dei and the frustrated families of current members.

According to ODAN, new members of Opus Dei agree to commit themselves to the group before it is explained to them what that commitment entails. When they do learn the extent of their commitment, they are told that they made a promise and not to keep it would be "turning their back on God." Those who decide to leave Opus Dei are told "that they will surely live a life without God's grace, and may even be damned."

See also PRIORY OF SION.

The Order   See SKULL & BONES.

Order of American Knights   Spin-off of the Knights of the Golden Circle.

Order of Malta   See THE SOVEREIGN ORDER OF SAINT JOHN OF JERUSALEM.

Order of Oriental Templars   See OTO.

Order of the German Houses   See TEUTONIC KNIGHTS.

The Order of the Gold and Rosy Cross   See ROSICRUCIANS.

Order of the Golden Dawn   See ROUND TABLE.

Order of the New Templars   The founder of this group was Jorg Lanz von Liebenfels, a Cistercian monk who published the black magic and erotica magazine called *Ostara*. Liebenfels, it is said, was a great influence on Adolf Hitler, and it was this group's use of the swastika that led Hitler to choose that symbol as the emblem of the Nazi party. Liebenfels used the swastika because it had been a symbol used by the Teutonic Knights of the medieval age.

See also KNIGHTS TEMPLAR; THULE SOCIETY.

The Order of the Rose and the Cross See ROSICRUCIANS.

Oriental Templars See OTO.

Order of the Temple of the East See OTO.

OTO (Ordo Templi Orientis) OTO believes in no rules governing human behavior. Their one law is: "Do what thou wilt shall be the whole of the Law."

According to the OTO website, "The letters O.T.O. stand for Ordo Templi Orientis, the Order of Oriental Templars, or Order of the Temple of the East. O.T.O. is an Outer Thelemic Order which is dedicated to the high purpose of securing the Liberty of the Individual and his or her advancement in Light, Wisdom, Understanding, Knowledge, and Power through Beauty, Courage, and Wit, on the Foundation of Universal Brotherhood."

The founder of OTO was Carl Kellner, a wealthy German industrialist and an initiated Mason who, in the late nineteenth century, was initiated into OTO's ancient tradition of *magick* (spelled with a *k* to distinguish it from the tricks performed by stage magicians) and mysticism by three wise men while he was in Asia seeking self-knowledge. Because of this knowledge, Kellner created his own secret society, which he called the Hermetic Brotherhood of Light. The sect eventually became known as OTO.

The group differed from the Freemasons in that they allowed women to join as full-fledged members, a necessity because many of the sect's rituals involved heterosexual orgies. Kellner's partner in the creation of OTO was Theodor Reuss, a former spy for the Prussian Secret Service who was experienced with secret societies. Reuss was a professional singer, a Grand Master Mason, and a Rosicrucian, who had attempted to create a modern version of the Illuminati.

Politically, OTO was extremely right-wing. Kellner and Reuss shared an interest in "sex magick" and together translated Asian Tantric sex manuals. They had a theory that sex fluids could be useful in alchemy, with the correct combination of male and female juices used to create a magickal child known as a homunculus. When Kellner died in 1905, Reuss took over as OTO's leader.

Aleister Crowley was OTO's most famous member. He joined the group in 1910, and, being another sex magick aficionado, quickly rose through OTO's lower degrees. The lower degrees of OTO are referred to as M:.M:.M:., with both a colon and a period between the letters. He rose to the top of the organization.

The "acid tests" in the mid-1960s in which youngsters would get together in a school gymnasium or other large space and take LSD together, then listen to psychedelic music, were thought to be very modern and innovative at the time. But, in reality, the same sort of psychedelic drug group experiments had been held by Aleister Crowley as far back as 1910. Crowley would gather people together in one place, such as Caxton Hall—in Salford, England—and give everyone a drink that contained psychedelic mushrooms. He called this experiment the Rites of Eleusis.

By 1912, Crowley—who called himself the "Great Beast"—was the OTO grand master in England and Ireland. He claimed to have learned his knowledge through the Knights Templar, the Gnostics, the Illuminati, the Knights of Malta, the Holy Grail, the Rosicrucians, the Masons (all Rites), and the Golden Dawn (and all Hermetic traditions).

Reuss died in 1921, leaving Crowley as OTO's sole leader. (OTO's leader is referred to as the "Caliph." Crowley publicly declared himself the priest of a religion called Thelema, which he had learned of near the turn of the century through channeling. Crowley introduced to OTO the "Gnostic Mass," which is based on the Catholic Mass. However, his ceremony features a nude woman sitting on the altar as well as groping among the congregation. Communion consists of swallowing "symbolic" semen.

Under Crowley's guidance, OTO spread into the United States. In the U.S., OTO opened the Agape Lodge, which was led by a man named Jack Parsons, a California Institute of Technology rocket pioneer who claimed to be the "anti-Christ." Parsons, a science fiction addict who was one of the first Americans to report seeing a UFO, was friends with L. Ron Hubbard, who is said to have used elements of Thelema when devising his own religion, Scientology.

Dr. John Whiteside Parsons' work in rocket fuel laid the groundwork for manned space travel. Parsons was a founding member of the Jet Propulsion Laboratory (JPL), and later founded the Aerojet Corporation. Parsons chose as the site for the new JPL an area in the Arroyo Seco section of Pasadena known as "Devil's Gate." JPL opened on Halloween night, 1936. Because of a suggestion by the International Astronomical Union in 1972, a crater on the moon was named after him. He was a descendant of one of the founders of the Hell-Fire Club in Great Britain.

For those looking to link modern secret societies with those of long ago, here's the route in this case, with the fewest degrees of separation: Parsons' Jet Propulsion Laboratory was derived from CalTech's Guggenheim Aeronautical Laboratory, which had been headed by Professor Theodore von Karman, who claimed to be a direct descendant of Rabbi Judah Loew, who had been the teacher of John Dee, who has been called the founder of Freemasonry and was said to have designed for Queen Elizabeth I the creation of the British Empire.

Parsons was born in Los Angeles on October 2, 1914. His mother was a wealthy woman who took part in occult activities, Ruth Virginia Whiteside, and his father was Marvel H. Parsons, who came from an Irish family involved in making telescope lenses. Parsons was born Marvel Whiteside Parsons but later became known as Jack. He was raised in Pasadena, California. Parsons' name in OTO was Frater Belarion, the "Anti-Christ, consort of Babalon." Parsons was once filmed having sex with his mother and also partook in acts of bestiality. Despite this, Parsons possessed a top secret security clearance and was employed by the National Defense Research Council, U.S. Navy, U.S. Army, the Los Angeles Superior Court, the Los Angeles Police Department, and the Israeli government. In 1950, Parsons was caught by the Propulsion and Research Development Laboratory of Hughes Aircraft giving secret documents regarding U.S. rocket and defense technology to the Israelis, but he was not prosecuted because of the intervention in 1951 of FBI director, and Mason, J. Edgar Hoover.

A Dr. Frankenstein wannabe, Parsons was, according to his own claims, trying to create life out of lifelessness through "magick." He referred to his creation as a homunculus. Parsons was killed in 1952 at the age of 37 in an explosion at JPL headquarters in Pasadena.

There are other connections between OTO and outer space. OTO established one of its first temples on Mount Palomar, which later became the site of CalTech's observatory with its 200-inch telescope.

OTO became close to dormant during World War II. Crowley grew ill and the job of running the organization went to Karl Germer (also known as Frater Saturnus X), who declared that OTO would no longer accept new members. In-fighting between factions of OTO broke out. In 1947, Crowley died. The infighting worsened in the 1960s when Germer died.

A period of chaos in OTO followed, which lasted until a man named Grady McMurty, Crowley's friend, took over in 1969. McMurty opened the organization up to new members, but it remained factionalized.

According to mindcontrolforums.com (accessed March 2, 2004): "The OTO's Solar Lodge in San Bernardino was founded by Maury McCauley, a mortician, on his own property. McCauley was married to Barbara Newman, a former model and the daughter of a retired Air Force colonel from Vandenberg. The group subscribed to a grim, apocalyptic view of the world precipitated by race wars, and the prophecy made a lasting impression on Charles Manson, who passed through the lodge. In the L.A. underworld, the OTO spin-off was known for indulgence in sadomasochism, drug dealing, blood drinking, child molestation, and murder. The Riverside OTO, like the Manson Family, used drugs, sex, psycho-drama, and fear to tear down the mind of the initiate and rebuild it according to the desires of the cult's inner-circle."

When McMurty retired as Caliph, his successor was elected. The next and current leader of OTO is believed to have the given name William Breeze, but is known officially only by his "magick name," Hymenaeus Beta. As of 1996, OTO had branches around the world (in forty-two countries) and was said to have a worldwide membership of about three thousand.

OTO's governing body in the U.S. is the U.S. Grand Lodge, which has hundreds of members and local branches in forty-five communities spread out over twenty-six states.

OTO membership is private. Names and addresses of members are kept secret. There are two types of membership: associate and initiate. Associates can be members by correspondence only. For a fee these members can get the OTO publication, called *The Magickal Link*. Those interested in becoming associate members can write to:

Ordo Templi Orientis
Associate Memberships
P.O. Box 430
Fairfax, CA 94978

Initiate members must undergo a physical ceremony to gain that status. From the bottom of the organization to the top, there are eighteen degrees for initiate members. Eleven have numbers, seven do not.

The bottom degree, the zero degree, is known as the Minerval Degree. Advancement is by invitation only. The first degree is known as "Man and Brother." The second degree is Magician. The third is Master Magician. The first three degrees are known as the Man of Earth Triad. The Man of Earth degrees are based on the stages of Kundalini Yoga and represent the Individual's Path in Eternity.

The fourth degree is called Perfect Magician and companion of the Holy Royal Arch of Enoch, Perfect Initiate, or Prince of Jerusalem. The fifth, sixth, and seventh degrees are known as the Lovers' Triad. The fifth degree is called Sovereign Prince Rose-Croix, and Knight of the Pelican and Eagle, Knight of the Red Eagle, and Member of the Senate of Knight Hermetic Philosophers. The sixth degree is called Illustrious Knight (Templar) of the Order of Kadosch, and Companion of the Holy Grail, Grand Inquisitor Commander, and Member of the Grand Tribunal, Prince of the Royal Secret. The seventh is called Very Illustrious Sovereign Grand Inspector General and Member of the Supreme Grand Council.

The eighth, ninth, and tenth degrees are called the Hermit Triad. The eighth degree is known as Perfect Pontiff of the Illuminati and Epopt of the Illuminati. The ninth is called Initiate of the Sanctuary of the Gnosis. And the tenth is Rex Summus Sanctissimus. The tenth degree is for a national grand master.

During membership in the higher degrees, there is instruction in Hermetic Philosophy, Qabalah, Magick, and Yoga, all aimed at preparing the Initiate for the revelation and application of one Supreme Secret.

See also SCIENTOLOGY.

P

P2   See Propaganda Due.

Palo Monte   See Palo Mayombe.

Palo Mayombe   Like Santeria, Palo Mayombe (also known as Palo Monte) is an African religion that was practiced in secret and in camouflaged forms in Central and South America by slaves of African origin. Today, it is practiced by both those of African and Hispanic descent. Palo Mayombe originated in Central Africa among Bantu-speaking people, in the region today called the Congo and Angola. Today it is practiced most extensively in Cuba, Suriname, and Brazil.

Palo teaches that all that exists is inhabited by spirits and that the rituals of Palo offer its members a method for direct communication with the spirits. Palo mediums channel messages from other worlds, from the dead, and from nature. The highest spirits, they believe, inhabit man and the major forces of nature, such as the sea, the wind, and lightning.

The centerpiece of Palo rituals is a cauldron called the Nganga or Prenda, which is filled with sacred bones, sticks (which are called palos), and earth. The cauldron is the home of the spirits of the dead, who act as intermediaries between man and the other spirits.

In order to practice Palo Mayombe in a Christian world, many of the original symbols have been replaced by Christian symbols. Images of Christian saints and the cross are used. Saints are used most frequently in the Palo rituals of Colombia and Venezuela.

Initiation into Palo involves a ceremony called *Rayamiento* (scratching), during which special marks are scratched onto the skin and the new member becomes protected by a particular spirit, usually the same spirit that protects his or her Godfather. Members then graduate to the next level when they receive their own cauldron, thus becoming a Tata or Yaya (father or mother).

Where do the bones in the cauldron come from? Well, in at least some cases, they come from the nearest graveyard. According to an Associated Press report of March 5, 2004, "A woman was charged with leading a cult that stole bodies from city cemeteries and used them in religious ceremonies, police said. Miriam Mirabel, 60, of Irvington, [New Jersey,] was arrested Monday by Essex County authorities. Police had been looking for her since one of her followers was arrested in August after being found with skulls and other human remains. Authorities said Mirabel told her followers to steal two bodies from Mt. Pleasant Cemetery in 2001 and one body from Holy Sepulchre Cemetery in 2002. Some of the remains were taken to a religious store in Newark, where they were used in religious ceremonies, police said. Mirabel was a priestess in the Palo Mayombe cult, which originated among West African slaves. She pleaded innocent at an arraignment Tuesday to charges of burglary, theft of human remains and conspiracy. She was ordered held on $500,000 bail. Her attorney, John Convery, called the case ghoulish, but said the large bail amount was excessive."

Peacock Angel, The Order of the   Devil-worshipping society, with the Peacock Angel being a euphemism for the (Judeo-Christian) devil. Peacock Angel initiation rites (Yezidis), according to Arkon Daraul's *Secret Societies*, included "a holy thread, of intertwined black and red wool . . . put around the neck. Like the sacred thread of the Parsis and other ancient Middle Eastern cults, this must never be removed; and it sounds like the cord that the Templars were accused of wearing when the Order was suppressed as heretic."

The Order believes that the Yezidis may have existed as long as four thousand years ago, although there are great gaps in its history. Anthropologist Sami Said Ahmed completed a massive study of the Yezidis in 1975. He concluded that Yezidism, which may have considered literacy to be taboo, is "the mother of all Eastern religions," and may have been the group that originated Egyptian society, religion, and culture—that is, the point at which the prehistoric becomes historic. Yezidism, it is believed, originated the systems of magick, occult rites that were later practiced by groups such as OTO and the Sufis.

According to the Yezidis myth, the Yezidis can trace their heritage back to the beginning of humankind. It is believed that the Yezidis, whereas the rest of mankind was descended from Adam and Eve, were descended from Adam alone, although it is unclear how this is possible.

The Yezidis, the Order of the Peacock Angel believes, are descendants of a son born to Adam of his spittle—perhaps a reference to ancient cloning. The Yezidis sprung from the King of Peace, a man named Na-'umi, also known as Melek Miran. The group, it is believed, did not become known as Yezidis until many generations later, when they were led by a miracle worker named Yezid.

See also ANUNNAKI; OTO; SUFIS.

Penitentes New Mexico-based flagellants. According to the 1914 *Catholic Encyclopedia*: "The Hermanos Penitentes are a society of individuals, who, to atone for their sins, practice penance which consists principally of flagellation, carrying heavy crosses, binding the body to a cross, and tying the limbs to hinder the circulation of the blood. These practices have prevailed in Colorado and New Mexico since the beginning of the nineteenth century. Up to the year 1890, they were public; at present they are secret, though not strictly. The Hermanos Penitentes are men; in the latter half of the nineteenth century they admitted women and children into separate organizations, which, however, were never numerous. The society had no general organization or supreme authority. Each fraternity is local and independent with its own officers. The chief officer, *hermano mayor* (elder brother), has absolute authority, and as a rule holds office during life. The other officers are like those of most secret societies: chaplain, sergeant-at-arms, etc. The ceremony of the initiation, which takes place during Holy Week, is simple, excepting the final test. The candidate is escorted to the *morada* (dwelling), the home, or council house, by two or more Penitentes where, after a series of questions and answers consisting in the main of prayer he is admitted. He then undergoes various humiliations. First, he washes the feet of all present, kneeling before each; then he recites a long prayer, asking pardon for any offence he may have given. If any one present has been offended by the candidate, he lashes the offender on the bare back. Then comes the last and crucial test: four or six incisions, in the shape of a cross, are made just below the shoulders of the candidate with a piece of flint."

When New Mexico was under Mexican rule, the flagellation took place in the streets and in church. After the Americans took over, flagellation occurred mostly in the *morada* and was self-administered with a short whip made from *amole* weed leaves called a *disciplina*.

During the mid-nineteenth century, the Penitentes would parade from their *morada* naked from the waist up, whipping themselves. The parade would be led by *acompanadores* (escorts) who would drag heavy crosses. The procession would also be accompanied by singers of hymns. There would also be a wooden wagon that carried a figure representing death, about to shoot with a bow and arrow. The parade made its way through the streets to the church. The Penitentes would go into the church and pray, then would re-emerge and parade back to the *morada*.

On Good Friday one member of the group would be tied to a cross. By the end of the nineteenth century the mock crucifixions had stopped, and flagellation was conducted in secret. When a member of the group died, his corpse was still held in the *morada* for a few hours and whipped.

Self-abuse in the form of flagellation, as part of religious rituals, first occurred in 13th-century Italy, then Spain and Latin America in the 1500s. The development of secret societies based upon these rituals, it is thought, didn't occur until the nineteenth century. These organizations are thought still to exist in certain parts of Mexico, Central, and South America. The Catholic Church does not condemn flagellation but has tried to regulate and control the practice, first during the reign of Pope Leo XIII.

The Penitentes of New Mexico derived from a previous Franciscan group known as the Third Order of St. Francis, which first appeared in the 1600s. Though these Franciscans used flagellation, they did not purposefully break the skin with the whipping. They paraded barefoot to and from church, but carried only small crosses. The severity of the whipping and the heaviness of the crosses increased over the years. In 1886, Archbishop Salpointe of Santa Fe ordered them in the name of the Church to abolish flagellation and the carrying of the heavy crosses. The archbishop advised the elders of the organization to stick to the rules of the Third Order of St. Francis, but the Penitentes disregarded the orders and continued with their ways. Three years later, Archbishop Salpointe ordered the group to disband, which forced the Penitentes to practice their rituals in secrecy.

Philadelphians   Quasi-Masonic society established in the early eighteenth century. Among its members were Chevalier Andrew Ramsay, who was born in Scotland in 1680 and served as a mouthpiece for Charles Radclyffe. It was Radclyffe who established the first Freemason Lodge in Paris in 1725.

In 1737, Ramsay delivered an "Oration" regarding Freemasonry that remains a seminal document for that society.

Another member of the Philadelphians was Sir Isaac Newton. Both Radclyffe and Newton are listed as grand masters of the Priory of Sion.

See also FREEMASONS; PRIORY OF SION.

PI-40   See MJ-12.

Prince Hall Shriners   See SHRINERS.

Priory of Sion   Completely unknown until the mid-twentieth century, the Priory (Religious House) of Sion may have predated the Knights Templar and been the true template for the secret societies that followed. The group claimed to possess the true history of Christ.

Centuries passed between the life of Jesus and the first extant written mention of him. There are two possible reasons for this. One is that Jesus never existed and was created in order to form a religion around him. The other is that, once the religion was formed, all contemporary reports of Jesus were destroyed so that the Church's version of his biography could be the one and only version.

News of the Priory's existence first reached the public in 1956 when a slew of published works appeared on the subject in France. The information came in well-timed news leaks and appeared to be emanating from a single source. Among the information released were documents called the *Dossiers secrets*, which gave a history of the group and included a list of the group's grand masters. The *Dossiers secrets* amount to genealogical trees and were researched, they claim, by a man named Henri Lobineau.

The Priory of Sion, the documents say, was founded in 1090 by Godfrey de Bouillon, a descendant of Charlemagne who led the First Crusade into the Holy Land to expel the Muslims from Jerusalem. The original name of the group was the Knights of the Order of Notre Dame de Sion, with Sion being the Hebrew name for Jerusalem. The order was named after an abbey called Notre Dame du Mont de Sion, which was built on Mount Sion, a high hill to the south of Jerusalem, which in turn was built over the ruins of a Byzantine basilica and was known at the time as "the Mother of All Churches." According to one nineteenth-century report, the abbey was inhabited by Augustinian canons.

In 1178, Pope Alexander III wrote a document that lists the "Ordre de Sion's" possessions. According to Baigent, Leigh, and Lincoln, these possessions included "houses and large tracts of land in Picardy, in France (including Saint-Samson at Orléans), in Lombardy, Sicily, Spain, and Calabria; as well . . . as a number of sites in the Holy Land, including Saint Léonard at Acre. Until the Second World War, in fact, there were in the archives of Orléans no less than twenty chapters specifically citing the Ordre de Sion. During the bombing of the city in 1940 all but three of these disappeared."

Some believe the Priory may have created the Knights Templar—that the Priory and the Templars were one and the same for many years, not separating until 1188, the year after Jerusalem was retaken by the Muslims. The occasion for that separation is referred to as "the cutting of the elm." According to some tales there was actually an elm tree that was cut down, causing the separation of the two groups. The tree is said to have stood in a sacred field adjacent to a fortress at Gisors. During a meeting in this field, the story goes, between Henry II of England and Philip II of France, the sun was harsh and the elm tree provided the only shade. Henry II and his entourage arrived first for the meeting and took the choice shady spot. When Philip arrived he was forced to stand in the sun. Hostilities commenced. A battle was fought over the tree, which the French won. Philip, in anger, had his men cut down the tree. Many, however, believe that the name "cutting of the elm" is meant to be symbolic. Even in the Dark Ages, fighting a bloody battle over a shade tree seems silly, leading historians to believe that something has been left out of the story, perhaps something that was never made public in the first place.

According to Priory of Sion documents, however, the Knights Templar ceased to be under the control of the Priory following the cutting of the elm. Until 1188, the Templars and the Priory shared the same grand master. Following the incident, the Priory had its own grand master, separate from that of the Templars. The first of these was Jean de Gisors. It is also in 1188 that the order's name was officially changed from *Ordre de Sion* to *Prieuré de Sion*. At the same time, the Priory established a pair of subtitles for their group. The first of these was "Ormus," the meaning of which is unknown. The second was *"l'Ordre de la Rose-Croix Veritas,"* or the Order of the Real Rose Cross. This is more than five centuries before any other evidence of an organization calling itself Rosicrucian.

The Templars were persecuted by the Church and ended up in England and Scotland. The Priory of Sion stayed in France. The largest contingent of Priory of Sion members was founded in Orleans, France, in the twelfth century and sanctioned by King Louis VII.

Some believe that while the Priory of Sion and the Knights Templar were part of the same organization, the Templars served as the Priory's public arm—its military and business force. Some also believe that the goal of the Priory of Sion is to restore the Merovingian dynasty, whose bloodline still exists and can be traced directly back to Dagobert II, and perhaps as far back as Jesus of Nazareth.

Here's how the secret of the Priory of Sion was revealed: In 1885, a thirty-three-year-old priest named François Bérenger Saunière was assigned to the Rennes-le-Château parish. The village was isolated in the eastern foothills of the Pyrenees. In prehistoric times the area was considered sacred by Celtic tribes who inhabited the region. The village had been captured by the Church during the Albigensian Crusade of the early thirteenth century that eradicated the Cathars from the region. During the 1360s, the area's population was decimated by the plague.

The population at the time of Saunière was about 200. Only a few miles to the southeast of the village were the ruins of a medieval fortress which had once served as a headquarters for the Knights Templar. About a mile to the east of the town were the ruins of the home of Bertrand de Blanchefort, who had served as the fourth grand master of the Templars.

His church had stood since 1059, dedicated to Mary Magdalene. Beneath the church lay Visigoth ruins that dated back to the sixth century. Six years after his arrival, Saunière decided to refurbish the old church. When he removed the altar stone, which rested on two Visigoth columns, he found four parchments in sealed wooden tubes.

Two of the parchments contained genealogies (family trees). One dated from 1244, the same year that the treasure—thought to be gold, silver, and coin—of the Cathars was last seen in Montségur, only a half day's horseback ride from Rennes-le-Château. The other dated from 1644.

The other two parchments contained the writings of Antoine Bigou, the personal chaplain of the Blanchefort family. These parchments had been written in the 1780s. One of those parchments had words that ran together and letters that had been inserted between words, seemingly without meaning, or a code.

Saunière continued his restoration and in time found a carved flagstone from the seventh or eighth century. According to some sources, there was a crypt with human skeletons beneath the flagstone. In the churchyard were headstones dating from the seventh and eighth century. One of these marked the grave of Marie, Marquise d'Hautpoul de Blanchefort. The engravings upon the headstones contained seemingly purposeful errors: more codes. If the letters on the Marquise's grave marking are rearranged, they read, when translated into English: "To Dagobert II King and to Sion belongs this treasure and he is there dead." This message was repeated in the codes on the parchments Saunière had discovered.

Yale's Skull & Bones is a supersecret society whose members include some of the most powerful men in the world—including George W. Bush, shown here—and whose initiation rites involve nude wrestling and lying in a coffin in only underwear while recounting adolescent sexual experiences. These rites take place in the windowless crypt within the Skull & Bones mausoleum-like meeting house on the Yale campus. Sounds silly, but the influence of the group is anything but. (AP/WideWorld Photo)

John F. Kerry, like George W. Bush, is a member of the elite secret society Skull & Bones. The *New York Times* called that fact a "field day for conspiracy theorists." Kerry became a Bonesman in 1966. Bush was initiated two years later. (AP/WideWorld Photo)

On October 16, 1978, Pope John Paul II—the former Karol Wojtyla of Krakow, Poland—makes his first public appearance as the 265th pope, leader of the Roman Catholic Church and its headquarters at the Vatican. The Roman Catholic Church at one time ruled the Western world. The occupants of the Vatican comprise the only secret society to be recognized by most of the world as an independent nation. (AP/WIDEWORLD PHOTO)

Member of the Bilderbergs, the Fabian Society, the Council on Foreign Relations, the Tri-lateral Commission, the Bohemian Grove, and former chairman of the board of the Chase Bank, David Rockefeller was presented in 2002 with the George C. Marshall Award for his exceptional leadership in the international community during times of global crisis. With Rockefeller is former President George H. W. Bush, member of Skull & Bones and former Director of Central Intelligence. (AP/WIDEWORLD PHOTO)

A spin-off of the Knights of the Golden Circle, the Ku Klux Klan has been a leading white supremicist group since the end of the American Civil War. A domestic terror group, the members wear white robes and hoods to keep their identities secret, and burn crosses to protest racial integration. (AP/WIDEWORLD PHOTO/*VICKSBURG EVENING POST*)

On March 10, 2004, bombs exploded inside the three-story Masonic Temple in the Kartal district of Istanbul, Turkey. Suicide bombers were believed to be behind the blasts, which killed two and injured six. One of the victims was a Turkish waiter whose coffin is seen here carried by friends and family. (AP/WIDEWORLD PHOTO)

High Priestess of the Church of Satan, Kara LaVey, holds hands with a wax figure of her father, Anton LaVey, who founded the devil-worshipping society in 1966, and who died in 1997 in the San Francisco church's ritual chamber. (AP/WideWorld Photo)

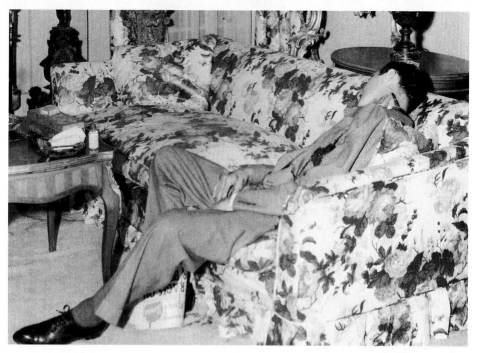

Mobster Benjamin "Bugsy" Siegel takes the big sleep on the chintz sofa in the living room of a friend's Beverly Hills home, on June 21, 1947. The shots came through the window. Mafia violence is often internal, as factions, or "families," make war against one another. (AP/WIDEWORLD PHOTO)

The Mafia boss in Chicago during the Cold War was San Giancana, shown here with his girlfriend, singer Phyllis McGuire of the McGuire Sisters. In the early 1960s, Giancana helped the CIA (with money and personnel) in covert operations within Cuba to rid that country of Castro. (AP/WIDEWORLD PHOTO)

As Secretary of State during the 1970s, Henry Kissinger dominated the
National Security Council. Kissinger mingles in several secret societies,
including the Bohemian Grove, the Council of Foreign Relations, and the
Trilateral Commission. (AP/WIDEWORLD PHOTO)

Five years after he began refurbishing the church, the formerly poor priest began to spend enormous amounts of money. He built a tall tower overlooking the nearby mountain and named it the Tour Magdala.

The refurbishment of the church had been completed, but in a strange way. The inscription over the main entrance read TERRIBLIS EST LOCUS ISTE or "This Place Is Terrible." A hideous statue stood just inside the main entrance. It was of the demon Asmodeus, the so-called custodian of secrets. Like many churches, the walls were decorated with depictions of the Stations of the Cross, but these depictions were unlike others. Each had bizarre errors. Jesus' body was carried into the tomb during the night instead of the day, as was accepted by the Church as fact. In one carving, a child wore Scottish plaid.

In addition to suddenly having money, Saunière also began to receive important guests, such as the Archduke Johann von Hapsburg, a cousin of the Austrian emperor.

On January 17, 1917, Saunière suffered a stroke. A priest was summoned to take Saunière's final confession and administer the Last Rites. The priest refused to administer the last rites and emerged from this session looking greatly shaken. According to the legend, the priest never smiled again. Five days after suffering the stroke, Saunière died. His longtime housekeeper and confidant Marie said that she knew a powerful secret and would share it before her death. But she was felled by a stroke in 1953 and rendered speechless, unable to divulge the great secret.

During World War II, German troops excavated in the Rennes-le-Château area, but it is unknown what their reasons or results were.

Extant evidence that the Priory of Sion actually existed includes a charter for the Ordre de Sion at Orléans from King Louis VII. There is also a papal bull confirming the order's possessions. It is believed that further proof existed before 1940, when Orléans was bombed by the Germans.

Many researchers have noted that the history of Europe makes more sense if we believe in the Priory of Sion and the secrets regarding Christ that they are said to have held. Previously mysterious events such as the attempt by the Church to wipe out the Cathars, the attempts to suppress the Knights Templar, and the assassination of the Merovingian king Dagobert become understandable. All were attempts by the Church to destroy Jesus' bloodline, which presented a direct threat to the Church's power.

Although some of the names on the list of Priory of Sion grand masters are of famous people, some are obscure. After the discovery of the list, long and hard research was needed to learn more about some of the Priory leaders. Yet, when the research was completed, not only did all of the names exist historically, but most of their biographies interconnected.

Here is a list of the grand masters of the Priory of Sion as they are listed in the *Dossiers secrets*. The years they supposedly ruled the organization are listed, followed by known biographical information:

- **Jean de Gisors** (1188–1220). Born 1133, died 1220, he was a wealthy landowner and vassal of the king of England. He was the first independent ruler of the Priory of Sion following the "cutting of the elm." He was a descendant of the Merovingian dynasty and was, theoretically, a descendant of Jesus.

- **Marie de Saint-Clair** (1220–66). Little is known about this woman, other than that she was a descendant of Henry de Saint-Clair, Baron of Rosslyn in Scotland, who fought in the First Crusade. Rosslyn is the site of the Rosslyn Chapel, which was built in the 1400s and contains many Freemason and Rosicrucian symbols. Some have suspected that she may have been Jean de Gisors' second wife, although this cannot be proven. Marie's mother was named Isabel Levis.

- **Guillaume de Gisors** (1266–1307). Born in 1219, grandson of Jean de Gisors who supposedly organized the Priory of Sion into a "Hermetic Freemasonry." A deed dated 1244 states that he was a knight. He apparently fought in the Sixth Crusade, probably in Egypt, as he was inducted into the Order of the Ship and Double Crescent (for veterans of that Crusade) by Louis IX (Saint Louis).

- **Edouard de Bar** (1307–36). Born 1302, so—according to the Priory documents—he took over as grand master at the age of five. He was the grandson of Edward I of England and nephew of Edward II. His daughter married into the house of Lorraine. At age six, Edouard is said to have gone into battle with the Duke of Lorraine. He was captured and held for six years, released when he was twelve years old. He died in 1336 in a shipwreck. The fact that Edouard took over as grand master at such an early age would seem to indicate that grand masters were chosen because of bloodline rather than other qualifications.

- **Jeanne de Bar** (1336–51). Elder sister of Edouard, born 1295, granddaughter of Edward I, niece of Edward II. She married the Earl of Warren in 1310, and divorced him in 1315 after he was excommunicated for adultery. Although she lived at a time when England and France were at war (the Hundred Years' War), she was friendly with both sides, and traveled between the two countries. She died in London in 1361.

- **Jean de Saint-Clair** (1351–66). Very little is known about this man, who was born about 1329 and whose grandfather was married to Jeanne de Bar's aunt.

- **Blanche d'Evereux** (1366–98). Born in 1332, Blanche d'Evereux was also known as Blanche de Navarre, the King of Navarre's daughter. In 1349, she married Philip VI, king of France. In 1359, she became the Countess of Gisors. She died near Gisors in 1398.

- **Nicolas Flamel** (1398–1418). Famous alchemist. Flamel is the first of the Priory of Sion's grand masters who appears not to be part of the bloodline of his predecessors. He was born around 1330 and his first job was as a scrivener in Paris, copying rare books. Along with alchemy he had an interest in Hermetic and Cabalistic thought. In his own writings, Flamel says that the book that changed his life, when he was in his early thirties, was called *The Sacred Book of Abraham the Jew, Prince, Priest, Levite, Astrologer and Philosopher to that Tribe of Jews who by the Wrath of God were Dispersed amongst the Gauls*. Flamel read that book for the next twenty-one years. In

1382, he met a Jew in Léon who explained parts of the book that had been mystifying him. On January 17—the same month and day upon which Sauniér suffered his stroke—in 1382, Flamel claimed he first changed lead into gold. (Although many others have studied the book with the long title, no proven transformations of lead into gold have taken place.) It is strongly suspected that Flamel did not actually change lead into gold either, but he did at that point in his life suddenly acquire great wealth. By the time of his death in 1418 he owned thirty houses in Paris, and founded fourteen hospitals. He had built ten churches and chapels in Paris and the same number in Boulogne.

- **René d'Anjou** (1418–80). Born in 1408, nicknamed "Good King René," he was the father of Marguerite d'Anjou, who married England's Henry VI and became an important figure in the War of the Roses. He may have been associated with Joan of Arc, and was the one-time employer of Christopher Columbus. René is said to have been preoccupied with the Holy Grail. He was one of the players in the start of the Renaissance.

The list of Priory grand masters is, for the most part, feasible. Most names on the list can be biographically linked to the names that precede and follow it on the list. But that is not the case with René d'Anjou and Nicolas Flamel. If there was a connection between these two men, it is lost to history.

René d'Anjou had many titles during his life, including King of Hungary, Naples, Sicily, Aragon, Valencia, Majorca, and Sardinia; Duke of Calabria, Anjou, and Lorraine; and Count of Bar, Provence, Piedmont, and Guise.

René d'Anjou apparently became grand master of the Priory of Sion at age ten. That same year he was inducted into the Order of the White Greyhound (l'Ordre du Levrier Blanc). Nothing is known about this order, or even if it is separate from the Priory. He was also, during his lifetime, a member of l'Ordre de la Fidelité, and the Order of the Crescent, which he established himself. The Order of the Crescent incurred the disfavor of the Pope.

René was known for his staged shows called *pas d'armes*, which were performed at the court of Tarascon. These were combinations of plays, in which the actors wore masks and the plots were purposefully confusing, and tournaments in which knights pretended to tilt at one another.

It was René d'Anjou who created the Cross of Lorraine, a symbolic cross that had two horizontal bars. The symbol was used by the French resistance movement during the Nazi occupation of World War II.

- **Iolande de Bar** (1480–83). René d'Anjou's daughter, born approximately 1428. In 1445, Iolande was wed to Ferri, Lord of Sion-Vaudémont, a charter knight of the Order of the Crescent. When Ferri died, Iolande turned Sion-Vaudémont into a sacred pilgrimage center for all of Lorraine. This was the second time the site had enjoyed sacred status, the first being in the pagan past. This was known because a statue of a pagan Gallo-Teutonic mother goddess named Rosemerhe was found there. Iolande's son René, named after his grandfather, became the Duke of Lorraine. Educated in Florence, he was tutored by Georges Antoine Vespucci, chief sponsor of the Renaissance artist Botticelli.

- **Sandro Filipepi** (1483–1510). Born in 1444, a famous artist, better known as Botticelli. Like Nicolas Flamel, an earlier name on the list of Priory of Sion grand masters, Sandro Filipepi does not appear to have any blood lineage with the other names on the list—although he was friends with the families who dominate this list. He was the tutor of the son of Iolande de Bar, the future Duke of Lorraine. He studied alchemy and Hermetic thought under teachers such as Verrocchio, who also taught Leonardo da Vinci. Leonardo's name follows Sandro's on the list. Botticelli is said to be the designer of one of the first decks of tarot cards. Though historically he has not been associated with esoteric ideas, recent art historians have noted esoteric themes in some of his major works—such as "Primavera," which is said to communicate the esoteric notion of the "underground stream."

- **Leonardo da Vinci** (1510–19). Born in 1452, Leonardo became one of the Renaissance's best-known artists. He was a classmate of Botticelli, who preceded him as Priory grand master, under the tutelage of Verrocchio. He is further connected to the list by Ludovico Sforza, who was a good friend of René d'Anjou, and a sponsor of Leonardo's. It is believed that Leonardo was an early Rosicrucian and that his belief system was considered by the Church to be intrinsically heretical. Among his suspected beliefs is that Jesus had a twin. There is evidence of this belief in his work (a sketch called "The Virgin with Saint John the Baptist and Saint Anne" for example), although the possibility certainly exists that the "twin" was meant to be symbolic only, and with uncertain meaning.

  In "The Last Supper" Leonardo suggests that the bread turning into Christ's body and the wine turning into his blood is symbolic only. The chalice Christ was said to have used during this miracle, the Holy Grail, is missing in the painting. Instead, Leonardo paints a feminine figure directly to Christ's right, suggesting Mary Magdalene, and arranges the figures at the center of the painting so that they form an M.

  Between 1515 and 1517, Leonardo worked as a military engineer for the army of Charles, Connétable de Bourbon, who follows him on the list of Priory grand masters.

- **Charles, Connétable de Bourbon** (1519–27). Born in 1490, Charles was France's most powerful lord at the beginning of the sixteenth century. Like the great majority of the names on the list of Priory grand masters, Charles is related by blood to many of the others. He was the great-grandson of René d'Anjou, and the grandson of Iolande de Bar. In 1521, he was forced to flee France because he became an enemy of French king Francis I. Charles became the commander of the imperial army of the Holy Roman Emperor, Charles V. He made Francis I rue the day he turned on Charles when he, as commander of the imperial army, captured the French monarch in 1525 at the Battle of Pavia. Charles, Connétable de Bourbon died in 1527 while besieging Rome.

- **Ferdinand de Gonzague** (1527–75). Better known as Ferrante de Gonzaga, he was the son of the Duke of Mantua and Isabella d'Este. His parents were patrons of Leonardo da Vinci. Although the *Dossiers secrets* state that he was Priory grand master until his death in 1575, other sources state that he died in 1557, and that his son César died in 1575. Either Ferdinand's death in 1557 was faked, or the Priory documents are in error.

- **Louis de Nevers** (1575–95). Nephew of Ferdinand de Gonzague, Louis de Nevers was better known as Louis de Gonzaga. Louis' brother married into the Hapsburg family. His daughter married the Duke of Lorraine. Known to be closely associated with members of secret societies—such as John Dee, the Queen's conjurer, astrologer, and secret agent—Louis was superintendent of finances for Henry IV of France and was in contact with Sir Thomas Fludd, who was the treasurer for the British army sent by Queen Elizabeth I to help France. Sir Thomas Fludd was the father of Robert Fludd, the man who follows Louis on the list of Priory grand masters.

  Dee (1527–1608) has been called the Founder of Freemasonry. He was a mathematician and a Cabalist. Queen Elizabeth, who was a Protestant and therefore anti-Catholic, awarded Dee high office in her government. Dee is often given credit for planning the creation of the British Empire. He believed in clandestine methods and is considered an early-day secret agent (with the code number 007, a symbol later borrowed by author Ian Fleming for his spy hero James Bond). Dee learned of sophisticated espionage methods by studying a fifteenth-century text called *Steganography*, written by a Cabalist named Johannes Trithemius. England was not a world power when Dee went to work for the queen, but quickly became one thereafter. Christopher Marlowe wrote a play purportedly about Dee called *Doctor Faustus*, about a human who seeks to perfect the world by tampering in God's domain. The play was clearly critical of Renaissance philosophy. It portrayed government as treacherous, with rulers in league with secret societies. At the conclusion of the play there is this warning: "Whose deepness doth entice such forward wits, to practice more than heavenly power permits." Marlowe was murdered in 1593 at age twenty-nine by Ingram Frizer, who was pardoned by the queen. After Marlowe's death, the government released false information about him, saying he was an "atheist and blasphemer" and died in a brawl in a tavern.

- **Robert Fludd** (1595–1637). Born in 1574, Fludd was a philosopher, esteemed physician, and spokesman for Hermetic thought which he called "Rosicrucianism." He took over from John Dee the role of England's top esotericist. Although it is unknown if Fludd belonged to the Rosicrucians, he did publicly praise the group. Fludd, from 1596 to 1602, traveled around Europe discussing esoteric subjects with the intelligentsia. Among those with whom he discussed Rosicrucianism was Janus Gruter, friend of Johann Valentin Andrea, the man whose name follows Fludd's on the Priory list. In 1602, Fludd became tutor to Charles, the son of Henry of Lorraine.

  Fludd was dedicated to "regeneration of the world," the manipulation of nature through human intellect.

- **Johann Valentin Andrea** (1637–54). Born in 1586, Andrea was a German theologian and esotericist, believed to be the pen behind the works of "Christian Rosenkreuz," which in turn gave birth to Rosicrucianism. Andrea was the creator of the secret societies known as the Christian Unions.

- **Robert Boyle** (1654–91). Born in 1627, son of the Earl of Cork, Boyle was the creator of the "invisible college," which evolved into the Royal Society of London for the Promotion of Natural Knowledge, a Freemason organization that took in scientific thinkers who had fled from the Inquisition and found refuge with the Christian Unions. During the 1670s, Boyle published two works about alchemy. They were called *Incalescence of Quicksilver with Gold* and *A Historical Account of the Degradation of Gold*.

- **Isaac Newton** (1691–1727). Born in 1642 in Lincolnshire, Newton was said to have descended from ancient Scottish nobility. He was elected to the Royal Society in 1672. Newton

is said to have worked as a spy against Louis XIV. He was not
a known Mason but was a member of the Gentlemen's Club of
Spalding, an organization that has been described as "semi-
Masonic." (Modern pop culture enthusiasts will note that the
Gentlemen's Club of Spalding was Bob Dylan's backup band
on the 1988 bootleg album *Secret Dossiers*.) In 1689, Newton
wrote *The Chronology of Ancient Kingdoms Amended*, which
attempted to trace royal lineage back to the dawn of history.
He believed that the dimensions and configuration of the
Temple of Solomon were encoded alchemical formulae.
During his life, Newton repeatedly read the writings of Nicolas Flamel, a previous Priory of Sion grand master who
claimed to have mastered alchemy. Newton did not believe in
the Holy Trinity or the divinity of Christ, and he believed that
the New Testament had been corrupted in the fifth century.
During his later years, Newton expressed sympathy toward
the Camisards, a Cathar-like group in early eighteenth-century
London. Days before his death, Newton is said to have burned
many of his personal papers and manuscripts.

- **Charles Radclyffe** (1727–46). Born in 1693, the son of Charles
  II's illegitimate daughter. A grandson of the next-to-last Stuart
  monarch, Radclyffe focused much of his energy on supporting
  the Stuart cause. He founded the first Masonic lodge on the
  continent of Europe in 1725, in Paris. He was the grand
  master of all of France's lodges until at least 1736. Radclyffe
  became an enemy of the new royal family with his efforts to
  return the Stuarts to the throne. He was captured in a French
  ship in 1746 and a few months later was beheaded in the
  Tower of London. The Stuarts were supporters of Freemasonry and are said to be the originators of the form of
  Freemasonry known as Scottish Rite. This form of Freemasonry consisted of degrees higher than those practiced in
  other lodges. These higher degrees featured the teaching of
  ancient mysteries known only in Scotland.

- **Charles de Lorraine** (1746–80). Born in 1744—and therefore,
  according to the Priory documents, became grand master of

the Priory of Sion at age two. He was the brother-in-law of empress Maria Theresa (a Hapsburg who was wife of Holy Roman emperor Francis, duke of Lorraine, thus starting the Hapsburg-Lorraine dynasty) and wartime field marshal. Despite apparent military skills, Charles lost repeatedly in battles against Prussian armies led by Frederick the Great. When his military career was over, he lived in Brussels and became a patron of the arts. In 1761, Charles became grand master of the Teutonic Order. Charles was followed as grand master of the Teutonic Order in 1770 by his nephew Maximilian. According to the Priory documents, Maximilian also followed his uncle as grand master of the Priory of Sion, although ten years later. On January 17, 1775—January 17 being a very important date to the Priory—Maximilian was in attendance as a statue of his uncle Charles astride a horse was raised in Brussels.

- **Maximillian de Lorraine** (1780–1801). Born in 1756, the nephew of Charles de Lorraine, who precedes him on the list of Priory grand masters. Also known as Maximilian von Hapsburg, he was the brother of Marie Antoinette. Maximilian's dreams of a military career were dashed when he was a boy and severely broke a leg falling off a horse. Instead, he became a bishop. He was, like his uncle Charles, a patron of the arts. Among the artists he helped finance were the classical composers Beethoven, Mozart, and Haydn. During the French Revolution, he gave refuge to aristocratic outlaws. He claimed not to be a Freemason.

- **Charles Nodier** (1801–44). Historically a minor essayist, but in his own time a major cultural figure. Nodier wrote extensively about the Merovingian dynasty in France and about the Knights Templar. His writings even in his own time were secondary to his flamboyant personality. He knew how to attract a crowd and hold its attention. Among his devoted followers was a young writer named Victor Hugo, who would succeed him as leader of the priory. In 1802, Nodier wrote about his own participation in a secret society that he did not name but described as "Pythagorean" and "biblical." In 1816, he published an essay entitled *A History of Secret Societies in the Army under Napoleon*. The book purports to be fiction but describes in detail how conspiracies by secret societies caused the downfall of Napoleon. In this work of "fiction," Nodier says that there are many secret societies in the world but the leading one is known as the "Philadelphes" (Brotherhood). Whether Nodier's writing consists of facts or, in modern terminology "disinformation"—statements designed to purposefully mislead—he built a myth around secret societies in the world that greatly changed the way people thought about power and history in nineteenth-century Europe.

- **Victor Hugo** (1844–85). Author of *The Hunchback of Notre Dame*. Born in 1802 of aristocratic descent, Hugo's family was originally from Lorraine. His father was a general in Napoleon's army, but apparently was also friends with Napoleon's enemies. By the time he was a teenager, Hugo was a follower of Charles Nodier, the man who precedes him on the Priory list. Hugo and Nodier operated a publishing house and traveled together with their wives. Hugo was one of the pallbearers at Nodier's funeral. Hugo had unorthodox religious views. He did not believe in the Holy Trinity or in Jesus' divinity. Hugo belonged to the same Rosicrucian order as Eliphas Lévi.

- **Claude Debussy** (1885–1918). Born in 1862, to a poor family, he began associating with rich people at a young age because of his skills as a pianist. A child prodigy, Debussy as a teenager performed at the home of the French president's mistress. At the age of eighteen, he was adopted by the same Russian noblewoman who had been the patron of Tchaikovsky. He did much traveling, although it is impossible to determine if he was ever associated with the other people on the Priory of Sion list. He did set to music some of the works of Victor Hugo, who precedes him on the list, and may have known Hugo through a common acquaintance, Symbolist poet Paul Verlaine. Debussy was also associated during his lifetime with Oscar Wilde, William Butler Yeats, and Marcel Proust.

- **Jean Cocteau** (1918–63). French filmmaker and playwright, Cocteau may have left clues as to his status in the Priory of Sion in his films and plays. Born in 1889 to a politically prominent family, he remained in contact with powerful people even as he lived a bohemian lifestyle. During the Nazi occupation of France, Cocteau is said to have remained uninvolved in the resistance movement, but did associate with Charles de Gaulle when World War II was over.

In 1984, the authors of *Holy Blood, Holy Grail* received a two-page letter signed by A. Robert Abboud, Gaylord Freeman, John E. Drick, and Pierre Plantard. A logo for *Prieure de Sion* was at the top of the page along with a crest containing the letters R and C. With the exception of Plantard, all of the men who had supposedly signed the letter were associated with the First National Bank of Chicago. The letter was a warning to anyone who might be considering faking Priory of Sion documents. The authenticity of the letter was put seriously into question by the discovery that Drick had died two years before the letter was written. An attempt had been made to link the Priory with a midwestern bank that did much business with the Rockefeller family.

According to a February 22, 2004, *New York Times* article, the story of the ancient Priory of Sion being the descendants of Jesus, for that matter the existence before the 1950s of the Priory of Sion at all, is so much "rank nonsense." The *Times* article suggests that the entire story, as presented in *Holy Blood, Holy Grail*, and then repeated in Dan Brown's novel *The Da Vinci Code*, was "planted in the Bibliotheque Nationale by a man named Pierre Plantard. As early as the 1970s, one of Plantard's confederates had admitted to helping him fabricate the materials, including genealogical tables portraying Plantard as a descendant of the Merovingians (and, presumably, of Jesus Christ) and a list of the Priory's past 'grand masters.' . . . Plantard, it eventually came out, was an inveterate rascal with a criminal record for fraud and affiliations with wartime anti-Semitic and right-wing groups. The actual Priory of Sion was a tiny, harmless group of like-minded friends formed in 1956. Plantard's hoax was debunked by a series of (as yet not translated) French books and a 1996 BBC documentary."

See also CATHARS; CHRISTIAN UNIONS; KNIGHTS TEMPLAR; PYTHAGORE-ANS; ROSICRUCIANS.

The Process The Process Church evolved out of a self-help group (Scientology). It was founded in London, England, by Robert de Grimston, who is known to Process members as "The Teacher." The Process of the group's name refers to changes believed necessary to avoid the end of the world. The group grew and spread during the 1960s and 1970s, both in Europe and in North America. Their U.S. headquarters are in Washington, D.C. During this time The Process was involved in anti-Vietnam protests. In addition to other activities, each chapter used funds to feed the poor. Women were allowed to conduct ceremonies.

In 1974, the Church and Robert de Grimston parted ways. He was dismissed as the group's "chief theologian." De Grimston returned to England. In the meantime the group reorganized itself in Massachusetts. In 1988, The Process was renamed the Society of Processeans and became largely a secular organization.

Process expert B. A. Robinson (www.religioustolerance.org; "The Process—Church of the Final Judgment"; accessed March 7, 2004) writes: "Assemblies were held in a room that had a Christian cross on one wall and, on the opposite side of the room, a Goat of Mendes (a goat's head in a pentagram) which symbolizes Satan. The Process version of this symbol had the pentagram placed upright. The Goat of Mendes was later removed as part of Process symbolism. A round altar was in the center of the room, covered with a Process motif. Candles were arranged on the altar pointing to the four cardinal directions; this symbolized their unity with all of creation. Frankincense was burned in the center of the altar as a symbol of Christ being at the heart of The Process. Members attending the ritual sat on cushions on the floor in concentric circles around the altar. To the rear was a music section usually with guitars, singers, sitar, piano, and drums. Because Saturday was the traditional Sabbath (Sunday being the Christian day of rest), the main service of the week was called the Sabbath Assembly. It was held Saturday evening at 7:00 P.M. The Christmas Assembly was held on Christmas Eve. Weddings occurred in all Chapters. The Process married same-sex couples in the same fashion as opposite-sex couples (however, registries tended to differ on the legal part of same-sex weddings). Chapters were closed on Sundays and Christmas Day."

According to W. S. Bainbridge, in his book *Satan's Power: A Deviant Psychotherapy Cult*, "The Church taught that Love conquers Evil, and thereby eliminates conflict. The basis of their religion was the book of Matthew in the Christian Scriptures (New Testament). They believe in a single unknowable God; God simply 'is.' Jesus Christ was seen as a Unifier; Satan as a separator, perhaps created by God to test mankind. They believe in the 'Law of the Universe' which is 'as you give, so shall you receive.' All matter is seen as sacred, because it stems from God. In its earlier days, ministers wore large surrounding black capes to promote their 'mourning the death of the world unless we change' message. Christ's teachings to 'love your enemies' became their prime rule of behavior. They love the individual, but not his/her evil deeds. These beliefs led to a love for Satan—not to his acts but to Satan, the Being."

Bainbridge says that Satan was added to the Process mix during the 1960s when the Processeans were traveling around the United States and crossed paths with Anton LaVey, who had recently started his Church of Satan.

Books such as *The Ultimate Evil* by Maury Terry and *The Family* by Ed Sanders have claimed that murderers such as the Manson Family and the "Son of Sam" were members of, or influenced by, The Process. It is believed that Manson and The Process crossed paths in 1967. One known fact is that they were neighbors.

According to the article "The Process Church of the Final Judgment" at charlesmanson.com (accessed March 7, 2004): "Manson lived on the same street (Cole Street in San Francisco) that The Process had its local chapter (two blocks apart at 636 and 407, although according to another source at different times). Given Manson's philosophical leanings, it's easy to imagine him engaging Processeans in debates or even lifting ideas from them. Manson did have a Scientology background and The Process was formed by two former Scientologists (Robert and MaryAnne de Grimston)."

The website then adds, "The Process connection has been oft repeated but never proven."

The Process points out various pieces of misinformation involved in both claims, and strongly denies any involvement with either Berkowitz or Charles Manson. Sanders was sued by The Process and was forced to remove material connecting Manson with The Process from future editions of the book.

See also SCIENTOLOGY.

Propaganda Due A lodge, also known as P2, that infiltrated the Italian government and, when that infiltration was revealed in 1981, brought about the government's downfall. The lodge, which had been in existence since 1895 and had a history of being seeded with business and political interests, was under the Masonic Grand Orient of Italy. The Masons disassociated themselves from Propaganda Due in 1976 because it was under the influence of special interests. The government downfall incident caused Italy, on July 24, 1981, to ban all secret societies.

The grand master of Propaganda Due was Licio Gelli. Born in 1919, Gelli was seventeen years old when he volunteered to fight in Spain for Mussolini's Fascist expeditionary force. During World War II, Gelli was a liaison officer for the Third Reich. After the war, he was recruited by the U.S. CIA. While working as an intelligence officer he accrued great wealth. During the 1981 revelations, it was discovered that Gelli was a co-conspirator with Roberto Calvi, the President of Banco Ambrosiano of Milan, who was incarcerated at the time, convicted of illicit export. Gelli also counted among his protégés one Michele Sindona, a banker associated with the Mafia who had handled accounts for the Vatican and was later charged with embezzlement. One inspector investigating him was killed. Sindona fled to the United States, where he was later sentenced to twenty-five years in prison for falsely filing for bankrupcy. Gelli was expelled from Freemasonry, along with his lodge, in 1976.

Propaganda Due, as would be expected because of its Fascist

leadership, was strongly anti-Communist, and was troubled by the fact that Communists had won 35 percent of the vote in the 1976 Italian parliamentary elections. In 1977, Communists were given a voice in policymaking by the Italian government. The decade was a violent one in Italy as the country was plagued by terrorist acts. Anti-Masonic forces took advantage of the fact that the public was slow to distinguish between Freemasonry and Propaganda Due, and used yellow journalism—that is, sensationalism—to heat up anti-Masonic fervor. Newspapers blamed the Masons for the assassination attempt on Pope John Paul II. A bomb attack on the Bologna railway station in which eighty persons were killed was likewise blamed on Freemasonry. A government investigation following the 1981 revelations resulted in a forty-eight-page report that compared Propaganda Due to the Ku Klux Klan, yet many Italians continued to blame Freemasonry for the actions of a lodge that it had banished years before.

See also FREEMASONS; MAFIA; THE VATICAN.

Prophets of Cevennes   See CAMISARDS.

Protocols of the Learned Elders of Zion   See ROSICRUCIANS.

Pure Ones   See CATHARS.

Pythagoreans   The Pythagoreans, a group of mystic mathematicians active in Greece circa 350 B.C., were the first known secret society to have a graded system, whereby members underwent a series of initiations, and with each new grade the member learned an additional portion of the society's secret doctrine. It is suspected that Plato learned geometry from the Pythagoreans. The secrets of the group became public with the writing of the book *Elements of Geometry* by Euclid in about 300 B.C.

The Pythagoreans got their name from Pythagoras, a mathematician who lived sometime before 500 B.C. It is known only that Pythagoras lived after Homer but before Socrates. Today's geometry still includes a formula for determining the length of a right triangle's hypotenuse ($a^2 + b^2 = c^2$), known as the Pythagorean Theorem. Pythagoras, it is said, learned geometry during his travels in Egypt.

The members of the group were known to correspond in mathematical terms, seeing their theorems and equations as expressions of philosophical mysteries. In the days of the Pythagoreans, religion, science, and magic were all considered part of the same thing—a pathway to understanding the ways of the gods. Therefore, while today we draw an obvious distinction between priests and mathematicians, in those days that line didn't exist.

See also PRIORY OF SION.

R

Red Army Faction   See BADER-MEINHOF.

Regla de Ocha   See SANTERIA.

Roshaniya   Sixteenth-century society in Afghanistan under the leadership of Bayezid Ansari. Roshaniya means "Illuminated Ones." This society is said to have been an offshoot of an eleventh-century society in Egypt called the Grand Lodge of Cairo.

See also ASSASSINS; GRAND LODGE OF CAIRO.

Rosicrucians   According to some documents, the first historical reference to something resembling Rosicrucianism came in 1188 when "The Order of the Real Rosy Cross" became a subtitle for the group known as the Priory of Sion under a grand master named Jean de Gisors. He was a vassal of Henry II of England. Long associated with Freemasonry, Rosicrucianism and Freemasonry merged only during the late eighteenth century. The group claimed to trace their lineage back to prehistoric times and the building of the Pyramids. De Gisors taught his followers that Rosicrucianism was the ancient secret tradition passed down from ancient Egypt through the great Greek philosophers.

The group remained completely secret for hundreds of years. The public first became aware of their existence with the publication in 1614 of Christian Rosenkreuz's *Report of the Rosicrucian Brotherhood*, in which the author, already dead for more than one hundred years at the time of publication, claimed to have formed a new Order of the Rosy Cross after gaining esoteric Eastern knowledge during a trip through the Holy Land.

It is now generally assumed that Christian Rosenkreuz never existed, and it is suspected that the man behind these works was Johann Valentin Andrea, who was the grand master of the Priory of Sion from 1637 to 1654. Rosenkreuz's legend states that he was born in 1378 and died in 1484 at the age of 106. He was said to have written his papers during the fifteenth century. The papers written by "Rosenkreuz" were said to have come from a secret underground brotherhood from Germany and France who wanted to transform the world by expanding human knowledge. The manifestos were heavily critical of the Catholic Church and the Holy Roman Empire. They called for mankind to release itself from the chains of religious faith, and to embrace scientific thought, which it referred to as unlocking the "secrets of nature."

The third and last of Rosenkreuz's manifestos was published in 1616 and was called *The Chemical Wedding*. It was a comedic allegory that tells the story of a princess who has had her domain wrongfully taken from her by Moors. Abandoned in the ocean inside a wooden chest, she is washed ashore and has adventures. She eventually marries a prince who helps her get her kingdom and her throne back.

The name Rosicrucian has been open to multiple interpretations. Is it a direct reference to Christ's crucifixion? Does it refer to the red crosses that were painted on the shields of the Knights Templar? Is it possible that the Rosicrucians are merely the Knights Templar after a name change made necessary when their group was outlawed? Or, is the name simply derived from Christian Rosenkreuz's *nom de plume*?

A sect called the Order of the Gold and Rosy Cross joined the Freemasons as the Freemason Strict Observance Lodge and, under this name, absorbed the Illuminati into the Freemasons.

Since at least the eighteenth century, the Rosicrucians' version of history has stated that Moses from the Old Testament and the Egyptian Pharaoh Amenhotep IV (a.k.a. Akhenaton) were one and the same individual. The theory is that the Hebrew stories of the Old Testament were just rewrites of the Egyptians' history that pre-existed them, and that both used as the basis for their stories of creation versions of that written by the first known civilization, the Sumerians, who lived in what is present-day Iraq.

It was a French lawyer, a Rosicrucian, named Maurice Joly, who wrote *Protocols of the Learned Elders of Zion*, first published in 1864 in France. A portion of the Protocols reads: "We are the chosen, we are the only true men. Our minds give off the true power of the spirit; the intelligence of the rest of the world is merely instinctive and animal. They can see, but they cannot foresee; their inventions are merely corporeal. Does it not follow that nature herself has pre-destined us to dominate the whole world? Outwardly, however, in our 'official' utterances, we shall adopt an opposite procedure, and always do our best to appear honorable and cooperative. A states-man's words do not have to agree with his acts. If we pursue these principles, the governments and peoples which we have thus pre-pared will take the IOUs for cash. One day they will accept us as benefactors and saviors of the human race. If any State dared to resist us, if its neighbors make common cause with it against us, we will unleash a world war." Joly went on to write that world domina-tion could be achieved through (1) control of what the public thinks; (2) creating war; (3) spreading hunger and disease; and (4) "dis-tracting and seducing the youth." With anti-Semitic material later added, the *Protocols* have been floating around secret society circles ever since. They have been taken seriously by Czar Nicholas II of Russia, Kaiser Wilhelm II and Adolf Hitler of Germany, and auto-mobile maker Henry Ford of the United States.

Alchemy became a key factor in Rosicrucian lore, a practice that the group called Hermetic science. But, like many secret societies, Rosicrucianism is more than a group with mystical and pseudo-scientific beliefs. They were also extremely influential.

Historian Jim Marrs sees the group as "a major force in the ongoing struggle between scientific rationalism and church dogma that resulted in the breakup of the Holy Roman Empire, the cre-ation of Protestantism, and the resulting Church of England, as well as the Renaissance."

Like the Knights Templar before them and other secret societies, the Rosicrucians were forced underground by the Vatican. By the early eighteenth century, the Rosicrucians had hidden themselves within the ranks of the Freemasons.

In the present-day United States there exists two separate and competing groups calling themselves Rosicrucians, both of which claim to possess secrets known to the ancient Egyptians. They are the Ancient Mystical Order Rosae Crucic (AMORC) and the Rosicrucian Fellowship. Both are based in California.

The AMORC uses for recruiting a list of great men from the past who were Rosicrucians. According to authors Michael Baigent, Richard Leigh, and Henry Lincoln, the modern organization has, in a sense, padded its résumé. The list of past members, they say, includes "every important figure in Western history and culture whose values, even if only tangentially, happened to coincide with the order's own. An often haphazard overlap or convergence of attitudes is misconstrued as something tantamount to 'initiated membership.' One thus is told that Dante, Shakespeare, Goethe, and innumerable others were 'Rosicrucians'—implying that they were card-carrying members who paid their dues regularly." For example, this is from the AMORC website: "Famous Rosicrucians included: Dante Alighieri, author of *The Divine Comedy*, Christopher Wren, Sir Francis Bacon, Robert Fludd, who translated the King James version of the Bible, and author Victor Hugo."

What is it like being a Rosicrucian? According to Rosicrucian expert Franz Hartmann in his book *Rosicrucian Symbols*, "The place or state wherein the true Rosicrucian lives is far too exalted and glorious to be described in words." Nonetheless, he gives it a shot: "When we enter the vestibule of the temple of the Rose Cross, we enter into a region of unalloyed bliss and happiness. There is an effulgence of superterrestrial light, where all laborious thinking and exercise of the imagination for the purpose of drawing logical inferences about the unknown, ceases; for in that light is the realm of pure knowledge; to live there is to perceive, and to perceive is to know. Into that paradise of celestial consciousness nothing impure can enter. No room is there for terrestrial flesh and blood; but the spiritual beings which inhabit that realm are made of the flesh and body of Christ in other words, of the substance of the spiritual soul."

According to the website "Rosicrucian Philosophy" (www.rosy-cross.org/Rosicrucians_Philosophy.html; accessed January 9, 2004), "The cross represents the thorns where the rose grows. Unless these thorns, the negative tendencies are changed, by the '*Process of*

Progressive Transmutation of Self,' the Rose or the Soul, cannot be immersed in the *Supreme Light*. The rose represents the *'Spiritual Arcanum'* of Regeneration or the *'second birth'* of *Saint John*. The Rose-cross has the same meaning as the Ansata Cross of the Egyptians, symbolizing *Regeneration* by way of a perfect balance between the masculine nature and the feminine nature. This Spiritual being or Soul, of pure and divine nature, *'crucified'* on the Cross, represents the physical and temporary body, the *'prison'* of the Soul, which in turn, represents material limitations. This 'temporary prison' through ignorance, forces the spiritual *inner being*, to suffer constantly, afflictions such as the ignorance, selfishness, sadness, avarice, deceit, envy, resentment, wrath, evilness, etc. The thorns of the rose."

Here are the "Rosicrucian Rules":

1. Love God above all.
2. Devote your time to your Spiritual advancement.
3. Be entirely unselfish.
4. Be temperate, modest, energetic, and silent.
5. Learn to know the origin of the Metals contained within the self.
6. Beware of those who teach what they do not know.
7. Live in constant adoration of the highest good.
8. Learn the theory before you attempt the practice.
9. Exercise charity towards all beings.
10. Read the ancient books of wisdom.
11. Try to understand their secret meaning.

There is a twelfth rule, called the Arcanum, but it is against the rules to speak of it. The rule is only given to Rosicrucians who have earned it. According to Franz Hartmann, the Arcanum is "inexpressible in the language of mortals, and it can, therefore, only be communicated heart to heart."

The "Duties of a Rosicrucian" are:

1. To alleviate suffering and to cure the sick without accepting any renumeration.

2. To adopt the style of their clothing to the customs of the country wherein they reside for the time being.

3. To meet once a year in a certain place.

4. Each member has to select a proper person to be his successor.

5. The letters R.C. are the emblem of the order.

6. The existence of the Brotherhood is to be kept secret for one hundred years, beginning from the time when it was first established. Nor will the "hundred years" be over until man has awakened to the consciousness of his own divine nature.

The Secret Signs of the Rosicrucian are:

1. The Rosicrucian is Patient.

2. The Rosicrucian is Kind.

3. The Rosicrucian knows no envy.

4. The Rosicrucian does not boast.

5. The Rosicrucian is not vain.

6. The Rosicrucian is not disorderly.

7. The Rosicrucian is not ambitious.

8. The Rosicrucian is not irritable.

9. The Rosicrucian does not think evil of others.

10. The Rosicrucian loves justice.

11. The Rosicrucian loves the truth.

12. The Rosicrucian knows how to be silent.

13. The Rosicrucian believes that which he knows.

14. The Rosicrucian's hope is firm.

15. The Rosicrucian cannot be vanquished by suffering.

16. The Rosicrucian will always remain a member of the Order.

There are thirteen jewels that have symbolic importance to the Rosicrucians. The most important is the diamond, often shown in the center of the rose, which represents wisdom. The other twelve are jasper (dark green, representing the power of active light), hyacinth (yellow, representing love), chrysolite (white, princely wisdom), sapphire (blue, truth), smaragd (green, blooming spring time), topaz (golden, peace), amethyst (violet, impartiality), beryl (diverse colors, humility), sardis (light red, faith), chrysoprase (light green, invisible power and strength), sardonyx (striped, joy), and chalcedony (striped, the glory of victory).

Rosicrucians study a series of seventy-two "Signs from the Heart of the Celestial Mother," which are symbols with inscriptions in Latin that represent allegories. They say that a member who understands the meaning of all of them truly has his eyes open. They are numbered 1–70, with a Prœnesis and an Epilogus. The allegories are:

Prœnesis) A ship in the open sea, with a floating anchor and a star shining overhead. The inscription reads: "*Hac monstrante viam.*"

1. An open book with the name Maria, and a heart transfixed by a sword. The inscription reads: "*Omnibus in omnibus.*"

2. A seven-headed monster menaced by a club. The inscription reads: "*In virtute tua.*"

3. A closed and sealed door with an angel trying to open it. The inscription reads: "*Signatur ne perdatur.*"

4. The landscape of an island with the sun rising and the stars shining. The inscription reads: "*Aurora ab lacrymis.*"

5. An orange tree bears fruit. The inside of the fruit is sweet but the skin is bitter. The inscription reads: "*Dulce amarum.*"

6. A fire burns upon an altar. Inside the fire a heart burns, creating a sweet odor. The inscription reads: "*In odorum suavitatis.*"

7. A white lily in a flower pot standing in a garden. The inscription reads: "*Virginei laus prima pudoris.*"

8. An angel uses a sieve to separate wheat from chaff. The inscription reads: "*Dimittit inanes.*"

9. A jeweled ring sits upon a table. The inscription reads: "*Honori invincem.*"

10. A globe is illuminated by a full moon. The inscription reads: "*Plena sibi et alis.*"

11. Jacob's ladder with seven steps linking Heaven and Earth. The inscription reads: "*Descendendo ascendendo.*"

12. On the wall of a tower is a sun-dial. The inscription reads: *"Altissimus obnumbrat."*

13. All of the signs of the Zodiac are represented. The Sun is in the sign of Virgo. The inscription reads: *"Jam mitius ardet."*

14. A hen broods over eggs in a stable. The inscription reads: *"Parit in alieno."*

15. Two palm trees lean inward toward one another. The inscription reads: *"Blando se pace salutant."*

16. A grapevine weeps, having been cut from the trunk. The inscription reads: *"Ut gaudeas mero."*

17. A plant representing myrrh. The inscription reads: *"Amara sed salubris."*

18. A painter's easel is blank. The inscription reads: *"Qua forma placebit."*

19. A heart transfixed by a sword. The inscription reads: *"Usque ad divisionem animœ."*

20. Two doves peck at one another. The inscription reads: *"Amat et castigat."*

21. A passion flower. The inscription reads: *"Delectat et cruciat."*

22. Eagles and bats, wolves and sheep, bask together under the sun. The inscription reads: *"Non possentibus offert."*

23. A bird sits between thorns and thistles. The inscription reads: *"Hic ego sustentor."*

24. Ivy winds around a dead tree. The inscription reads: *"Nec mors separavit."*

25. Two hearts in a winepress. The inscription reads: *"Cogit in unum."*

26. A crocodile cries while eating a man. The inscription reads: *"Plorat et devorat."*

27. A wolf eats a sheep. The inscription reads: *"Non est qui redimat."*

28. Tulip leans toward the rising sun. The inscription reads: *"Languexit in umbra."*

29. Two stringed musical instruments. A hand plays one of them. The inscription reads: *"Unam tetigis se sat est."*

30. A white lily grows between thorns. The inscription reads: *"Transfixum suavius."*

31. Jonah is thrown into an angry sea. The inscription reads: *"Merger ne mergantur."*

32. The setting sun and the evening star. The inscription reads: *"Sequitur deserta cadentum."*

33. A snake winds itself around a cross. The inscription reads: *"Pharmacumnon venenum."*

34. An eagle flies toward the sun. The inscription reads: *"Ad te levavi oculos."*

35. A log floats in the water. A squirrel stands on it, rowing. The inscription reads: *"Ne merger."*

36. A light tower illuminates the ocean. The inscription reads: *"Erantibus una micat."*

37. A rock protrudes from a stormy sea. The inscription reads: *"Non commovebitur."*

38. A diamond lies upon a table. The inscription reads: *"In puritate pretium."*

39. Grafting a tree. The inscription reads: *"Accipit in sua."*

40. A man hangs onto a tree. The inscription reads: *"Non est hac tutior umbra."*

41. A flock of sheep. Each sheep bears the letter T on its forehead. The inscription reads: *"Non habel redargutionem."*

42. A chandelier with seven lights upon it. The inscription reads: *"Non extinguetur."*

43. A solar eclipse. The inscription reads: *"Morientis sideris umbra."*

44. A rainbow cries as the sun sets. The inscription reads: *"Desinit in lacrymas."*

45. A cypress tree is blown by winds from the four quarters of the world. The inscription reads: *"Concussio firmat."*

46. Two hearts are surrounded by thorns, a dagger, and nails. The inscription reads: *"Vulneratum vulnerat."*

47. Instruments of torture and a heart transfixed by a sword. The inscription reads: *"Supereminet omnes."*

48. A beehive and bees flying around flowers. The inscription reads: *"Currit in odorem."*

49. A chemical furnace with retorts, from which drops are falling. The inscription reads: *"Calor elicit imbres."*

50. A man sows grain into furrows. The inscription reads: *"Ut surgat in ortum."*

51. A cloth spread upon a field and sprinkled with water. The inscription reads: *"A lacrymis candor."*

52. A bird flies between ocean waves. The inscription reads: *"Mersa non mergitur."*

53. Noah's dove carries an olive branch. The inscription reads: *"Emergere nuntiat orbem."*

54. A flying eagle carries a lamb. The inscription reads: *"Tulit proedeam tartari."*

55. Rain falls upon flowers. The inscription reads: *"Dulce refrigerium."*

56. A level and a plumb-line. The inscription reads: *"Recta a recto."*

57. A hot iron upon an anvil. The inscription reads: *"Dum calet."*

58. A bird sits alone in a cave. The inscription reads: *"Gemit dilectum suum."*

59. An elephant drinks blood from a grape. The inscription reads: *"Acuitar in proelium."*

60. A bird escapes from a nest. The inscription reads: *"Ad sidera sursum."*

61. Sunrise rays shine into an adamant heart. The inscription reads: *"Intima lustrat."*

62. A flying bird is attached to a string. The inscription reads: *"Cupio dissolvi."*

63. A pair of Birds of Paradise fly upwards. The inscription reads: *"Innixa ascendit."*

64. A triple crown made of gold, iron, and silver. The inscription reads: *"Curso completo."*

65. A broken statue of Dagon and a corpse. The inscription reads: *"Cui honorem honorem."*

66. The Israelites are allowed to pass as the Red Sea divides. The inscription reads: *"Illue iter quo ostendum."*

67. A human figure lost inside a labyrinth. A hand coming down from Heaven holds a thread dangling down to the figure. The inscription reads: *"Hac duce tuta via est."*

68. In a camp of tents, there is a standard bearing the image of a man. The inscription reads: *"Præsidium et decus."*

69. A clock showing two o'clock. The inscription reads: *"Ultima secunda."*

70. A ship at sea has a light that is attracting fishes and birds. The inscription reads: *"Venient ad lucern."*

Epilogus) Noah's Ark floats on a calm sea. The inscription reads: *"Non mergitur, sed extollitur."*

Rosicrucians study a second set of fifty-two symbols representing allegories which are called "Signs Referring to the Divine Child." These are:

Prœnesis) A hen protects her chicks with her wings as a hawk circles above. The inscription reads: *"Sub umbra alarum tuarum."*

1. A figure kneels holding a book that shows a fiery heart. The inscription reads: *"Tolle lege."*

2. A ray of sunshine ignites a fire upon an altar. The inscription reads: *"Extinctos suscitat ignes."*

3. A ray of sunshine travels through a lens and sets a ship on fire. The inscription reads: *"Ignis ab Primo."*

4. The sun shines upon a lambskin spread out over the Earth. The inscription reads: *"Descendit de cœ is."*

5. A chrysalis upon a leaf. The inscription reads: *"Ecce venio."*

6. (There is no emblem number six.)

7. The sea and the rising sun. The inscription reads: *"Renovabit faciem terræ."*

8. A rising sun eclipsed by the moon. The inscription reads: *"Condor ut exorior."*

9. A chicken and an eagle in the air. The former is protected against the latter by a shield. The inscription reads: *"A facie persequentis."*

10. A rose in the midst of a garden. The inscription reads: *"Hæc mihi sola placet."*

11. A lamb burning upon an altar. The inscription reads: *"Deus non despicies."*

12. Dogs hunting. The inscription reads: *"Fuga salutem."*

13. A lamb dying at the foot of a cross. The inscription reads: *"Obediens uaque ad mortem."*

14. The ark of the covenant. Bolts of lightning. The inscription reads: *"Procul. este profani."*

15. Sun in the midst of clouds. The inscription reads: *"Fulgura in pluvium fruite."*

16. Sun shining upon sheep and wolves. The inscription reads: *"Super robos et malos."*

17. A well and a pitcher. The inscription reads: *"Hauriar, non exhauriar."*

18. Animals entering the ark. The inscription reads: *"Una salutem."*

19. Shepherd carrying a lamb. The inscription reads: *"Onus meum leve."*

20. Sheep drinking at a well. The water is stirred by a pole. The inscription reads: *"Similem dant vulnera formam."*

21. A dove sitting upon a globe. The inscription reads: *"Non sufficit una."*

22. Light penetrating the clouds. The inscription reads: *"Umbram fugat veritas."*

23. A vineyard and the rising sun. The inscription reads: *"Pertransiit beneficiendo."*

24. Three hearts with a sieve floating above them. The inscription reads: *"Cælo contrito resurgent."*

25. Swan cleaning his feathers before proceeding to eat. The inscription reads: *"Antequam comedum."*

26. A hungry dog howling at the moon. The inscription reads: *"Inanis impetus."*

27. Ark of the covenant drawn by two oxen. The inscription reads: *"Sancta sancte."*

28. A winepress. The inscription reads: *"Premitur ut exferimat."*

29. An opening bud. The inscription reads: *"Vulneribus profundit opes."*

30. Amor shooting arrows at a heart. The inscription reads: *"Donee attingam."*

31. Cross and paraphernalia for crucification. The inscription reads: *"Præbet non prohibet."*

32. A sunflower looking towards the rising sun. The inscription reads: *"Usque ad occasum."*

33. Drops of sweat falling down in a garden. The inscription reads: *"Tandem resoluta venit."*

34. Sword protruding from the clouds. The inscription reads: *"Cædo noncedo."*

35. Hammer and anvil, a forge and a fire. The inscription reads: *"Ferendo, non feriendo."*

36. A ram crowned with thorns upon an altar. The inscription reads: *"Victima coronata."*

37. A sheep carrying animals. The inscription reads: *"Quam grave portat onus."*

38. A crucified person and a snake upon a tree. The inscription reads: *"Unde mors unde vita."*

39. A tree shedding tears into three dishes. The inscription reads: *"Et Iæsa medelam."*

40. A spring fountain. The inscription reads: *"Rigat ut erigat."*

41. A heart offered to an eagle. The inscription reads: *"Redibit ad Dominum."*

42. A heart upon a cross surrounded by thorns, crowned with a laurel. The inscription reads: *"Pignus amabile pacis."*

43. Bird persecuted by a hawk seeks refuge in the cleft of a rock. The inscription reads: *"Hoc tuta sua sub antro."*

44. Target with a burning heart in the center; Amor shooting arrows at it. The inscription reads: *"Trahe mi post te."*

45. Pelican feeding her young ones with her own blood. The inscription reads: *"Ut vitam habeant."*

46. (There is no emblem number forty-six.)

47. Phoenix sinking into the flames. The inscription reads: *"Hic mihi dulce mori."*

48. Blood from a lamb flowing into a cup. The inscription reads: *"Purgantes temperat ignis."*

49. Clouds emitting bolts of lightning. The inscription reads: *"Lux recto fatumque noscenti."*

50. Eagle flying towards the sun. The inscription reads: *"Tune facie ad faciem."*

Epilogus) A hedgehog, having rolled in fruits, is covered with them. The inscription reads: *"Venturl providus ævi."*

See also ANUNNAKI; GOLDEN DAWN SOCIETY; FREEMASONS; KNIGHTS TEMPLAR; PRIORY OF SION.

Rosslyn Chapel   This chapel is featured in Dan Brown's best-selling novel *The Da Vinci Code*. Some believe that the roots of Freemasonry as a secret society date back as far as the mid-fifteenth century with the construction of Rosslyn Chapel near Edinburgh, Scotland. There are many legends regarding Rosslyn Chapel and the secrets it is said to keep.

According to *The Sword and the Grail* by Andrew Sinclair, the most famous legend is about a pillar at the chapel's east end called "The Apprentice Pillar." Sinclair wrote: "An account of this remarkable story was printed in 1774 and speaks of a tradition that has prevailed in the family of Roslin from father to son, which is, that a model of this beautiful pillar having been sent to Rome, or some foreign place; the master-mason, upon viewing it, would by no means consent to work off such a pillar, till he should go to Rome, or some foreign part, to take exact inspection of the pillar from which the model had been taken; that, in absence, whatever might be the occasion of it, an apprentice finished the pillar as it now stands; and that the master, upon his return, seeing the pillar so exquisitely well finished, made enquiry who had done it; and, being stung with envy, slew the apprentice. Above the west door of the chapel, there is a carved head of a young man with a gash on his right temple. This is said to be the head of the murdered apprentice. Opposite him is the head of a bearded man, the master who killed him. To his right, there is another head, that of a woman, called 'the Widowed Mother.' It is thus made clear that the unnamed precocious youth was, to use a phrase familiar to all Freemasons, a 'Son of the Widow.'"

The chapel was built by William Saint-Clairs, who not only knew the original Knights Templar, but also became Scottish Freemasonry's first grand master. The chapel is in the village of Roslin (spelled differently), which consists of one street of shops with a few houses at one end. The village is built at the edge of a wooded gorge called the Valley of North Esk. Seven miles outside the village is the Temple, formerly known as the Templar Preceptory of Balantrodoch.

According to *The Temple and the Lodge* by Michael Baigent and Richard Leigh, "The valley of the North Esk is a mysterious, seemingly haunted place. Carved into a large, moss-covered rock, a wild pagan head gazes at the passer-by. Further downstream, in a cave behind a waterfall, there is what appears to be another huge head with cavernous eyes, perhaps a weathered carving, perhaps a natural product of the elements. The path leading through the valley is crossed by numerous ruined stone buildings and passes by a cliff-face with dressed stone windows. Behind this window is a veritable warren of tunnels, sufficient to conceal a substantial number of men and accessible only by a secret entrance: one had to be lowered down a well. According to legend, Robert the Bruce found refuge here during one of the many crises that beset his campaigns. Perched on the very edge of the gorge is an eerily strange edifice, Rosslyn Chapel. One's first impression is that it appears to be a cathedral in miniature. Not that it is particularly small. But it is so overloaded, so dripping with Gothic carvings and floridly intricate embellishments, that it seems somehow to be a truncated part of something greater, like a fragment of Chartres, transplanted to the top of a Scottish hill. It conveys a sense of amputated lushness, as if the builders, after lavishing their most dazzling skills and costly materials upon the structure, simply stopped abruptly. In fact, they did. They ran short of money. Rosslyn Chapel was originally intended to be part of something much greater, the 'Lady Chapel' of a vast collegiate church, a full size cathedral on the French scale. In the absence of funds, the project was never completed. From the existing west wall, massive blocks of stone jut forth, awaiting others which never arrived."

The chapel took forty years to build. The foundations were laid in 1446. Work started four years later. It was completed in the 1480s by Sir William St. Clair's son Oliver Sinclair.

According to Christopher Knight and Robert Lomas in *The Hiram Key: Pharoahs, Freemasons and the Discovery of the Secret Scrolls of Jesus*: "William St. Clair himself masterminded the whole construction of the building from its inception to his own death in 1484, just two years before its completion; furthermore, he personally supervised every tiny detail of the work. . . . William St. Clair had brought some of Europe's finest masons to Scotland for this great project, building the village of Rosslyn to house them. From the outside, Rosslyn is a representation in stone of the Heavenly Jerusalem as depicted in Lambert's copy, with towers and a huge central curved, arched roof. Inside the Rosslyn shrine, the layout is a reconstruction of the ruin of Herod's Temple, decorated with Nasorean and Templar symbolism. In the north-east corner we found a section of the wall carved with the towers of the Heavenly Jerusalem complete with the Masonic compasses, styled exactly as they are shown on Lambert's scroll. As we looked directly upwards from the organ loft, we could see that the arched roof had a running series of keystones down its length, just like the one the Royal Arch degree describes as found in the ruins of Herod's Temple!"

See also FREEMASONS; PRIORY OF SION.

Round Table   Named after the legendary meeting place of King
Arthur's knights, this group was formed by diamond tycoon Cecil
Rhodes. Rhodes has been called by author Jim Marrs in his book
Rule by Secrecy, "the progenitor of the modern secret societies." And
this group was called by Dr. John Coleman, "a maze of companies,
institutions, banks and educational establishments."

Rhodes was owner of the de Beers Consolidated Mines, Ltd. of
South Africa (de Beers being the original owner of the land). Rhodes
was born in 1853, the son of a vicar, and as a boy studied Greek
philosophy.

Rhodes, already active in British Freemasonry, was inspired as a
young man by fine arts professor John Ruskin, a habitually auto-
erotic pedophile, who studied secret societies (such as the occult
Theosophy Society), as well as the writings of Plato. Ruskin believed
that the world was better off when governed by a ruling class.

By the time he was forty, Rhodes controlled 90 percent of the
world's diamonds.

According to Marrs, "The Round Tables started out as a collection of semi-secret groups formed along the lines of the Illuminati
and Freemasons with 'inner' and 'outer' circles and a pyramid hierarchy. The inner circle was called the Circle of the Initiates (or the
Elect) while the outer circle was called the Association of Helpers.
Two members of Rhodes's inner circle of Initiates were British
financiers Lord Victor Rothschild and Lord [Alfred] Milner." The
Round Table group realized that "one needn't wait for crisis and tur-
moil. Social upheaval could be created and controlled to their own
benefit. Hence came the cycles of financial booms and busts, crises
and revolutions, wars and threats of war, all of which maintained a
balance of power."

Rhodes died in 1902 of heart disease. His will called for "the
establishment, promotion, and development of a Secret Society, the
true aim and object whereof shall be the extension of British rule
throughout the world [including] the United States of America."

By World War I, Round Table meetings were being held in seven
nations. In addition to Rhodes' money, the group was sponsored by
the Carnegie United Kingdom Trust, J.P. Morgan, the Rockefellers,
and the Rothschilds. After World War II, this group evolved into the
Royal Institute of International Affairs.

See also INSTITUTE FOR ADVANCED STUDY; ROYAL INSTITUTE OF INTER-NATIONAL AFFAIRS.

Royal Institute of International Affairs (RIIA) British branch of a secret society the American branch of which is known as the Council on Foreign Relations, formed at a meeting in Paris on May 30, 1919, as a first step toward forming a post-World War I global government. Some have called their intent a desire to perpetuate British power globally. The group was the concept of an adviser to President Woodrow Wilson named Colonel Edward Mandell House and a group of internationalist bankers. This group incorporated the pre-existing secret society known as the Round Table group.

The RIIA held their meetings in London's Chatham House in Saint James Square. Much of the money and influence behind this group, as had been true of the Round Table group, came from Cecil Rhodes—of Rhodes Scholarship fame—who had owned the majority of the diamond mines in South Africa.

See also COUNCIL ON FOREIGN RELATIONS; ROUND TABLE.

Rule of the Orisha See SANTERIA.

S

Santeria The practices of Santeria are not discussed outside of the group. The beliefs and practices differ greatly, it is believed, depending on the leaders involved. Santeria is known by various names. Its official name is Regla de Ocha, which means The Rule of the Orisha. Those who use this name refer to it as Ocha for short. Another name is La Regla Lucumi. Santeria means "The Way of the Saints" and is the most common name for the group. In Brazil, the group is known as Candomble Jege-Nago. A derogatory synonym for Santeria is Macumba, which also means evil witchcraft.

Santeria is a religion that combines an African religion (the worship of the Orisha—meaning "head guardian"—and beliefs of the Yoruba and Bantu people in southern Nigeria, Senegal and Guinea Coast) with Catholic practices. Slaves brought their religion with them when they were forcibly moved to other parts of the world and, over the years, the religion combined with Christianity. Slaves were baptized by the Roman Catholic Church upon arrival and their native practices were suppressed. They hid their actual religious practices by changing the names of their elements of worship to those of Catholic saints.

A few examples: Babalz Ayi became St. Lazarus (patron of the sick). Shangs became St. Barbara (controller of thunder, lightning, fire). Eleggua (sometimes called Elegba) became St. Anthony (controller of roads, gates, etc.). Obatala became Our Lady of Las Mercedes, and the Resurrected Christ (father of creation; source of spirituality). Oggzn became St. Peter (patron of war). And Oshzn became Our Lady of Charity (controller of money, sensuality).

Santeria is most common in the Caribbean, especially in Cuba. For decades, because of the Communist ban on religion in Cuba,

Santeria was practiced in secret. The bans were lifted during the 1990s, and Santeria is now practiced openly in Cuba.

It is also common in the Hispanic population in Florida, Puerto Rico, New Jersey, New York City, Los Angeles, Argentina, Brazil, Colombia, Mexico, Venezuela, France, and the Netherlands.

Estimates of how many members the group has vary widely, from 22,000 to 800,000.

God is known as Olorun, or Olódùmarè, the "owner of heaven." He is the supreme deity. Beneath him are the lesser guardians, called Orisha. Each of these has an associated Christian saint. Orishas need nourishment. Worshippers feed them through animal sacrifice, prepared dishes, and human praise. During the ritual sacrifices (usually chickens are the victims) an animal's blood is collected and offered to the Orisha. Sacrifices, it is believed, bring forgiveness for sins. Santeria has been criticized for alleged mistreatment of animals, but members say that the animals are always killed in a humane manner (quickly) and are often eaten afterwards.

Priests are called Santeros or Babalochas. Priestesses are called Santeras or Iyalochas. They are trained for many years, then endure a period of solitude before being initiated. They learn dance, songs, and healing methods.

During Santeria ceremonies, the names of one's dead ancestors are called out. This is called Veneration of Ancestors. Members dance rhythmically and feverishly, becoming possessed by Orisha. The possessed then channel messages from the Orisha.

Botanicas are stores that provide Santerian supplies, such as charms, herbs, potions, and musical instruments. Santeria has no book, like a Bible, but is passed down from generation to generation through oral tradition only.

Santeria acquired an evil connotation in 1989 when the bodies of more than a dozen murdered men were found in Matamoros, Mexico, not far from the Texas border. The killings were initially blamed on Santeria. The murders were eventually found to be the responsibility of an individual hired by a criminal gang of drug runners. The gang did include members whose practices were based on those of Santeria, but these killings are not evidence that Santeria encourages or condones human sacrifice.

This isn't to say that actual Santeria rituals can't be dangerous—even deadly. On February 23, 2004, an HIV-infected forty-one-year-old woman named Minerva Perez from the Bronx, New York, went to a friend's apartment for a Santeria "cleansing" (*una limpleza*). During the ritual, sixty-two-year-old Mildred Sanchez lit candles and covered Perez with a highly flammable liquid used in Santeria rituals called "Florida water." Florida water is a nineteenth-century alcohol-based cologne which is mixed with herbs and is thought to seal the body from bad energy. The candles are white votive candles which are lit during rituals to honor an orisha, or spiritual guardian.

Other items frequently used in Santeria cleansing rituals include white flowers; herbs such as *espanta muerto* and *quita maldición*, which are used to take away a curse or to "scare away death"; and coconuts. Coconuts are cut in half and then thrown. The future can be predicted, it is believed, by how the coconuts fall. Police found halved coconuts outside the apartment building where Perez died.

Perez caught fire when Sanchez made the sign of the cross over her body with one of the candles and the Florida water ignited. Police outside the apartment building heard the screams and burst into the apartment. They found Perez dead, badly burned and with a gash on her forehead. Sanchez was suffering from burns on her hands and arms, apparently caused when she attempted to put out the fire. A neighbor told reporters that, according to beliefs, Santeria rituals can purge the seven deadly sins.

"It can be beautiful but it can also be dangerous," the neighbor said. "You've got to be careful."

Scientology   The Church of Scientology was founded by Lafayette Ron Hubbard, better known as L. Ron Hubbard. Hubbard was friends with Jack Parsons, a key figure in OTO, a secret society in which Hubbard was trained.

A year after the end of World War II, Jack Parsons wrote a letter about Hubbard to well-known Satanist Aleister Crowley in which he said, "About three months ago I met [Naval Intelligence officer] Captain L. Ron Hubbard. . . . Although Ron has no formal training in Magick, he has an extraordinary amount of experience and understanding in the field. . . . He is the most thelemic person I have ever met and is in complete accord with our own principles. He is also interested in establishing the New Aeon. . . . We are pooling our resources in a partnership that will act as a limited company to control our business ventures."

The bible of Scientology is L. Ron Hubbard's book *Dianetics: The Modern Science of Mental Health*.

According to Scientology's official website:

> Scientology is about the individual man or woman. Its goal is to bring an individual to a sufficient understanding of himself and his life and free him to improve conditions in the way that he sees fit.
>
> Which brings up this relevant question: What is Scientology? Scientology is an applied religious philosophy.
>
> The fastest growing religious movement on Earth, Scientology has become a firmly established and active force for positive change in the world in less than half a century.
>
> The Scientology religious philosophy contains a precise system of axioms, laws, and techniques, exhaustively researched and documented as workable. As such, it provides the individual with the ability to dramatically improve conditions, not only in his own life but in the world around him.

Scientology's critics, however, strongly disagree with Scientology's self-description as a religious self-help organization. They say it is a secretive money-hungry cult. According to the somewhat hysterical anti-Scientology website, "What's Wrong With Scientology" by Kristi Wachter, "The risks American soldiers are facing in the Middle East has renewed my disgust that L. Ron Hubbard lied about his navy record and Scientology continues to propagate those lies. In fact, Hubbard's service record ranged from mediocre to poor. Repeating Hubbard's lies may not be the worst thing Scientology's ever done, but I still find it despicable. Why do people protest Scientology? Scientology locks people up. There are over two dozen allegations that Scientology has held individuals against their will. These illegal acts were not committed by rogue Scientologists— they were in accordance with Scientology policy. Scientology held Lisa McPherson against her will for seventeen days, according to

Scientology's own logs. She died in their custody. The state of Florida has decided not to prosecute the two felony charges filed against Scientology in her death after Scientology used relentless pressure to get the medical examiner to make a partial change in the cause of death, but her estate has sued Scientology for wrongful death and false imprisonment."

She goes on to accuse the Church of Scientology of lying and attacking free speech.

According to David S. Touretsky, author of the "Secrets of Scientology" website,

> The Church of Scientology is a rich and vengeful religious cult, or as one critic puts it, "a cross between the Moonies and the Mafia." But it would be a mistake to dismiss its underlying technology as harmless or ineffective. Scientologists know a great deal about thought control, social control, rhetorical judo (defeat by misdirection, deft use of logical fallacies) and high pressure sales, though as victims of their own technology, they wouldn't characterize it that way.
>
> Despite its extensive advertising campaign, including half-hour TV infomercials for Dianetics, the Church has been careful to maintain a veil of mystery about its teachings, in part by outlawing any meaningful discussion or analysis of them. (See the policy bulletin prohibiting verbal tech.) To learn the inner secrets of the cult requires years of strict obedience and large monetary donations.
>
> In return, Scientology promises its adherents "total freedom." The Internet, through sites like this one, is going to make good on that promise. This web site is dedicated to exposing the various technical tricks behind Scientology, until all its secrets have been laid before the public at no charge.

Today, Scientology does much of its recruiting through celebrity endorsements. Celebrities such as John Travolta and Tom Cruise seldom get through a talk-show appearance without singing the virtues of Scientology.

See also OTO.

The Seasons   French society said to be a branch of the Illuminati and closely affiliated with the Knights of the Golden Circle.

See also ILLUMINATI; KNIGHTS OF THE GOLDEN CIRCLE.

Shickshinny Knights   See SOVEREIGN ORDER OF SAINT JOHN OF JERUSALEM.

Shriners   The Shriners of North America, a half million strong, have branches in the United States, Mexico, Canada, and Panama. They are known for wearing fez hats. They are a charitable organization and fund the Shriners Hospitals for Children, a network of twenty-two hospitals that provide orthopedic and burn care for children under eighteen years of age at no cost. They are famous as the sponsor of the East West Shrine Game, a college all-star football game held each January. Their leader is referred to as the Imperial Potentate.

According to the Shriners' website: "Back through the days of the Middle Ages and into the early Christian period runs the history of the Nobles of the Mystic Shrine. The shores of the Mediterranean gave this Order birth, and fostered it for thirteen hundred years. There it prospers as of old, but now serving largely a different purpose. Originally it was used for the propagation of the Muslim faith and to aid in the enforcement of the laws, rendering justice where the usual means were too slow or too uncertain. The Order of today—the Order as we know it in this country (United States)—practices the virtues of Charity and Brotherly love. No longer Muslim, nor yet Christian, it is built upon the broader plane that receives all men alike if they believe in a Deity and are of character such as will pass the strict qualifications for membership. The modern Order of the Nobles of the Mystic Shrine insists upon the highest Masonic qualifications, thus insuring that none but men of unquestioned character may cross its portals, but the ancient Order required a firm belief in the teachings of the Prophet Mohammed (PBUH) and obeisance to Allah."

The Order, they claim, was founded in Mecca in 644 A.D., and over the next millennium spread throughout North Africa. The

Order crossed the Mediterranean in 1698, when it made its way into Italy. By the eighteenth century it was in England, and the first Shriners organized in the United States in 1872. The first American Shriner was William J. Florence, a well-known comedian. He was initiated in France and received instruction in Egypt before introducing the Order to the New World.

Only Masons of the highest rank are allowed to become Shriners. You must be either a Thirty-Second Degree Scottish Rite Mason, or a Knight Templar in good standing. Shriners refer to their members as Nobles, and the rules say that every Noble must be a "God-fearing man." Members must be right-living, for remaining vice-free is necessary for combating their enemies: atheism, intolerance, bigotry, and excess.

The Shriners, they say, have many members in the Orient, and are proud of the fact that Jews, Christians, and Muslims all have been known to become Shriners, since all of those religions worship the same God. The affiliation with the Masons came about only after the Shriners first organized in the United States. This was a screening process since the Masons were considered to be among the best men in North America.

At the start of the twentieth century, there were Masons who did not approve of the Shriners. According to Shriner literature, "Many high men in Masonry opposed Shrinedom, fearing it would be to the detriment of Masonry, to which nothing can be added or taken away. In time however, they saw that the Order had nothing to do with Masonry except the very high compliment it payed the Ancient and Accepted Order of receiving only its most honored members; but finally they had to admit that the Order of the Mystic Shrine was a monument to Masonry."

According to Shriner historian Frank J. Butler, "In character, the Order of the Mystic Shrine may be said to be the broad plane of religion and the enforcement of the laws, whether based upon the Koran, the Books of Moses, or the Scriptures of the Christian apostles. The Order of the Mystic Shrine was founded when Kalif-Alec, cousin-german and son-in-law of the Prophet Mohammed himself, conceived the idea of a superior court. Strictly Arabian in its composition, this court was to deal out justice to violators of the law where the ordinary process would not reach—to break down corrupt influence, to form respect for and support of the law, to be an inquisition, if you will, the founders of the unwritten law."

Butler further wrote: "There are two characteristics prevalent in the maintenance of Shrinedom: First, trust in God—for Masons must be trusted to keep faith. . . . Secondly, trust in one's fellow-man, for one's faith in his fellow-man must endure, whenever possible, good council, abolish error, and aid in reformation, because one is a poor Mason when he fails to offer the friendly rebuke where it is needed with just as much admiration as he gives the means of praise and commendation."

One of the Shriners' most important temples is known as the "Damascus Shrine," a reference to a domed shrine in Damascus, Syria, said to contain the severed head of John the Baptist.

Skull & Bones   Yale's Skull & Bones is a super-secret society whose members include some of the most powerful men in the world (including both George H.W. and George W. Bush) and whose initiation rites involve nude wrestling and lying in a coffin in only underwear while recounting adolescent sexual experiences. These rites take place in the windowless crypt within the Skull & Bones mausoleum-like meeting house on the Yale campus. It sounds silly, but the influence of the group is anything but that.

Members of Skull & Bones are called Bonesmen. Only fifteen new members are inducted each year. Among the early influential Bonesmen were the sons of railroad magnate Edward H. Harriman, William Averell, who joined in 1913, and Edward Roland Noel, who joined in 1917. The elder President Bush's father, Prescott Bush, also became a Bonesman in 1917. Bonesman McGeorge Bundy, who joined in 1940, was national security adviser to president John F. Kennedy and Lyndon B. Johnson, as well as the president of the Ford Foundation from 1966 to 1979. Later members have included Frederick Smith, the founder of Federal Express, and Richard Pershing, the grandson of General John J. Pershing, who was killed during the Tet offensive in the Vietnam War. Many Bonesmen have gone on to become officials for the Central Intelligence Agency.

Skull & Bones began in 1832 at Yale University. (Though more than 170 years old, there have been fewer than two thousand Bonesmen in total.) Its founders were Alphonso Taft and General William Huntington Russell. Taft was the father of William Howard Taft, who was also a Bonesman and the only man to serve both as president of the United States and as Chief Justice of the Supreme Court. Alphonso Taft served as Secretary of War and Attorney General under President Ulysses S Grant. He also served as U.S. minister (ambassador) to Austria-Hungary and Russia under President Chester Arthur. The Tafts, of Cincinnati, Ohio, were not a religious family. If pressed, the family said that it was "Unitarian," which merged various parts of different religions.

General Russell came from one of Boston's most respected families and served with the Connecticut legislature. The Russells, it is said, initially made their fortune in the slave trade and by smuggling opium into the country, which is the reason the new secret society adopted the pirates' symbol, the skull and the crossbones— although the use of the symbol can be found in secret societies long before the birth of Skull & Bones, or the Russell family's businesses. The pirate symbol was used as the flag of the Knights Templar. It has been suggested that the Skull & Bones chapter opened at Yale in 1832 was merely a new chapter of a pre-existing society in Germany, the German Illuminati. Many of Skull & Bones' initiation rituals and symbols are similar to those of Freemasonry.

Although Skull & Bones does not officially exist, it was incorporated in 1856 under the name "Russell Trust." Not all of the group's Thursday and Sunday meetings take place on the Yale campus. Some meetings of Skull & Bones are said to be held at Deer Iland (*sic*), which is in the Saint Lawrence River. The "s" was left out of the word "Island" for unknown reasons at the request of a Bones member. To become a member you have to be a junior at Yale University. Each year, only fifteen new members are chosen. New members are called Knights. Older members are called Patriarchs. Although there are hundreds of living members, only about thirty different families are represented. Obviously, the proper breeding is a key factor in being chosen as a member.

According to Ron Rosenbaum, a *New York Observer* columnist

writing in *Esquire* magazine, "You get the feeling there's a lot of intermarriage among these Bones families. Year after year there will be a Whitney Townsend Phillips in the same Bones class as a Phelps Townsend Whitney. In fact, one could make the half-serious case that functionally Bones serves as a kind of ongoing informal Establishment eugenics project."

Which leads to the question: Is there aristocracy in the United States? Did the American Revolution really deliver us from the domination of nobility? Not necessarily. According to Gary Boyd Roberts of the New England Historic Genealogical Society, nineteen U.S. Presidents have descended from Edward III. Bonesman George W. Bush, leader of the Free World, can trace his heritage back to Charlemagne and Alfred the Great.

Rosenbaum, who lived next door to the Skull & Bones tomb during his years at Yale, goes on to say: "What Skull & Bones does is take preppy Prince Hals and give them a sense of mission." Rosenbaum is referring to the carefree Shakespeare character who goes on to become the heroic Henry V.

One Bones ritual involves kissing a skull. Rosenbaum says, "The rituals emphasize a sense of mortality, that life is short, and you have a mission to make something of your life."

According to conspiracy theorist and sometimes-politician Lyndon LaRouche, "Skull & Bones is no mere fraternity, no special alumni association and added mumbo-jumbo. It is a very serious, very dedicated cult-conspiracy against the U.S. Constitution. Like the Cambridge Apostles, the initiate to the Skull & Bones is a dedicated agent of British intelligence for life."

Bonesmen who are also part of the Council on Foreign Relations constitute a secret society inside a secret society, and it is said that the Bonesmen wield the real power in the CFR.

Apparently one of the matters of foreign policy of great interest to Skull & Bones is China. Since the U.S. developed a relationship with China during the Nixon administration, many of the U.S. ambassadors to that country have been Bonesmen, including the elder George Bush. Some feel this is because of the huge amount of opium China produces. And, historians note, the relationship between Communist China and Yale dates back to 1903, when Yale Divinity School set up a program of schools and hospitals and future Chairman Mao Zedong was among the staff.

Skull & Bones has several synonyms. They have been called simply Bones, or The Order. Other names include Chapter 322 and The Brotherhood of Death.

During the winter of 2004—as it became increasingly likely that John Kerry would become the Democratic nominee for President, to run against incumbent George W. Bush—it also became public knowledge that Kerry, like Bush, was a Bonesman. *The New York Times* (February 2, 2004) called the news a "field day for conspiracy theorists." Kerry became a Bonesman in 1966. Bush was initiated two years later. The story goes that the younger Bush was at first reluctant to join Skull & Bones.

"I'd rather join Gin & Tonic," he reportedly said.

But his father, then a Congressman, said, "Do the right thing and join Skull & Bones. Become a good man."

According to Kerry's spokesman, David Wade, "Rest assured, there are no pictures of them dancing together naked."

The two men were students at Yale at the same time. In addition to being a Bonesman, Kerry was president of the Yale Political Union, a group of ambitious young men. In contrast, before becoming a Bonesman, George W. Bush was the president of the fraternity Delta Kappa Epsilon, which was better known at Yale by its nickname "Animal House," after the movie about a hard-partying frat.

According to New York Governor George Pataki, who attended Yale at the same time as Bush and Kerry: "The fact that they were both in Skull & Bones is a sign of respect that their classmates held for each of them."

NBC's Tim Russert, host of *Meet the Press*, asked both Bush and Kerry about Skull & Bones on separate episodes of the Sunday morning talk show.

Noting that the leaders of both political parties were members of the same secret society, Russert asked, "What does that tell us?"

Kerry responded: "Not much, because it's a secret."

"Is there a secret handshake? Is there a secret code?" Russert asked.

"I wish there was something secret I could manifest here," Kerry replied.

Russert asked President Bush the same question about the leaders of both political parties.

"It's so secret we can't talk about it," the President said.

"What does that mean for America? The conspiracy theorists are going to go wild," Russert said.

"I'm sure they are," the President agreed.

On March 11, 2004, the Bush Administration released a list of the guests who had slept overnight at the White House between June 2002 and December 2003. Among the names were at least three belonging to Bonesmen: Donald Etra, Ken Cohen, and Muhammad Saleh.

Originally an all-white, all-male club, Skull & Bones now admits women, minorities, and gay members.

According to Thomas R. Dye and L. Harmon Zeigler, in their book, *The Irony of Democracy*, "Elites, not masses, govern America. In an industrial, scientific, and nuclear age, life in a democracy, just as in a totalitarian society, is shaped by a handful of men. In spite of differences in their approach to the study of power in America, scholars—political scientists and sociologists alike—agree that 'the key political, economic, and social decisions are made by tiny minorities.'"

See also COUNCIL ON FOREIGN RELATIONS; ILLUMINATI; KNIGHTS TEMPLAR.

Snake Heads   See TRIADS.

Society of Jesus   See JESUITS.

Society of Processeans   See THE PROCESS.

Sons of Liberty   Spin-off of the KNIGHTS OF THE GOLDEN CIRCLE.

The Sovereign and Military Order of Malta   See KNIGHTS OF MALTA.

The Sovereign Order of Saint John of Jerusalem   Secret Society formed about 1070, before the First Crusade. The original members were Italian merchants who, a generation before Jersusalem was taken from the Muslims, established a hospital in that city. After the First Crusade, the hospital workers—known as Hospitallers—formed an order similar to the Knights Templar and elected a grand master.

The Hospitallers did not start out as a military group but later developed into one. In 1291, after the Muslims regained control of the Holy Land, the Sovereign Order of Saint John of Jerusalem moved, along with the Knights Templar, to the island of Crete. When the Templars were decimated by orders of the Pope, the Hospitallers acquired much of the Templar empire. In the sixteenth century, a Turkish raid forced the Hospitallers to move their headquarters to Malta, and they became known as the Sovereign and Military Order of Malta (a.k.a. the Knights of Malta).

In the modern world, this group is a right-wing fraternal organization more popularly known as the "Shickshinny Knights," because they are headquartered in Shickshinny, Pennsylvania. The group claims to be the original Knights of Malta, the same fraternal order that dates back to 1070.

One of the most famous members of this secret society was General Charles Willoughby. General Willoughby was born in 1892 in Heidelberg, Germany, as Adolf Tscheppe-Weidenbach and came to the United States in 1910. In the U.S., Willoughby became a Counter Intelligence Corps agent, a major general in the U.S. Army and General Douglas MacArthur's chief of intelligence during the Korean War. After the war, Willoughby worked out of a Washington, D.C., headquarters.

Author Dick Russell, in his book *The Man Who Knew Too Much*, writes that, during the Cold War, Willoughby's "domestic associations extended from the Cuban exile community to the H. L. Hunt family." Willoughby reportedly ran Dallas, Texas, oil tycoon H. L. Hunt's private intelligence network. MacArthur reportedly referred to Willoughby as "my little Fascist." Willoughby formed the ultra-secret intelligence agency known as FOI, which theoretically specialized in rooting out Communist spies. Willoughby worked with "Japanese Warlords," "German Nazis," and CIA director—and later Warren Commissioner—Allen Dulles in an attempt to establish a "global anti-Communist alliance."

According to Korean War historian Bruce Cumings: "Willoughby was a thoroughly loathsome person whose entire world view consisted of piles of ethnic stereotypes; he was apparently capable of anything." Cumings writes that, after World War II, Willoughby retained his ties with Japanese militarists, including germ-warfare specialist General Ishii.

Cumings also says: "After MacArthur's sacking by U.S. president Harry Truman, Willoughby frequently visited Spain and claimed to have been involved in the American military base negotiations with Francisco Franco. He set up a kind of right-wing *internationale* called the 'international *comité*,' using money from the Hunt brothers in Texas, linking Spain and Portugal together with German right-wingers, the Hargis Crusade, and others. He was an agent for Hunt Oil in seeking offshore rights in the Portuguese colony of Mozambique."

Willoughby knew and worked with Nazi intelligence mastermind Reinhard Gehlen during the Cold War.

According to historian Peter Dale Scott, in his book *Deep Politics and the Death of JFK*, "In late 1963 the most conspicuous transnational feature of the Hunt-Willoughby network was their close identification with Madame Nhu, the widow of the recently assassinated Ngo Dinh Nhu in Vietnam."

The Sovereign Order of Saint John of Jerusalem is also known as Hospitallers, Knights Hospitallers, Knights of John, Brothers of the Hospital, Hospitallers of Jerusalem, Knights of Saint John, the Sovereign Order, The Religion, Knights of Jerusalem, Knights of Cyprus, Knights of Rhodes, Knights of Malta, Order of Malta, Knights of Russia. Under its original name, it still exists with headquarters in London as a Protestant group, and an offshoot of the Knights of Malta.

See also KNIGHTS OF MALTA; KNIGHTS TEMPLAR.

The SS (Schutzstaffel)   The knightly order of the Nazi Party, led by its high priest, Heinrich Himmler. The SS served as Adolf Hitler's bodyguards. Himmler joined the Nazi party in 1923 and was involved in the earliest attempts of Adolf Hitler to assume power in Germany. Himmler was associated with the *Germanenorden* (a secret society based on Freemasonry) and its spin-off, the Thule Society.

In 1924, Himmler renounced the Catholic Church, of which he had previously been a member. In 1929, Hitler made Himmler the head of the SS, which fashioned itself after the Teutonic Knights.

When the SS first formed, it was not yet a powerful organization and spent much of its time organizing search parties to find Christian artifacts such as the Holy Grail, the Ark of the Covenant, and the Spear of Longinus, the spear that wounded Christ on the cross. The SS believed that Jesus was an Aryan and his father Joseph was a Roman.

Himmler told his senior SS men in 1942: "This Christendom, this greatest pestilence which could have befallen us in history, which has weakened us for every conflict, we must finish with." His plan was to replace Christianity with a celebration of Aryan history, using solstice celebrations as the holidays.

An SS wedding ceremony was created. Himmler himself described the matrimonial ceremony: "If there was a girl in a village who had reached marriageable age and not found a man, the father went out on a moon-dark night, that is at new moon, with the girl and the villagers. The girl was placed on the dolmen or ancestral burial, the villagers stood in a wide circle around this stone, face outward. The father had spoken beforehand with a villager, thus with one of the blood-community. This man took himself from the ring to the ancestral burial and coupled with the girl. The love and sexual act took place on the ancestral burial. . . . What was done was no casual act, but took place in the sight of the ancestors and on the grave of the ancestors."

About Himmler, Hitler is supposed to have said, "What nonsense! Here we have at last reached an age that has left all mysticism behind it, and now he wants to start all over again. We might just as well have stayed with the church. . . . To think that I may some day be turned into an SS saint! I would turn over in my grave. . . ."

Starting in 1932, by which time there were 52,000 members, the SS wore an all-black uniform. By June 1944, there were more than 800,000 members.

Headquarters for the SS was the castle of Wewelsberg near Paderborn in Westphalia, which Himmler had acquired in 1934. Reconstruction work was done by labor supplied by concentration camps. The twelve senior members of the SS sat in high-backed chairs made of pigskin around a huge round oak table inside the castle. Each chair had mounted upon it a silver disc, with the name of the SS member who sat there engraved upon it. Each of the twelve members had his own quarters inside the castle. Himmler's room was dedicated to the tenth-century Saxon king Henry the First (also known as Henry the Fowler).

Himmler, of course, believed in mass killing as an expedient way of acheving social change. He once said, "You only need to look up the Germanic Sagas. If they proscribed a family and outlawed them, or if there was a blood feud in the family, then they were drastically thorough. . . . They said, 'This man is a traitor, the blood is bad, there is bad blood in them, that will be eradicated.' And in the case of a blood feud it was eradicated down to the last member. . . ."

During World War II, the SS Death's Head Units were put in charge of Germany's concentration camps. The SS also followed the German Army into the Soviet Union, where they had the responsibility of murdering Jews, Gypsies, Communists and partisans. Following World War II, at the Nuremberg War Crimes Trial, the SS was declared a criminal organization and many of its leaders were executed.

See also Teutonic Knights; Thule Society; Vril Society.

Sufis   Illuminist sectarians with orders in East Africa, North Africa, Indonesia, Malaysia, Afghanistan, Kurdistan, Russia, Turkmenistan, and the Balkans. Orders are Islamic, quasi-Islamic and non-Islamic.

According to the website "What is Sufism?" (www.nimatullahi. org/us/WIS/WIS1.html; accessed March 8, 2004): "The substance and definition of Sufism: the substance of Sufism is the Truth and the definition of Sufism is the selfless experiencing and actualization of the Truth. The practice of Sufism: the practice of Sufism is the intention to go towards the Truth, by means of love and devotion. This is called the *Tariqat*, the Spiritual Path or way towards God. The definition of the sufi: the sufi is one who is a lover of Truth, who by means of love and devotion moves towards the Truth, towards the Perfection which all are truly seeking. As necessitated by Love's jealousy, the sufi is taken away from all except the Truth-Reality. For this reason, in Sufism it is said that, 'Those who are inclined towards the hereafter can not pay attention to the material world.

Likewise, those who are involved in the material world can not concern themselves with the hereafter. But the sufi (because of Love's jealousy) is unable to attend to either of these worlds.'"

According to A. A. Tabari in his online essay "The Other Side of Sufism" (www.qss.org/articles/sufism/toc.html; accessed March 8, 2004): "In response to those concerned Muslims on the North American Continent and elsewhere, that I present this critique on Sufism. It would, *In Sha' Allah*, prove useful to put in the hands of those Muslims who are unaware of the hidden dangers of Sufism, and who, due to their shallow knowledge of Islam, or for other reasons, are duped into believing that salvation is attained only by way of ascetic mystical doctrines, and that the relationship between man and Allah is maintained through a few self-appointed priests. Deviation from the right path led some Muslim rulers at certain stages of history to believe the perfection of thought could be reached by mixing Greek philosophies with Islamic beliefs. They contaminated the purity and simplicity of Islam as a way of life. This opened the door to esoterism, elitism, and mysticism, which later developed into a religion of its own. . . . Sufism is often, willfully or otherwise, referred to by Sufis themselves, or by orientalists, as 'Islamic mysticism,' in order to give the impression that Islam is either wholly or partly an esoteric religion, with a set of dogmatic rituals to be understood by the elite alone—in this case, the Sufis! Unfortunately, the lack of any sound critical analysis of the subject in the English language allows these orientalists to flood the English and North American book market with literature that stands unchallenged, and dupes naive Muslims into believing that true salvation can only be attained by pursuing a mystical order. Their vain goal strips Islam of its Universality. . . . If Sufis insist that they are Muslims, then what is the sense of identifying themselves with Sufism rather than with Islam? The word "Sufism" was not familiar to those who lived in the first and the best three generations of as-Salaf as-Salih (the pious predecessors) who were commanded by Allah the Exalted and His Messenger."

Swastika   The swastika, an archetype for "spin" set at right angles, is most famous as the emblem of the Nazi party of Adolf Hitler, before and during World War II. Since then it has been used as an emblem of neo-Nazi activity. The emblem, however, pre-existed Hitler. Hitler used the symbol because, during the late 1800s, the swastika began to symbolize Germanic culture and by the first decades of the twentieth century, the symbol had taken on distinctive anti-Semitic undertones.

The word swastika derives from "su" (Sanskrit for "well") and "asti" meaning "to be."

The swastika has appeared all over the world and has been used, with various meanings, by many civilizations. In Scandinavia, the symbol was long accepted to mean Thor's hammer.

Early Christians, seeking to avoid persecution, used it as a camouflaged cross. Ancient Asian, Egyptian, and Irish civilizations also used the symbol. In India it means good luck and is placed on door, shrines, and sometimes painted onto the human body. In North America, it served as a symbol for the Hopi tribe of Native Americans.

According to Frank Waters in his book *The Book of the Hopi*, "The swastika symbol represents the path of the migrations of the Hopi clans. The center of the cross represents Tuwanasavi or the Center of the Universe which lay in what is now the Hopi country in the southwestern part of the U.S. Tuwanasavi was not the geographic center of North America, but the magnetic or spiritual center formed by the junction of the North-South and the East-West axis along which the Twins sent their vibratory messages and controlled the rotation of the planet. Three directions (*pasos*) for most of the clans were the same: the ice-locked back door to the north, the Pacific Ocean to the west and the Atlantic Ocean to the east. Only seven clans—the Bear, Eagle, Sun, Kachina, Parrot, Flute, and Coyote clans—migrated to South America to the southern *paso* at its tip. The rest of some forty clans, having started from somewhere in southern Mexico or Central America, regarded this as their southern *paso*, their migration thus forming a balanced symbol. Upon arriving at each *paso* all the leading clans turned right before retracing their routes."

The symbol exists both in a clockwise version, the one used by the Nazis, and a counter-clockwise version, as is used by Buddhists.

Symbionese Liberation Army   See TERRORIST GROUPS.

T

Technocracy   Technocracy, a scientists-should-rule-all movement, was founded in 1918 by Howard Scott and a group of architects, engineers, and scientists. The word Technocracy was coined by an American engineer named W. H. Smith in 1919. It gained popularity in 1941 because of its use in James Burham's *Managerial Revolution*. Technocracy is the belief that government should not be run on political ideology, philosophy, and opinion—but rather on science.

Members must be North American. "Aliens" are not allowed to join. Nor are politicians—that is, those who currently hold public office.

The group originally called itself the Technical Alliance and described itself as a research organization. The society is divided into chartered sections, each consisting of at least fifty members. Dues are fifteen dollars per year. Members get to wear the chromium and vermilion insignia of Technocracy—the Monad, an ancient generic symbol signifying balance.

The organization was incorporated in 1934 in New York State. In 1934, Howard Scott made his first lecture tour. Most states in the United States and provinces in Canada have their own chartered section. Many members are in the military. As their propaganda reads, "So long as you are a patriotic North American you are welcome in Technocracy."

According to the website "What is Technocracy?", the movement is based on three conclusions of its founder: "(1) That there exists on the North American Continent a physical potential in resources to produce a high standard of goods and services for all citizens, and that the high-speed technology for converting these resources to use-forms in sufficient volume is already installed, and that the skilled personnel for operating it are present and available. Yet we have unprecedented insecurity, extensive poverty and rampant crime. (2) That our current economic and political model (called the Price System), can no longer function adequately as a method of production and distribution of goods. The invention of power machinery has made it possible to produce a plethora of goods with a relatively small amount of human labor. As machines displace men and women, however, purchasing power is destroyed, for if people cannot work for wages and salaries, they cannot buy goods. We find ourselves, then, in this paradoxical situation: the more we produce, the less we are able to consume. And (3) that a new distributive system must be instituted that is designed to satisfy the special needs of an environment of technological adequacy, and that this system must not in any way be associated with the extent of an individual's functional contribution to society."

The attributes of a Technocratic society are said to be:

- A scientific method of control of the technology of our continent.
- Democratic controls for all nontechnical issues and decisions.
- Removal of methods of scarcity such as money, debt, value, and interest.
- Replacement of these methods with an empirical accounting of all physical resources, products, and services.
- Productive capacity higher than currently possible, without requiring any new equipment.
- Decrease in human labor through proper use of automation.
- Higher standard of living for all citizens.
- Elimination or vast reduction of various social ills, such as poverty, crime, pollution, insecurity, and disease.

Templars   See KNIGHTS TEMPLAR.

Temple of Set   Group led by U.S. military intelligence officer Lt. Col. Michael Aquino. The Temple of Set was founded in 1975 as a splinter group of the Church of Satan. The founders of this group

disagreed with the management style and philosophy of the Church
of Satan, and so formed their own group.

The Temple of Set's philosophy is based on self-improvement
and self-creation, as represented by the Egyptian principle of
Xeper—which is sometimes spelled Khepher or Kefer. Set is an
ancient Egyptian god. Members of this group are called Setians.
Like most secret societies, members must be initiated, and then
move upward in the organization by levels called degrees. The group
is recognized as an incorporated religion by both the U.S. federal
government and the state of California.

Despite their status as a religion, the Temple of Set has no
church, and each member is allowed to follow the religion in any
place and in any manner of the individual's choosing. There are
priests who act as advisors. The priests represent both the group
and the entity called Set. Setians do not worship Set, nor do they
worship any other god or entity. Members believe that Set's very
being results in change in the universe and that members serve
the interests of Set—who is loved but not worshipped—through
self-betterment.

Setians follow what is called the "Left-Hand Path," which means
they feel the individual takes precedence over society—even if that
society is the Temple of Set itself.

The Temple of Set has been criticized, with most of that criticism directed at leader Michael Aquino. Aquino persists in using
Nazi imagery and symbolism, and references to Nazi ideology, in
his Temple of Set literature. Aquino, for example, has spoken in
favor of those who deny the Nazi holocaust as historical fact.

Aquino is not afraid to strike back at his critics. He has filed
lawsuits against some of them and others have claimed to become
the subject of his harassment.

See also CHURCH OF SATAN.

Terrorist Groups   Terrorism is defined in the Code of Federal Reg-
ulations as "the unlawful use of force and violence against persons
or property to intimidate or coerce a government, the civilian population, or any segment thereof, in furtherance of political or social
objectives." The primary goal of all terrorist acts is the creation of

terror. Here's a guide to foreign terrorist groups of the present and recent past:

Abu Nidal Organization (ANO)—Militant Palestinian group that split from the PLO in 1974. Has carried out terrorist acts in twenty countries—including the United States, United Kingdom, and Israel, claiming nine hundred lives.

Abu Sayyaf Group (ASG)—Islamic group fighting for an Islamic state on the island of Mindanao in the Philippines. One of the plotters of the 1993 World Trade Center bombing in New York City, Ramzi Yousef, is suspected of training terrorists for the Abu Sayyaf Group. In May 2000, this group kidnapped three Americans, one of whom was later found beheaded. Although ransom was paid to the kidnappers, the captives were not released and one of the remaining Americans was killed in crossfire during a rescue attempt by the Filipino Army.

Al-Jihad—Militant Islamic group operating in Egypt against the Egyptian government, as well as Christian, Israeli, and Western targets on Egyptian soil. Working in conjunction with Al Qaeda, this group is suspected of involvement in the 1998 bombing of the U.S. Embassy, in Kenya, and the U.S. destroyer *Cole*.

Al Qaeda—The terrorist group behind the terrorist attacks on The Pentagon in Washington, D.C., and the World Trade Center in New York on September 11, 2001, was *Al Qaeda*, an Arabic word meaning "the base." In approximately 1989, Osama bin Laden and Muhammad Atef founded Al Qaeda. Quoting from a U.S. government indictment handed down against the organization in November 1998, Al Qaeda was "an international terrorist group . . . which was dedicated to opposing non-Islamic governments with force and violence. One of the principal goals of Al Qaeda was to drive the United States armed forces out of Saudi Arabia (and elsewhere on the Saudi Arabian peninsula) and Somalia by violence. Al Qaeda had a command and control structure which included a *majlis al shura* (or consultation council) which discussed and approved major undertakings, including terrorist operations."

Both Atef and bin Laden sat on this council. Al Qaeda had ties to other "terrorist organizations that operated under its umbrella," including the al-Jihad group based in Egypt, the Islamic Group, formerly led by Shaykh Umar Abel al-Rahman, and other jihad groups in other countries.

Again quoting the indictment: "Al Qaeda also forged alliances with the National Islamic Front in Sudan and with representatives of the government of Iran, and its associated terrorist group Hezbollah, for the purpose of working together against their perceived common enemies in the West, particularly the United States." Other members of Al Qaeda "conspired, confederated and agreed to kill nationals of the United States." In furtherance of this conspiracy, bin Laden and others "provided training camps and guesthouses in various areas, including Afghanistan, Pakistan, Somalia, and Kenya for the use of Al Qaeda and its affiliated groups." Bin Laden and others provided currency and weapons to members of Al Qaeda and associated terrorist groups in various countries throughout the world.

Bin Laden established a headquarters for Al Qaeda in Khartoum, Sudan, in 1991, and established a series of businesses, including two investment companies, an agricultural company, a construction business, and a transportation company, all of which were "operated to provide income and support to Al Qaeda and to provide cover for the procurement of explosives, weapons, and chemicals and for the travel of Al Qaeda operatives."

Bin Laden issued a number of *fatwahs* (rulings on Islamic law) stating that U.S. forces stationed in Saudi Arabia, Yemen, and the Horn of Africa, including Somalia, should be attacked. Al Qaeda members "provided military training and assistance to Somali tribes opposed to the United Nations' intervention in Somalia. . . . On October 3 and 4, 1993, in Mogadishu, Somalia, persons who had been trained by Al Qaeda (and trainers who had been trained by Al Qaeda) participated in an attack on United States military personnel serving in Somalia as part of Operation Restore Hope, which attack resulted in the killing of eighteen United States Army personnel."

Bin Laden and others attempted to procure components of nuclear and chemical weapons. And that was *before* the events of 9/11.

In reaction to the 9/11 attacks, the U.S. committed military forces to the overthrow of the Taliban, the ruling government of Afghanistan who were playing host to bin Laden and the Al Qaeda terror training camps. The Taliban was removed from power but bin Laden, apparently, has so far survived the war, much to the chagrin of President George W. Bush, who had called for the capture of bin Laden "dead or alive."

Al-Zarqawi Network—Terror group operating in Iraq, led by one-legged mastermind Abu-Musab al-Zarqawi. Responsible for several suicide bombings across Iraq. According to letters written by al-Zarqawi in 2004, his group is plotting to join forces with Al Qaeda for future attacks and beheadings.

Ansar Al Islam—Kurdish group with ties to both Al Qaeda and the Al-Zarqawi Network. This group is suspected of carrying out the simultaneous suicide bombings of two Kurdish political party head-quarters in northern Iraq in February 2004. Before the U.S. invasion of Iraq in 2003, this group also reportedly operated a factory near the Iraq/Iran border that produced the poison ricin.

Armed Islamic Group (GIA)—Islamic extremist group fighting to replace the current regime in Algeria with an Islamic state.

Aum Shinrikyo (Aum)—Japanese religious sect. The name translates as "Supreme Truth." Carried out sarin gas attacks in the subways of Tokyo, Japan, in 1995. The attacks killed twelve and sickened thousands. The group has also been connected to a series of other murders. The leaders of the group preached doomsday messages and their followers tried to make the prophecies self-fulfilling. The cult also unsuccessfully tried to use biological weapons such as anthrax and botulism to kill people. On February 16, 2004, Japanese agents raided key facilities of the group—which now calls itself Aleph— in search of evidence of a terror plot. The raids involved more than two hundred police. Headquarters in Tokyo and elsewhere were searched. Police were expecting an attack because the group's leader, Shoko Asahara, was about to be sentenced for his role in the deadly attacks a decade earlier. On February 26, 2004, he was sentenced to death.

Democratic Front for the Liberation of Palestine: Hawatmeh Faction (DFLP)—Marxist-Leninist group supporting the birth of a Palestinian state through revolt of the masses.

Euzkadi Ta Askatasuna (ETA)—Basque group fighting Spain for an independent Basque state.

First of October Antifascist Resistance Group (GRAPO)—Armed wing of the Spanish Communist Party, which advocates the overthrow of the Spanish Government and replacement with a Marxist-Leninist regime. This strongly anti-American group was formed in 1975, and has killed more than eighty persons and injured more than two hundred.

Gama'a al-Islamiyya (Islamic Group, IG)—Militant Islamic group seeking Islamic rule in Egypt by force. The leader of this group, Shaykh Umar Abd al-Rahman, was arrested for the 1993 World Trade Center bombing.

Hamas (Islamic Resistance Movement)—The word "hamas" means "zeal" in Arabic. Hamas is also an acronym for the Arabic translation of Islamic Resistance Movement. This group, founded in 1987, is an outgrowth of the Muslim Brotherhood, and believes in establishing a Palestinian state through violent means. Hamas is known for its suicide bombers. In recent years, Iran has increased shipments of guns and explosives to this Palestinian extremist group. On March 22, 2004, the spiritual leader and founder of Hamas, Sheik Ahmed Yassin, was killed, along with two bodyguards, by an Israeli rocket, as he was leaving a mosque in Gaza City. The leader, who was wheelchair-bound and spent the years 1989–1997 in an Israeli prison, was struck in the chest by the rocket and blown to pieces. In response, Palestinians began burning tires in the streets and demonstrators chanted for revenge. In defending the action, the Israeli military said that Yassin was "responsible for numerous murderous terror attacks, resulting in the deaths of many civilians, both Israeli and foreign."

Harakat ul-Ansar (HUA)—Islamic group based in Pakistan and operating in Kashmir against Indian troops.

Hezbollah (Party of God)—Group of Lebanese Shi'ite Muslims fighting Israel since the 1982 Lebanon War. According to a Justice Department letter to a Senate Committee released to the press in November 2002, the Iranian-backed jihad group Hezbollah had cells in the United States and was prepared to make an attack on U.S. soil. The terrorist group had been called the most sophisticated in the world.

The letter stated: "They're here. FBI investigations to date indicate that many Hezbollah subjects based in the United States have the capacity to attempt terrorist attacks here, should this be a desired objective of the group. [Hezbollah members] have been tasked with surveillance of potential targets in the United States."

Hezbollah was responsible for driving the Israelis from southern Lebanon. They are also responsible for the 1983 truck bombing of the Marine barracks in Beirut that killed 241 U.S. Marines. They have provided explosives training to Al Qaeda. The FBI has twice arrested Hezbollah members in the U.S., both times for illegal money-making schemes, the selling of bootleg cigarettes and videotapes.

Irish Republican Army (IRA)—Formed in 1969 as a clandestine armed wing of Sinn Fein, a legal political movement dedicated to removing British forces from Northern Ireland and unifying Ireland. The IRA is a Marxist organization which is divided into small, tightly knit cells. They have used bombings, assassinations, kidnappings, punishment beatings, extortion, and robberies to target senior British Government officials, British military and police in Northern Ireland, and Northern Irish Loyalist paramilitary groups.

Islamic Movement of Uzbekistan—Terrorists fighting for an Uzbek Islamic state who fought alongside the Taliban in Afghanistan against U.S. forces. In 2000, this group kidnapped four American mountain-climbers who subsequently escaped after pushing one of the terrorists off a cliff.

Japanese Red Army (JRA)—International terrorist group dedicated to the overthrow of the Japanese government and world revolution. The leader lives in Lebanon and supports militant Islamic causes.

Jemaah Islamiyah—Southeast Asian group, associated with Al Qaeda, accused of the 2002 Bali bombing that killed two hundred people, and the 2003 car bombing in Jakarta, Indonesia, that killed thirteen.

Kach—Radical Israeli group seeking overthrow of Israeli government and restoration of the biblical state of Israel.

Kahane Chai—Offshoot of Kach (see above).

Khmer Rouge—Radical Cambodian political group. Their attempt to purify the "Khmer race" resulted in millions dead.

Kurdistan Workers' Party (PKK)—Communist group of Turkish Kurds seeking an independent Kurd state in southeastern Turkey.

Lashkar I Jhangvi—A Kashmiri separatist group allegedly tied to Al Qaeda and Jaish-e-Mohammed. This group is suspected of involvement in the February 2002 kidnapping and murder of *Wall Street Journal* reporter Daniel Pearl.

Liberation Tigers of Tamil Eelam (LTTE)—Revolutionaries in Sri Lanka.

Manuel Rodriguez Patriotic Front Dissidents (FPMR/D)—Armed wing of the Chilean Communist Party that has attacked U.S. businesses in Chile, mostly fast-food restaurants.

Mujahedin-e Khalq Organization (MEK, MKO)—Radical Iranian revolutionaries based in Iraq.

National Liberation Army (ELN)—Marxist guerrilla group operating out of Colombia. They kidnap foreign businessmen for ransom.

Palestine Islamic Jihad/Shaqaqi Faction (PIJ)—Militant Palestinians originally based in the Gaza Strip, now operating throughout the Middle East.

Palestine Liberation Front/Abu Abbas Faction (PLF)—Conducts attacks against Israel. Attacked cruise ship *Achille Lauro* in 1985, murdering U.S. citizen Leon Klinghoffer. The group's leader, Abul Abbas, died in U.S. custody in Iraq in 2004.

Popular Front for the Liberation of Palestine (PFLP)—Group based in Syria, Lebanon, and Israel. They attack Israeli and moderate Arab targets.

Popular Front for the Liberation of Palestine–General Command (PFLP-GC)—Based in Syria, and active since 1968. Believes in the violent destruction of Israel.

Revolutionary Armed Forces of Colombia (FARC)—Military wing of the Colombian Communist Party which has since 1964 committed terrorist acts against Colombian targets.

Revolutionary Organization 17 November (17 November)—Based in Greece, named after the 1973 student uprising in Athens. Supports radical causes in Greece through assassinations and bombings.

Revolutionary People's Liberation Party/Front (DHKP/C)—Offshoot of the Turkish People's Liberation Party/Front. This radical anti-U.S. group attacks Turkish military targets (as well as U.S. targets during the Gulf War).

Revolutionary People's Struggle (ELA)—Greek leftist group. Bombs Greek government and economic targets.

Salafist Group for Call and Combat (GSPC)—Armed Algerian group, perhaps several hundred in number, that has gained some favor in

Algeria by pledging to avoid civilian targets, and usually hits government and military targets, often in rural areas. Despite their pledges, there have been civilian casualties. There have been reports that this group maintains contacts with North African extremists sympathetic to Al Qaeda.

Salifiya Jihadia—Moroccan terrorist group named by the CIA as responsible for five bombings in Casablanca in May 2003.

Shining Path (Sendero Luminoso, SL)—Maoist group in Peru. Conducts bombings and assassinations. Has claimed thirty thousand lives in Peru.

Tupac Amaru Revolutionary Movement (MRTA)—Radical Peruvian group seeking to rid Peru of imperialism through kidnapping, assassinations, and commando-style military operations.

There are also terrorist groups right here in the United States. The most notorious example of domestic terrorism is the April 1995 truck bombing of the Alfred P. Murrah Federal Building in Oklahoma City, which killed 168 people and injured more than 500. Allegations have been made that the right-wing extremist group known as the Aryan Republican Army was involved in this attack. The FBI classifies domestic terrorist threats mostly by political motive, dividing them into three main categories: left-wing, right-wing, and special-interest. Religious sects, sometimes using what is called *leaderless resistance*, have also been connected with terrorist incidents. Leaderless resistance entails a general endorsement of terrorist violence by movement leaders but leaves planning and executing operations to individuals or small groups. Right-wing terrorism groups tend to be motivated by opposition to federal taxation and regulation, the United Nations, other international organizations, and the U.S. government itself, as well as by a hatred of racial and religious minorities. Left-wing terrorism consists of anti-capitalist revolutionary groups. These groups were most active during the 1960s and the Vietnam era. The only such groups still active, experts say, are Puerto Rican separatists. There are also special-interest terrorists that focus on single issues such as abortion, the environment, or animal rights.

Here is a brief rundown of present and recent-past domestic terror groups:

Armed Forces for Puerto Rican National Liberation (FALN)—Called the *Fuerzas Armadas de Liberación Nacional* (FALN) in Spanish, this Puerto Rican clandestine terrorist group advocates complete Puerto Rican independence. In 1950, members of the FALN attempted to assassinate U.S. President Harry S Truman. FALN was also responsible for more than fifty bomb attacks on U.S. political and military targets between 1974 and 1983.

Earth Liberation Front—"Eco-terrorists" who commit acts of terror, usually arson, to protest the destruction of the world's ecology. About the organization, leader Katie Fedor said, "There's no central hierarchy, there's no membership list. ELF works in small groups of closely connected colleagues that they trust, literally, with their freedom." In 1998, the group took responsibility for the destruction of two Elks Lodges on Vail Mountain in Colorado, an act designed to protest the destruction of the natural environment of the North American lynx. This group is a splinter group of Earth First!, a radical environmental activist movement whose participants endorse "front-line, direct action to get results."

Symbionese Liberation Army—"Symbionese" means "joined together." American underground radical group of the 1970s best known for turning Patty Hearst into Tanya. They used a serpent as their emblem.

Weather Underground—Anti-racist and anti–Vietnam War group active in the U.S. during the 1960s and '70s. They used bombings and violent protests as their *modus operandi*. Their announced intention was to overthrow the U.S. government.

Teutonic Knights   Medieval brotherhood that used the swastika as a symbol. This group was similar to the Knights Templar, with one major exception: they conquered and ruled their own nation.

The country was called Ordenstaat and extended from Prussia to the Gulf of Finland. They were a military/religious order who answered only to the Pope. Members took vows of poverty, chastity, and obedience.

The Teutonic Knights formed in the early twelfth century in Jerusalem. The group formed following the construction in that city by a German couple of a hospital for poor German-speaking people. The hospital was called Hospital of St. Mary of the Germans in Jerusalem. Attached to the hospital was a chapel. Both structures were dedicated to the Virgin Mary. When Saladin conquered Jerusalem in 1187, all records of the hospital ceased in Jerusalem. Three years later, a field hospital with that name was constructed, using sails from ships as shelter, for wounded German soldiers during the Siege of Acre. The organization behind the hospital was transformed into a religious order responsible to the local bishop. It is written that Pope Clement III approved the Order on February 6, 1191, as Hospital of St. Mary of the Germans in Jerusalem. There is disagreement over whether the field hospital organization was the same as the actual hospital in Jerusalem in name only, or if there was a stronger connection. It is said that a ceremony was held on March 5, 1198, and that at that ceremony, attended by the patriarch of Jerusalem, the king of Jerusalem, the head of the crusading army, and the masters of the Templars, the Hospital of St. Mary was transformed into a military order. Like the Hospitallers, the new Order, called the Teutonic Order, would be in charge of caring for the sick, yet they would follow Templar rule and wear Templar white cloaks. To differentiate between Templar and Teutonic knights, the Teutonic Order was assigned to wear black crosses, rather than the red worn by the Templars.

The Teutonic Knights quickly developed a system of provinces when its first independent rule was adopted in 1264. They had a hierarchical chain of command with commanderies at the lowest level. Provinces or bailiwicks were parts of "countries" that composed the Order as a whole. In rising order, the Teutonic ranks were local commander, province commander, national commander, and grand master. Top leadership positions were elected by the general chapter. Membership remained predominantly German-speaking. Distinct classes made up the Order. These were knights, priests, brothers, peasants, and slaves. Women were employed for domestic help.

In the thirteenth century, under Grand Master Hermann von Salza, the wealth and possessions of the Teutonic Knights grew rapidly. In a space of twenty years, the Teutonic Order was invited into Greece, Hungary, and Prussia by secular rulers to perform military duties on their behalf. In Hungary, the Teutonics were expelled a few years after they were invited in by King Andrew II, who felt that their power had grown too great. By the end of the thirteenth century, members of the Teutonic Knights could be found in Cyprus, Sicily, Apulia, Lombardy, Spain, France, Alsace, Austria, Bohemia, the Low countries, Germany, and Livonia. Pope Honorius III gave the Teutonics the same power and privileges as the Templars and the Hospitallers in 1221.

By that time, they had moved their headquarters to Venice. In 1309, the headquarters moved to Marienburg in Prussia. In 1237, a knightly order in Livonia called the Brothers of the Sword joined the Teutonic Order, strengthening the Teutonic Order in the Baltic region.

More than two thousand villages were built by the Order during the fourteenth century. In the fifteenth century, the Order went to war against Poland and Lithuania. In 1410, the Order lost a battle against a coalition put together by their enemies and were decimated. The Teutonic Knights lost their financial, military, and political capabilities due to this military loss. But they did not cease to exist.

In 1525, Grand Master Albrecht von Brandenburg became a Lutheran, joining the cause of the rebellious Martin Luther, and was named Duke of Prussia by the Polish king. The Teutonic Knights thus ceased to be a German Order answering to the Roman Church. In the seventeenth century, the Order was still used occasionally for military purposes, such as when one thousand troops were raised by the Order to help the Austrians in a battle against the Turks.

The Order was again hit hard in the late eighteenth century by the Napoleonic Wars. In 1809, Napoleon dissolved the Order in all countries under his dominion. The Order functioned only under a thick veil of secrecy until 1839, when Austrian Emperor Ferdinand I reconstituted the Order as the Order of the Teutonic Knights. The

"Honorable Knights of the Teutonic Order" was founded in 1866, with Knights now making annual contributions for hospitals. During World War I, the Order took care of about three thousand wounded soldiers in their facilities.

In 1923, for the first time, masters of the Order were allowed to come from among the clerics rather than just from the "knighthood." Because of National Socialist rule, the Order was dissolved in Austria in 1938 and Czechoslovakia in 1939. A young Adolf Hitler had a fascination with the Teutonic Knights. Following World War II, the Order resumed operations in Germany, and in other locations in Europe. The Order's headquarters, treasury, and archives are now located in Vienna, Austria.

Also known as Hospital of St. Mary of the Germans of Jerusalem and the Order of the German Houses.

Theosophy Society   Theosophy means "God's divine wisdom." This society was founded in New York City in 1875 by a mystic from Russia named Helena Petrovna Blavatsky. She wrote books during the 1870s and 1880s that attempted to describe the scientific basis for religious beliefs. She felt this was necessary because the advancement of scientific knowledge—including the theory of evolution—was resulting in a new generation of religious skeptics. In 1878, Blavatsky and her lead disciple, U.S. Army colonel Henry Steel Olcott, moved the Theosophical Society's headquarters to Madras, India.

Six years later, in 1884, Blavatsky opened a branch of the Theosophical Society in Germany. It—complete with its beliefs in visitors from outer space, reincarnation, human media who can channel messages from the dead, and white superiority—became the philosophical basis for the Nazi party.

See also Round Table.

Third Order of St. Francis   See Penitentes.

Thuggees   One of the world's oldest organized crime gangs. Dating back to the early nineteenth century, this Indian secret society worships the goddess Kali. Members were known as Thugs. Thugs tended to be the sons of Thugs—which is the source of the English word thug, meaning hoodlum—and membership is considered hereditary. Thugs could be either Hindu or Muslim. Thugs preyed on travelers, robbing and often murdering their victims. As is the case with many organized crime groups, the men carried out the Thug activities while the women at home knew nothing about it.

According to the British Broadcasting Company (BBC), "A typical Thug killing was done by joining a group of travellers and entertaining and cooking for them so that the travellers were soon off guard. At a pre-arranged signal (the code phrase was *bring the tobacco*) the Thugs would strangle the male travellers and take everything of value. The Thugs kept the valuables themselves and dedicated the corpses to Kali."

Members of a Thug group had their own specialties. There were the *sothaees* who lured travellers; the *lughaees*, who dug the graves in advance; and the *bhuttotes*, who killed. The victims were strangled with a scarf called a *roomal*.

At their peak, Thugs were murdering forty thousand people per year. During the 1830s, the British rulers of India went to war with the Thuggees. The leader of this movement was William Sleeman, who established the Thuggee and Dacoity Department inside the Indian government.

According to the BBC, "Over three thousand Thugs were captured by William Sleeman during the 1830s. Four-hundred eighty-three Thugs gave evidence against the rest, 412 were hanged and the rest imprisoned or rehabilitated." Some, however, have described this anti-Thug movement as a witchhunt, with many non-Thugs and innocents being killed along with the guilty parties.

The Thuggee and Dacoity Department was the primary anti-Thuggee force until the beginning of the twentieth century when a new Central Criminal Intelligence Department replaced it. The anti-Thuggee movement was very successful, a fact that greatly benefited the British rulers.

Thugs became famous in the Western world because of the popularity of a book called *Confessions of a Thug*, written by Philip Meadow Taylor in 1839. More recently, the Thuggees were featured in George Bruce's 1968 book *The Stranglers: The Cult of Thuggee and its Overthrow in British India*, in the 1939 film *Gunga Din*, and in 1984 in *Indiana Jones and the Temple of Doom*.

Jules Verne described the Thugs in his 1872 book *Around the World in 80 Days*. Verne wrote: "The travellers crossed, beyond Milligaum, the fatal country so often stained with blood by the sectaries of the goddess Kali. . . . It was thereabouts that Feringhea, the Thuggee chief, king of the stranglers, held his sway. . . . These ruffians, united by a secret bond, strangled victims of every age in honour of the goddess Death, without ever shedding blood; there was a period when this part of the country could scarcely be travelled over without corpses being found in every direction. . . . The English Government has succeeded in greatly diminishing these murders, though the Thuggees still exist, and pursue the exercise of their horrible rites."

By 1890, the Thugs were all but extinct, although the Thuggee concept continues in India, sometimes under that name.

Thule Society   Known in Germany as the *Thule Gesellschaft*, or the *Germanorden* (German Order), this group started out near the end of World War I as a "literary discussion group," founded by Baron Rudolf Freiherr von Sebottendorff. It evolved into an anti-Semitic pro-Germany organization that believed in the occult. The Thule Society was greatly influenced by another occult group known as the Theosophy Society.

Critics of the society during the 1920s said that the Thules were not a study group but a propaganda group.

The group was named after a mythic and Arctic land called Ultima Thule, which was supposedly the original homeland for Germanic people. These people were superior to other humans, it is believed, because they were extraterrestrials who, over the years, had lost knowledge of their origins.

The Thule Society's emblem is a swastika over a sword. According to some, there is an inner core of Thule members who worship Satan and believe that an increased awareness of evil raises their consciousness.

There is also a story that the Thule Society was determined to return those of the Merovingian bloodline—supposedly descendants

of Jesus and Mary Magdalene—to the thrones of Europe. Adolf
Hitler and his Nazi party stepped in and prevented this from
happening.

In the years after World War II, it is believed that members of
this group continued Hitler's policies of ethnic cleansing under the
guise of "sacrifices," murdering hundreds of people believed to be
Jews or Communists. According to historian Trevor Ravenscroft, the
Thules are a "Society of Assassins."

According to Thule Society lore, a German writer named John
van Helsing discovered a crashed flying saucer in the Black Forest in
1936. He said the craft was back-engineered by members of the
Thule Society. This information, in combination with information
gathered by the Vril Society through channeling, allowed the first
German flying saucer, known as the Haunebu 1, to be flown in
August 1939. It is said that secret SS files contain details of the craft,
saying that it was seventy-five feet in diameter.

See also NEW TEMPLARS, ORDER OF THE; THE SS; THEOSOPHY SOCIETY;
VRIL SOCIETY.

Tong   Organized crime group in China, Taiwan, and Hong Kong.
The name, translated into English, means "meeting hall."

According to Hakim Bey in his essay "The Tong" (www.
eightwinds.org/tong-2.html, accessed February 10, 2004): "A Tong
can perhaps be defined as a mutual benefit society for people with
a common interest which is illegal or dangerously marginal—hence,
the necessary secrecy. Many Chinese Tongs revolved around smuggling and tax-evasion, or clandestine self-control of certain trades
(in opposition to State control), or insurrectionary political or religious aims (overthrow of the Manchus for example—several Tongs
collaborated with the Anarchists in the 1911 Revolution). A common
purpose of the Tongs was to collect and invest membership dues
and initiation fees in insurance funds for the indigent, unemployed,
widows and orphans of deceased members, funeral expenses, etc.
In an era like ours when the poor are caught between the cancerous
Scylla of the Insurance Industry and the fast-evaporating Charybdis
of welfare and public health services, this purpose of the Secret Society might well regain its appeal. (Masonic lodges were organized on

this basis, as were the early and illegal trade unions and 'chivalric orders' for laborers and artisans.) Another universal purpose for such societies was of course conviviality, especially banqueting—but even this apparently innocuous pastime can acquire insurrectionary implications. In the various French revolutions, for example, dining clubs frequently took on the role of radical organizations when all other forms of public meeting were banned."

Tong has existed in the United States since 1847, when the first groups were organized in San Francisco as extensions of merchant organizations. The groups were formed to provide a social outlet for its members and to protect their cultural identity. Although criminal elements were included in the Tong groups from the beginning, not all of the members were criminally inclined.

Originally concentrated in San Francisco, during the last fifty years Tong groups have spread out across the United States, and elements now exist in most major U.S. cities. Today, Chicago, Illinois, is a stronghold of Tong groups. According to Jim Brongiel, an Asian organized crime specialist for the Office of International Criminal Justice (a University of Illinois think tank that trains Chicago Police sergeants and lieutenants through an executive development program, as well as publishing *Criminal Justice International*): "We have seen large amounts of money being laundered through various Chicago banks from businesses that use the word 'international' in their dealings. Asian gangs, with close links to sophisticated criminal organizations like the 14K Triad, the largest triad on the Chinese mainland, are involved in money laundering, illegal gambling, counterfeiting, the theft of computer software, and the smuggling of illegal aliens into this country."

See also TRIADS.

Triads Popularly known as the Chinese Mafia, these groups have their hands in drug trafficking, prostitution, gambling, robberies, murders, and a particularly gruesome series of torture methods for those who cross their path.

The Triads were secret criminal societies organized in the 1800s to battle the rule of the Chinese dynasty. They continue to this day to flourish in Hong Kong, Malaysia, Singapore, Thailand (then called Siam), Burma, and Taiwan. Triads operate in Great Britain and Australia, having migrated from Hong Kong.

In 1889, a Triad war broke out in the Chinatown (Yaowarat) section of Bangkok, near the temple of Wat Yannawa. To stop the street battle, the Siamese army was brought in on horse-drawn trams of the Bangkok Tramway Company. The battling triads were the Tang Kong Xi triad (Techiew) and the Siew Li Kue triad (Fujian). The battle started on June 19, 1889, with both gangs pulling the roofs from houses to build street barricades. By the next day, twenty triad members were dead and more than one hundred were seriously wounded. On June 21, the army moved in. During the army's intervention, ten triad members were killed, twenty wounded. Eight hundred triad members, including eight leaders, surrendered.

One of the Triads' top businesses is the smuggling of illegal aliens. Triad members who engage in this activity are known as "snake heads." For a fifteen-thousand-dollar commission, a Chinese-based snake head will smuggle an illegal alien into the U.S. The alien is always promised a job when they arrive. Once the commission is paid, the alien learns that the conditions of the transfer to the U.S. involve no sanitation and cruel overcrowding. Those who survive the trip quickly learn that no job is waiting. Many of these illegal aliens, in order to survive, become Triad members in cities like Chicago, so the system feeds itself.

Another Triad business is the selling of drugs, in particular "ice," the smokable form of methamphetamine.

To form a new and more dangerous form of organized crime, there is evidence that the Chinese gangsters are working in conjunction with non-Asian gangs in the U.S. such as the "Bloods" and the "Crips."

See also TONG.

Trilateral Commission   The Trilateral Commission was first conceived in 1970 by the head of the Russian Studies Department at Columbia University, Zbigniew Brzezinski, who determined a greater need for cooperation between the governments of Asia, Europe, and

North America. In a world of global communications and global economy, he said the world would soon be in need of global government.

"National sovereignty is no longer a viable concept," he said. Brzezinski added that this global government would be funded by a "global taxation system."

Brzezinski first presented his ideas for a trilateral commission during the spring of 1972 at a meeting of the Bilderberg Group in Belgium. The meeting to organize the commission was held in July 1972 at the Rockefeller estate near Tarrytown, New York. The commission was formally founded on July 1, 1973. David Rockefeller was its chairman. Rockefeller had formerly been the chairman of the Council on Foreign Relations. Brzezinski was named founding North American director.

Befitting its name, the Trilateral Commission had three headquarters, in New York, Paris, and Tokyo. It is governed by an executive committee of thirty-five members. Meetings are held approximately once every nine months. The activities of the commission are funded by the Rockefeller Brothers Fund, the Ford Foundation, Time-Warner, Exxon, General Motors, Wells Fargo, and Texas Instruments.

The Trilateral Commission, by policy, feels that too much democracy can be a dangerous thing. A commission paper published in 1975 entitled *The Crisis of Democracy* said that democracy worked best in "moderation." The paper argued that too much democracy made countries unable to respond quickly enough to crises. To demonstrate the direct relationship between Trilateral Commission policy and national governmental policy, consider that one of the authors of that paper, Harvard political science professor Samuel P. Huntington, later became coordinator of security planning for the National Security Council serving President Jimmy Carter, and in that capacity helped to create the Federal Emergency Management Agency, a civilian group with the power to take control of the nation in cases of "emergency."

The Trilateral Commission has been called a "cabal" of powerful men who, through the use of multinational corporations, seek to rule the world. One who felt this way was Barry Goldwater, the Republican senator who lost to Lyndon Johnson in the 1964 presidential election.

Goldwater said, "What the Trilaterals truly intend is the creation of a worldwide economic power superior to the political government of the nation-states involved. As managers and creators of the system they will rule the world."

Among the members of the Trilateral Commission is Alan Greenspan, who had been, since the Ronald Reagan administration, the chairman of the Federal Reserve.

Speaking of Ronald Reagan, when Reagan was campaigning for the presidency in 1980, one of his competitors for the Republican nomination was George H.W. Bush. Reagan was highly critical of Bush's membership in both the Trilateral Commission and the Council on Foreign Relations (CFR). However, as we now know, when Reagan won the nomination he not only chose Bush as his vice presidential running-mate, but, after his election as president, Reagan's fifty-nine-member transition team included ten Trilateralists, ten members of the Bilderberg Group, and twenty-eight members of the CFR.

Although the commission publishes a list of its membership and papers telling its official position on various matters, much of its inner workings is top secret. Its meetings, for example, are securely private.

See also BILDERBERG GROUP; COUNCIL ON FOREIGN RELATIONS.

V

The Vatican The Vatican is the traditional home of the Pope, the leader of the Roman Catholic Church. It is built inside the city of Rome on the site of St. Peter's tomb—Peter being one of Jesus' apostles and the first Pope. The occupants of the Vatican comprise the only secret society to be recognized by most of the world as an independent nation.

The word "vatican" comes from the Latin *vates*, which means prophet. The site of St. Peter's Square, the heart of the Vatican, is located on the ancient site of the temple of the oracle of Apollo. Apollo's prophecies were called *vaticinia*. Writers such as novelist Dan Brown and secret society theorist Michael A. Hoffman, II, have speculated as to why St. Peter's Square is the site of Masonic symbolism, such as "Cleopatra's needle," an obelisk in the Piazza de San Marco. There are those who believe that today's Vatican, more than ever, has been infiltrated and corrupted by Freemasonry.

The U.S. Central Intelligence Agency's website (www.cia.gov; accessed March 10, 2004), reports: "Popes in their secular role ruled portions of the Italian peninsula for more than a thousand years until the mid-nineteenth century, when many of the Papal States were seized by the newly united Kingdom of Italy. In 1870, the pope's holdings were further circumscribed when Rome itself was annexed. Disputes between a series of 'prisoner' popes and Italy were resolved in 1929 by three Lateran Treaties, which established the independent state of Vatican City and granted Roman Catholicism special status in Italy. In 1984, a concordat between the Holy See and Italy modified certain of the earlier treaty provisions, including the primacy of Roman Catholicism as the Italian state religion."

The Vatican sits on the west bank of the Tiber River. The 109–acre

Vatican City was proclaimed an independent state in 1929 by the Lateran Treaty between Pope Pius XI and King Victor Emmanuel III. The piazza of St. Peter's Church sits in its southwest corner. A square containing Belvedere Park and administrative buildings is north of the piazza. To the west of the park are the Pope's palaces, and beyond these are the Vatican gardens. The western and southern boundaries of the Vatican City are marked by the Leonine Walls.

There are several buildings outside Vatican City that are considered technically part of the Vatican. These include the basilicas of San Giovanni in Laterno (St. John Lateran), Santa Maria Maggiore (St. Mary Major), and San Paolo fuori le Mura (St. Paul Outside the Walls); the palace of San Callisto at the foot of the Janiculum and the papal summer residence at Castel Gandolfo, in the Alban Hills outside Rome. The Vatican museums consist of the Museo Pio-Clementino, founded in the eighteenth century, which contains one of the world's great collections of antiquities; the Chiaramonti Museum, founded in the early 1800s, which contains a collection of Greek sculptures; the Braccio Nuovo, which many believe is the most beautiful of all the museums; the Egyptian Museum; the Etruscan Museum; and the Pinacoteca Vaticana, which opened in 1932 and contains paintings by Giotto, Guercino, Caravaggio, and Poussin.

Many of the Renaissance and modern paintings that comprise the Vatican's art treasures are found elsewhere than in the museums. There are galleries surrounding the various courtyards, such as the Cortile del Belvedere and the Cortile San Damasco. One of the most famous artistic monuments in the world adjoins the Cortile San Damasco. It is the building containing the Raphael rooms, which contain the works of Raphael and his followers. The single most famous piece of art in the Vatican is the ceiling of the Sistene Chapel, which was painted in 1508–12 by Michelangelo.

The Vatican dates back to the fifth century, when Emperor Constantine I built the basilica of St. Peter's (purportedly on the site of St. Peter's tomb) and Pope Symmachus built a palace nearby. During the fourteenth century schism, the pope lived in Avignon, France, but ever since the pope returned to Rome in 1377, he has resided at the Vatican. The priceless art collection at the Vatican was assembled by the Renaissance popes (Sixtus IV, Innocent VIII, Alexander VI, Julius II, Leo X, and Clement VII).

The Vatican maintains it own "Secret Archives"—which is what they call it. It contains documents and manuscripts dating back to the beginnings of the Roman Church. According to Matthew Bunson's *The Pope Encyclopedia*, the archives are "headed by a cardinal like the Vatican Library, another rumored storehouse of secrets." The archives are "partially open today to a few approved scholars who are let in only with specific purposes and with permission of the Pope. It is the most mysterious institution in the papal city, for in its more than thirty miles of shelving are reputed to be the accumulated records of scandals, secrets, and revelations of the most shocking and explosive kind, blithely boxed and filed away with the insouciance born of centuries of silence and discretion."

All bishops, when they are promoted to cardinals, swear an oath to preserve the secrets of the Church.

If we are to believe the letter of Catholic law, the Church is run and operated for the most part by men who have taken an oath of celibacy. In light of recent scandals, in which a frightening percentage of North American Catholic priests have been accused of sexually abusing their constituents, the world wonders now more than ever just what the "secrets of the Church" could be.

See also FREEMASONS; KNIGHTS OF MALTA; PROPAGANDA DUE; ROSICRUCIANS; V.M.R.D.; VODUN.

List of Popes
(name, dates served)

1. St. Peter (32–67)	9. St. Hyginus (136–40)
2. St. Linus (67–76)	10. St. Pius I (140–55)
3. St. Anacletus (Cletus) (76–88)	11. St. Anicetus (155–66)
4. St. Clement I (88–97)	12. St. Soter (166–75)
5. St. Evaristus (97–105)	13. St. Eleutherius (175–89)
6. St. Alexander I (105–15)	14. St. Victor I (189–99)
7. St. Sixtus I (115–25)—also called Xystus I	15. St. Zephyrinus (199–217)
8. St. Telesphorus (125–36)	16. St. Callistus I (217–22)
	17. St. Urban I (222–30)
	18. St. Pontain (230–35)

19. St. Anterus (235–36)
20. St. Fabian (236–50)
21. St. Cornelius (251–53)
22. St. Lucius I (253–54)
23. St. Stephen I (254–57)
24. St. Sixtus II (257–58)
25. St. Dionysius (260–68)
26. St. Felix I (269–74)
27. St. Eutychian (275–83)
28. St. Caius (283–96)—also called Gaius
29. St. Marcellinus (296–304)
30. St. Marcellus I (308–09)
31. St. Eusebius (309 or 310)
32. St. Miltiades (311–14)
33. St. Sylvester I (314–35)
34. St. Marcus (336)
35. St. Julius I (337–52)
36. Liberius (352–66)
37. St. Damasus I (366–83)
38. St. Siricius (384–99)
39. St. Anastasius I (399–401)
40. St. Innocent I (401–17)
41. St. Zosimus (417–18)
42. St. Boniface I (418–22)
43. St. Celestine I (422–32)
44. St. Sixtus III (432–40)
45. St. Leo I (the Great) (440–61)
46. St. Hilarius (461–68)
47. St. Simplicius (468–83)
48. St. Felix III (or II) (483–92)
49. St. Gelasius I (492–96)
50. Anastasius II (496–98)
51. St. Symmachus (498–514)
52. St. Hormisdas (514–23)
53. St. John I (523–26)
54. St. Felix IV (or III) (526–30)
55. Boniface II (530–32)
56. John II (533–35)
57. St. Agapetus I (535–36)— also called Agapitus I
58. St. Silverius (536–37)
59. Vigilius (537–55)
60. Pelagius I (556–61)
61. John III (561–74)
62. Benedict I (575–79)
63. Pelagius II (579–90)
64. St. Gregory I (the Great) (590–604)
65. Sabinian (604–06)
66. Boniface III (607)
67. St. Boniface IV (608–15)
68. St. Deusdedit (Adeodatus I) (615–18)
69. Boniface V (619–25)
70. Honorius I (625–38)
71. Severinus (640)
72. John IV (640–42)
73. Theodore I (642–49)
74. St. Martin I (649–55)
75. St. Eugene I (655–57)
76. St. Vitalian (657–72)
77. Adeodatus (II) (672–76)
78. Donus (676–78)
79. St. Agatho (678–81)
80. St. Leo II (682–83)
81. St. Benedict II (684–85)
82. John V (685–86)
83. Conon (686–87)
84. St. Sergius I (687–701)
85. John VI (701–05)
86. John VII (705–07)
87. Sisinnius (708)
88. Constantine (708–15)
89. St. Gregory II (715–31)

90. St. Gregory III (731–41)
91. St. Zachary (741–52)
92. Stephen II (752)
93. Stephen III (752–57)
94. St. Paul I (757–67)
95. Stephen IV (767–72)
96. Adrian I (772–95)
97. St. Leo III (795–816)
98. Stephen V (816–17)
99. St. Paschal I (817–24)
100. Eugene II (824–27)
101. Valentine (827)
102. Gregory IV (827–44)
103. Sergius II (844–47)
104. St. Leo IV (847–55)
105. Benedict III (855–58)
106. St. Nicholas I (the Great) (858–67)
107. Adrian II (867–72)
108. John VIII (872–82)
109. Marinus I (882–84)
110. St. Adrian III (884–85)
111. Stephen VI (885–91)
112. Formosus (891–96)
113. Boniface VI (896)
114. Stephen VII (896–97)
115. Romanus (897)
116. Theodore II (897)
117. John IX (898–900)
118. Benedict IV (900–03)
119. Leo V (903)
120. Sergius III (904–11)
121. Anastasius III (911–13)
122. Lando (913–14)
123. John X (914–28)
124. Leo VI (928)
125. Stephen VIII (929–31)
126. John XI (931–35)
127. Leo VII (936–39)
128. Stephen IX (939–42)
129. Marinus II (942–46)
130. Agapetus II (946–55)
131. John XII (955–63)
132. Leo VIII (963–64)
133. Benedict V (964)
134. John XIII (965–72)
135. Benedict VI (973–74)
136. Benedict VII (974–83)
137. John XIV (983–84)
138. John XV (985–96)
139. Gregory V (996–99)
140. Sylvester II (999–1003)
141. John XVII (1003)
142. John XVIII (1003–09)
143. Sergius IV (1009–12)
144. Benedict VIII (1012–24)
145. John XIX (1024–32)
146. Benedict IX (1032–45)
147. Sylvester III (1045)
148. Benedict IX (1045)
149. Gregory VI (1045–46)
150. Clement II (1046–47)
151. Benedict IX (1047–48)
152. Damasus II (1048)
153. St. Leo IX (1049–54)
154. Victor II (1055–57)
155. Stephen X (1057–58)
156. Nicholas II (1058–61)
157. Alexander II (1061–73)
158. St. Gregory VII (1073–85)
159. Blessed Victor III (1086–87)
160. Blessed Urban II (1088–99)
161. Paschal II (1099–1118)
162. Gelasius II (1118–19)

163. Callistus II (1119–24)
164. Honorius II (1124–30)
165. Innocent II (1130–43)
166. Celestine II (1143–44)
167. Lucius II (1144–45)
168. Blessed Eugene III
     (1145–53)
169. Anastasius IV (1153–54)
170. Adrian IV (1154–59)
171. Alexander III (1159–81)
172. Lucius III (1181–85)
173. Urban III (1185–87)
174. Gregory VIII (1187)
175. Clement III (1187–91)
176. Celestine III (1191–98)
177. Innocent III (1198–1216)
178. Honorius III (1216–27)
179. Gregory IX (1227–41)
180. Celestine IV (1241)
181. Innocent IV (1243–54)
182. Alexander IV (1254–61)
183. Urban IV (1261–64)
184. Clement IV (1265–68)
185. Blessed Gregory X
     (1271–76)
186. Blessed Innocent V (1276)
187. Adrian V (1276)
188. John XXI (1276–77)
189. Nicholas III (1277–80)
190. Martin IV (1281–85)
191. Honorius IV (1285–87)
192. Nicholas IV (1288–92)
193. St. Celestine V (1294)
194. Boniface VIII (1294–1303)
195. Blessed Benedict XI
     (1303–04)
196. Clement V (1305–14)

197. John XXII (1316–34)
198. Benedict XII (1334–42)
199. Clement VI (1342–52)
200. Innocent VI (1352–62)
201. Blessed Urban V (1362–70)
202. Gregory XI (1370–78)
203. Urban VI (1378–89)
204. Boniface IX (1389–1404)
205. Innocent VII (1404–06)
206. Gregory XII (1406–15)
207. Martin V (1417–31)
208. Eugene IV (1431–47)
209. Nicholas V (1447–55)
210. Callistus III (1455–58)
211. Pius II (1458–64)
212. Paul II (1464–71)
213. Sixtus IV (1471–84)
214. Innocent VIII (1484–92)
215. Alexander VI (1492–1503)
216. Pius III (1503)
217. Julius II (1503–13)
218. Leo X (1513–21)
219. Adrian VI (1522–23)
220. Clement VII (1523–34)
221. Paul III (1534–49)
222. Julius III (1550–55)
223. Marcellus II (1555)
224. Paul IV (1555–59)
225. Pius IV (1559–65)
226. St. Pius V (1566–72)
227. Gregory XIII (1572–85)
228. Sixtus V (1585–90)
229. Urban VII (1590)
230. Gregory XIV (1590–91)
231. Innocent IX (1591)
232. Clement VIII (1592–1605)
233. Leo XI (1605)

234. Paul V (1605–21)
235. Gregory XV (1621–23)
236. Urban VIII (1623–44)
237. Innocent X (1644–55)
238. Alexander VII (1655–67)
239. Clement IX (1667–69)
240. Clement X (1670–76)
241. Blessed Innocent XI
    (1676–89)
242. Alexander VIII (1689–91)
243. Innocent XII (1691–1700)
244. Clement XI (1700–1721)
245. Innocent XIII (1721–24)
246. Benedict XIII (1724–30)
247. Clement XII (1730–40)
248. Benedict XIV (1740–58)
249. Clement XIII (1758–69)

250. Clement XIV (1769–74)
251. Pius VI (1775–99)
252. Pius VII (1800–1823)
253. Leo XII (1823–29)
254. Pius VIII (1829–30)
255. Gregory XVI (1831–46)
256. Blessed Pius IX (1846–78)
257. Leo XIII (1878–1903)
258. St. Pius X (1903–14)
259. Benedict XV (1914–22)
260. Pius XI (1922–39)
261. Pius XII (1939–58)
262. Blessed John XXIII
    (1958–63)
263. Paul VI (1963–78)
264. John Paul I (1978)
265. John Paul II (1978–)

Vigilantes of San Francisco The Vigilantes were a secret group that used lynchings to "clean up" the American Barbary Coast. The "Barbary Coast" was the name given to the rough San Francisco waterfront between 1849, the beginning of the gold rush, to 1906, the San Francisco earthquake. The densely populated forty-square-block section of San Francisco on the waterfront was overrun with crime, drugs, saloons, and brothels. Police seemed helpless to prevent crime. The neighborhood's name came from the historical Barbary Coast, which is in North Africa and was known in the nineteenth century for its barbarians and pirates. The San Francisco neighborhood's boundaries were by East Street (now the Embarcadero) along the bay, Dupont Street (now Grant Avenue) to the west, Broadway north, and Commercial Street to the south. The most notorious section of the Barbary Coast was called "Devil's Acre." This area, between Broadway and Pacific Street, was so overrun with criminal types that it was said you could find ten men for any adventure in ten minutes. Cleaning up the neighborhood became the mission of self-appointed "justice-seekers" called the Vigilantes of San Francisco. Because crime tended to have the upper hand over government-sanctioned law enforcement in the Old West, vigilante groups were not uncommon, but the Vigilantes of San Francisco were the largest and most active group. Most of the Vigilantes were well-to-do family men, who therefore had something worth protecting. They were railroad owners, cattle barons, and bankers. Although they kept their identities secret, since they were breaking the letter of the law themselves, they made attempts not to punish innocent men by holding informal trials and deliberations, and they tried to make sure that the punishment fit the crime. Murderers and rapists were lynched. Petty thieves were not. Lesser criminals were forced to leave the city and told never to come back. The Vigilantes sought justice and did not persecute anyone because of race or other bias. Because the great majority of those in San Francisco supported the activities of the Vigilantes, little was done to stop them.

According to the Barbary Coast Vigilance Committee, "By all accounts, it was a terrible condition of affairs, some said it was the nearest approach to criminal anarchy that an American city had yet experienced, that ultimately brought about the formation of the first Vigilance Committee of San Francisco. In a secret meeting held early in June 1851 (in a building at Battery and Pine Streets owned by Samuel Brannan) after many hours of discussion and deliberation, a group of approximately two hundred prominent citizens formed the first Vigilance Committee."

They wrote "The Constitution of the Committee of Vigilance City of San Francisco—State of California."

It read, in part:

THEREFORE, the citizens, whose names are hereunto attached, do unite themselves into an association for the maintenance of the peace and good order of society, and the preservation of the lives and property of the citizens of San Francisco, and do bind themselves, each unto the other, to do and perform every lawful act for the maintenance of law and order, and to sustain the laws when faithfully and properly administered; but we are determined that no thief, burglar, incendiary or assassin, shall escape punishment, either by the quibbles of the law, the insecurity of prisons, the carelessness or corruption of the police, or a laxity of those who pretend to administer justice. And to secure the objects of this association we do hereby agree:

1. That the name and style of the association shall be the COMMITTEE OF VIGILANCE, for the protection of the lives and property of the citizens and residents of the city of San Francisco.

2. That there shall be a room selected for the meeting and deliberation of the committee, at which there shall be one or more members of the committee appointed for that purpose, in constant attendance, at all hours of the day and night, to receive the report of any member of the association, or of any other person or persons whatsoever, of any act of violence done to the person or property of any citizen of San Francisco; and if in the judgment of the member or members of the committee present, it be such an act that justifies the interference of the committee, either in aiding in the execution of the laws, or the prompt and summary punishment of the offender, the committee shall be at once assembled for the purpose of taking such action as a majority of the committee when assembled shall determine upon. . . .

3. That when the committee have assembled for action, the decision of a majority present shall be binding upon the whole committee, and that those members of the committee whose names are hereunto attached, do pledge their honor, and hereby bind themselves to defend and sustain each other in carrying out the determined action of this committee at the hazard of their lives and their fortunes.

The Vigilantes were successful. They met in secret and hit the streets in raids. Crime declined dramatically in San Francisco and the Vigilantes became heroes of the Old West.

V.M.R.D.   A Macedonian secret society operating in the 1930s who, like the Croatians, resented Serbian domination of the country then known as the "Kingdom of Yugoslavia." In an event that eerily mimicked the start of World War I, the V.M.R.D. became notorious when they were accused by the Croatians of the murders of Yugoslav King Alexander Karageorgević and French Foreign Minister Louis Barthou in October 1934 as the pair drove in a motorcade through the streets of Marseilles, the Yugoslavian king being on a state visit to France at the time. The shots came from a man in the crowd named Vlada Gheorghieff, who used a revolver. According to some sources, the assassin—who was attacked on the spot by the French police and died later that night, was a member of the Macedonia Revolutionary Organization. (Published stories that the assassin fled to and was given sanctuary by the Vatican are completely unfounded.)

According to an essay entitled *Croatia Myth & Reality* on the website mirror.veus.hr/myth/king.html: "The legacy of Serbia's kings, the oppression of Yugoslavia's nationalities and the wrath of those who escaped it came together on October 9, 1934, when the Yugoslav cruiser *Dubrovnik* steamed into the port of Marseilles, France, with Alexander on board. Under his tight-fitting Navy admiral's uniform the King wore his customary bullet-proof vest. Because of the size of the *Dubrovnik*, the ship anchored in the bay and Alexander came ashore on a smaller boat, leaving most of his ninety-man bodyguard behind. Alexander had been on French soil less than five minutes when Vlada Gheorghieff mounted the running board of Alexander's car and opened fire with a twenty-round Mauser machine pistol, killing the King, French Foreign Minister Louis Barthou and two bystanders. Gheorghieff, a Macedonian by birth and a Bulgarian citizen, was a member of the Macedonian Revolutionary Organization which sought to free Macedonia from Yugoslavia. French Colonel Piolet, mounted on horseback beside the car, immediately drew his saber and attacked Gheorghieff who died later that evening. The famed French defender Georges Desbonnes later recalled that 'out of respect for His Majesty, the physicians did not examine the king's whole upper torso, missing at first the mortal wound through Alexander's back.' The entire event was captured on film and covered by dozens of journalists and witnessed by hundreds of people. Alexander was among the most hated and feared dictators in Europe and a half-dozen or more other would-be assassins of various nationalities were waiting in Marseilles that day. Because

Alexander's mortal wound was in his back, and Gheorghieff at his front, Georges Desbonnes was sure that a bullet from one of Alexander's wildly firing bodyguards actually killed him. In any event, there is no historical question that a Macedonian-born Bulgarian citizen and member of the Macedonian Revolutionary Movement by the name of Vlada Gheorghieff mounted the running board, pulled the trigger, was struck down on the spot, died in custody that evening and was laid to rest in a Marseilles cemetery in the presence of two detectives and a grave digger."

According to Jasper Ridley in his book *The Freemasons*, "The assassin was probably one of the Ustase refugees in Hungary. . . . The Yugoslav government held Hungary responsible for Alexander's death, and Yugoslavia and her allies threatened to go to war but Mussolini supported Hungary. There were widespread fears that a European war might break out; but Mussolini was preparing to invade Abyssinia, and did not want a war in Europe. The dispute ended peacably."

Another theory has it that King Alexander was murdered by the Freemasons after the king, a Masonic grand master, resigned from his lodge after the Masons refused to pay for a railway he wanted built in Bosnia.

Vodun (Voodoo)   According to an article called "Pope Addresses Adherents of Voodoo: Church Recognizes 'Seeds of the Word' in Other Religions," in the February 10, 1993, edition of the Vatican publication *L'Osservatore Romano*, Voodoo is "a religion originating in West Africa . . . involving the spirits of the great God . . . marked by drums and songs accompanying an animal sacrifice. Ceremonies are conducted by a man (*hungan*) or woman (*mambo*), who are often knowledgeable about witchcraft as well."

The word Vodun—also known as Vodoun, Voudou, Vodou, Voodoo, Sevi Lwa—comes from a local African word for spirit. It is practiced today most extensively in Benin, the Dominican Republic, Ghana, Haiti, and Togo. In Benin and Haiti it is the country's official religion. It is classified by some as an animist, or nature-based, religion.

Like Santeria, Vodun practices, for many years, were kept secret.

The reason for the secrecy was that the practitioners were slaves who, like those who practiced Santeria, camouflaged the religion they brought with them from West Africa. The spirits that were worshiped (Lwas) were called by the names of Roman Catholic saints. This process of changing one's religion to better fit in with new surroundings is called syncretism. Today, Vodun is not just comprised of West African practices combined with Roman Catholic terminology. Over the centuries other influences have pushed their way into the mix as well. These include those of the Arawak Indians and native Haitians. Each practitioner of Vodun follows his or her own "Loa," or mysterious path, which in current form is represented by a Catholic saint. The main Loa is Olorub, whose enemy is Obatala.

Among the lesser spirits are:

Agwe: spirit of the sea
Aida Wedo: rainbow spirit
Ayza: protector
Baka: an evil spirit who takes the form of an animal
Baron Samedi: guardian of the grave
Dambala (or Damballah-wedo): serpent spirit
Erinle: spirit of the forests
Ezili (or Erzulie): female spirit of love
Mawu Lisa: spirit of creation
Ogou Balanjo: spirit of healing
Ogun (or Ogu Bodagris): spirit of war
Osun: spirit of healing streams
Sango (or Shango): spirit of storms
Yemanja: female spirit of waters
Zaka (or Oko): spirit of agriculture

Male priests are called *hungans* (a.k.a. hougans), females are called *mambos*. Vodun functions both as the church and the hospital, with most ceremonies concentrating on the healing of the sick. Vodun is practiced in the United States, mostly through Haitian immigration.

Vodun does involve dark magic. While *hungans* and *mambos* take part only in ceremonies that involve healing and the bringing of good luck, darker ceremonies are enacted by priests known as *bokors* or *caplatas*. Dark Voodoo is also known as "left-handed Vodun." Voodoo dolls are used in attempts to cause maladies to the practitioners' enemies, and, through the use of drugs, zombies are created and exploited. Voodoo dolls are actually stuck with pins. This practice is most common in New Orleans, Louisiana, in the United States, and in parts of South America. Practitioners also believe that dead people can be revived after burial and that these resurrected people, zombies, have no will of their own. In reality zombies have never died, but are under the influence of drugs.

Vril Society   Vril was supposedly the language, comprised of oral sounds and clicks, spoken by the people of Atlantis. (Atlantis being the mythical land in the Atlantic where a great civilization is said to have existed before it sank to the bottom of the ocean.) The Vril Society, also known as the Luminous Lodge, was a secret society that formed in Germany following the First World War. The story goes that the society traces its origin back to 1917, with the war still ongoing, when four people—three men and a woman who was a "spiritual medium"—met in secret and discussed a "magical violet black stone" and methods of making contact with worlds of far away and/or long ago. They believed that this could be achieved through the power of the "Black Sun," the light from which was real but could not be seen by the human eye. The emblem for the Vril Society was a Black Sun, although the idea did not originate with the Vril Society. Black Suns were part of the symbology of Babylon and Assyria.

According to Vril Society lore, the group—now working in conjunction with the Thule Society—was successful in channeling information from extraterrestrials. Because of this they were able to build a flying saucer that was first flown in 1939.

One believer in the Vril Society was a man named Kerry Thornley, who shows up in literature about President Kennedy's assassination in a variety of contexts. Thornley, a suspected Oswald look-alike (even though he was several inches taller than Oswald) was the only man to write a book (albeit a novel) about Lee Harvey Oswald *before* President Kennedy's assassination. He was in the Marines at the El Toro Annex in California in 1959 when he met Oswald. He wrote the novel *The Idle Warriors* in 1962, about a disgruntled Marine who defects to the Soviet Union. Thornley called his Oswald-based hero Private Johnny Shellburn. The book was not published until 1991. After the assassination, Thornley did publish a book about the assassination, but it was a nonfiction account.

After meeting Oswald, Thornley became obsessed with him, and from that point on their lives formed an interesting parallel. Thornley was stationed in Atsugi, Japan. So was Oswald (although not at the same time). Thornley was interviewed by agents of the FBI two days after President Kennedy's assassination. The FBI was drawn to him because of the manuscript he had been vigorously shopping to publishers.

Thornley testified for the Warren Commission and a copy of his manuscript was placed in the National Archives. He told the Commission that he was a "close acquaintance" but not a "good friend" of Oswald in the Marines. His testimony helped establish the accused assassin as having Marxist leanings.

Thornley moved to New Orleans after being discharged from the Marines, as had Oswald. Oswald and Thornley simultaneously lived in New Orleans. Thornley, however, claims he never ran into Oswald there. Regarding his and Oswald's proximity in New Orleans during the summer of 1963, Thornley wrote that Oswald "was even reputedly stopping in now and then at a bar where I hung out. We may have passed each other on the street but, if so, we didn't recognize each other. Only after the assassination did I realize that Oswald had been right under my nose for over two weeks. . . ."

New Orleans District Attorney Jim Garrison didn't believe this to be true. Garrison said there was at least one eyewitness—a woman named Barbara Reid—who placed Thornley and Oswald together in a New Orleans restaurant just weeks before the assassination.

Garrison called Thornley as a witness at the Clay Shaw trial and later charged Thornley with perjury. Garrison's claims against Thornley were: (1) Thornley and Oswald were involved together in covert CIA operations. (2) Thornley impersonated Oswald as early as 1961. (3) Thornley's writings about Oswald were actually CIA disinformation. Garrison eventually dropped the perjury charge, although his claim number 2 is worth considering, in light of the fact that Thornley made a short visit to Mexico City in September 1963, just as Oswald is supposed to have done.

Thornley, while living in New Orleans, became an admitted acquaintance of assassination suspects Guy Banister and David Ferrie. After living in New Orleans, Thornley moved to Los Angeles, where he got a job as a doorman at the building where mobster Johnny Roselli lived.

It was while living in Atlanta that Thornley told authorities that, back in New Orleans before the assassination, he had been told by a man named Gary Kirstein that President Kennedy and Martin Luther King, Jr. would be murdered. Thornley came to suspect that Kirstein was actually E. Howard Hunt. After telling this story, Thornley claimed he was pistol-whipped by ski-masked intruders at a friend's birthday party. The only thing the intruders stole was Thornley's identification.

According to the *New York Press*, Thornley believed, at least publicly, that "he and Lee Harvey Oswald were products of genetic tests carried out by a secret proto-Nazi sect of eugenicists, the Vril Society . . . that a bugging device was implanted in his body at birth, and that both he and Oswald were secretly watched and manipulated from childhood by shadowy, powerful Vril overlords."

On the February 25, 1992, edition of the television program *A Current Affair*, Thornley said that he was part of a conspiracy to assassinate President Kennedy and that his co-conspirators were men he called "Brother-in-law and Slim."

See also GREEN MEN SOCIETY; THULE SOCIETY.

W

White Greyhound, Order of the   See Priory of Sion.

Wicca   The church and school of witches and warlocks. The word witch derives from the Anglo-Saxon term *wicce*, which in turn derives from an Indo-European word that means "to do magic." Other words derived from *wicce* include wicker, wicked, wiggle, and vicar.

Because of the popular connotations of being a witch, today most Wicca continues to be practiced in secret. Wicca believes in the female side of divinity in addition to, and sometimes in place of, the more conventional image of a male God. Witches perform spells, which they call *magick*, adding the *k* to differentiate their practices from those of stage illusionists.

Today's Wicca has been called "a living, growing religious tradition," combining practices that pre-date the Inquisition with those only a few years old.

According to AmericanWicca.com (accessed March 9, 2004): "Witchcraft today may be seen as the sum total of all a Witch's practices, including but not limited to: spellcasting, divination (fortune telling), meditation, herbalism, ritual and ritual drama, singing and dancing to raise energy, healing, clairvoyance and other psychism, creative mythology, and more. As a religion, the Craft is a revival and/or reconstruction of the pre-Christian religions of Europe, especially northern Europe (giving us Celtic or Norse traditions), sometimes elsewhere giving us Greco-Roman, Egyptian, or Levantine traditions. Many of us have turned for inspiration to the still-living indigenous traditions of other lands, such as Australia, Asia, India, and the Americas. Some of us, recognizing that we are American Witches, work with deities and land-spirits of local Amerindian

[Native American] tribes, though we do not claim to be members of any Amerindian tradition. As Margot Adler, a Witchcraft authority, has written, 'The real tradition of the Craft is creativity.'"

A couple of well-publicized crime sprees have invoked the name of Wicca in their communications with authorities and/or the press. In 1977, the Son of Sam cult referred to itself in a letter as "Wicked King Wicker." The "Unabom," following a New Jersey bombing, referred to himself as "H. C. Wickle."

According to William J. Schnoebelen (www.nireland.com/ evangelicaltruth/fmwitch.html; "Freemasonry, the Orange Order, and Wiccan Witchcraft"; accessed March 10, 2004), Wicca and Free-masonry are alike in many ways. They are both built on a founda-tion system of three degrees, both groups meet in secret, and both have ceremonial initiations involving sworn oaths. He lists the more specific similarities as: "(1) Cause candidates to strip off all sec-ular clothing; (2) Cause the candidate to be divested of all metal; (3) Hoodwink (blindfold) the candidate and ceremonially tie ropes around him (though the form of the tying varies); (4) Cause the can-didate to stand in the Northeast corner of the 'temple' in the first degree; (5) Challenge the candidate by piercing their naked chest with a sharp instrument (witches use a sword, Masons, the point of a compass); (6) Challenge the candidate with secret passwords; (7) Lead the candidate blindfolded in a circumambulation (walking round) of the temple; (8) Require the candidate to swear solemn oaths of secrecy before being given custody of the secrets of the group. . . . (9) Both have a ceremonial unhoodwinking of the candi-date, following the oath, before lighted candles that is intended to bring 'illumination.' (10) Both convey to the new initiate the 'working tools' pertinent to that degree, and each of their uses are taught to them. (11) In both, the tools have correspondences both in the cere-monial realm and in similarities to human reproduction. (12) Both, in the higher degrees, take the initiate through a ritual death-and-rebirth experience in which the initiate acts the part of a hero (hero-ine) of the craft. (13) Both cause the candidate to endure (while being blindfolded) being picked up, spun around, carried around, being jolted or struck from person to person. This is supposed to produce an 'altered state of consciousness.'"

Y

Yakuza   A Japanese organized-crime group. The word "Yakuza" means eight-nine-three, for a total of twenty. This is symbolic of being a loser in society because it refers to a card game called Oichu-Kabu. This game is similar to our Blackjack, but in Oichu-Kabu, the perfect number is nineteen rather than twenty-one—therefore, twenty means you lose. Thus the name of the organization.

Yakuza dates back to the early seventeenth century, evolving from a group known as *kabuzi-mono* (crazy ones)—criminals known for their slang speech, long swords and distinctive clothing and hairstyles. The *kabuzi-mono* were bands of robbers who attacked villages and small cities, sometimes murdering for fun as they looted and pillaged. Today's Yakuza prefers to trace their ancestry back to a group known as *machi-yakko* (city servants), a Robin Hood-like band who were the enemies of the *kabuzi-mono*, and have been the heroes of many fictional stories.

The Yakuza, under that name, first appeared in the mid seventeenth century. They were gamblers and street vendors who were loyal to one another in times of conflict. Given a choice between loyalty to one's Yakuza comrades or one's own family, Yakuza would stand by Yakuza.

Today's Yakuza are almost all, like their predecessors, poor misfits of society, who have turned to crime because they lack more honorable opportunities. For these people, Yakuza becomes their family.

Yakuza members organize themselves like families, with the father-figure referred to as *oyabun* and the children called *kobun*.

Since the mid-1800s, the initiation ceremony into Yakuza involves the ceremonial drinking of sake.

Today's Yakuza are divided into three groups.

1. *Tekiya*: street vendors, who operate in Japan's markets and fairs. This group evolved from peddlers of questionable medicines, much like snake-oil merchants of the American Old West. The *tekiya* are known for their shoddy merchandise and con-man techniques. It is common for *tekiya* to pretend to be drunk so that customers buy products, thinking they are taking advantage. In reality, it is the other way around. Today's *tekiya* participate in protection rackets, and the harboring of criminals.

2. *Bakuto*: gamblers. The *bakuto* gained power when they were hired by government construction and irrigation firms to gamble with the firm's employees in an effort to get back a portion of the wages paid to the laborers. (A similar scheme is used in Atlantic City and Las Vegas, where show business personalities and boxers are paid by the casinos partially in chips in an attempt to get a portion of their payroll back in the casinos.)

   The *bakuto* originated the ceremonial cutting off of someone's fingers. This is called *yubitsume*. The top joint of the little finger is ceremoniously chopped off as an apology for an infraction, or as a punishment. This amputation signifies the weakening of the hand, which means the member of the *bakuto* can no longer hold his sword so tightly. If an individual must undergo *yubitsume* more than once, either the top joint of another finger is chopped off, or the next joint of the little finger.

   Bakuto are sometimes ceremoniously tattooed with a black ring around the arm as apology or punishment. The tattooing process, because it involves a solid black ring, can take up to one hundred hours.

3. *Gurentai*: hoodlums. This last group emerged as part of Yakuza only after World War II.

In the second half of the nineteenth century, Japan went through a modernization period, and the Yakuza modernized as well. They recruited construction workers and gained control of the rickshaw business. The police were cracking down on *bakuto* gangs, so the gamblers became more secret in their activities. The *tekiya* continued to operate in the open, and expanded their activities during this time period. Yakuza went into politics, supporting certain politicians and campaigning against others. The Yakuza became an important part of the nineteenth-century ultranationalist movement in Japan, which used a secret military to force Japan into adopting democracy. A reign of terror, using Yakuza as its henchmen, continued until the 1930s. During the ultranationalist movement, two prime ministers and two finance ministers were assassinated. There were several *coup d'etat* attempts. After the Japanese attack on Pearl Harbor, however, Japanese priorities changed. Many members of Yakuza joined the army.

After World War II, the Americans occupying Japan tried to wipe out Yakuza. But their attempts were unsuccessful. The Americans had rationed food, and Yakuza went into the black market, selling illegal food. Yakuza became wealthy and powerful during this period, and Japan's civil police, who were not allowed to carry weapons, were defenseless against them. The leaders of the black market were the *gurentai*. In 1950, the Americans admitted defeat and stopped their battle against the Yakuza. The Yakuza became increasingly violent during the 1950s. They stopped carrying swords and started carrying guns. They began to look like American gangsters, with dark suits and ties, crew cuts, and sunglasses. By 1963, it was believed that Yakuza had 184,000 members. Various Yakuza gangs went to war against one another over turf. During that time a man named Yoshio Kodama managed to convince the leaders of the various Yakuza factions that in-fighting helped no one, and that there were many benefits to operating as a single coalition. His plan worked. Kodama has been referred to as "the Japanese underworld's visionary godfather."

On March 1, 1992, the Japanese government passed the Act for Prevention of Unlawful Activities by Boryokudan (Yakuza and other criminal gangs). Legally, the definition of *boryokudan* is any group with a certain percentage or higher of members who have a criminal record. Although it is not illegal to be a member of these groups, the Act prohibits these groups from partaking in forms of extortion that are not specifically banned by previously existing laws. The Act was a blow against the Yakuza protection rackets. In order to avoid being classified as a *boryokudan*, the Yakuza has once again moved underground, using legitimate organizations as fronts. As the millenium began, almost eighty gangs have registered as businesses or religious organizations. There have been several public protests by Yakuza members, claiming that they are not criminals as they are publicly perceived, but these efforts were more than overshadowed by the murder of filmmaker Itami Juzo, who was making an anti-Yakuza film. Yakuza remains very powerful and rumors persist that they—through both legal and illegal means—continue to have an impact on Japanese elections. There are also rumors that, since it is more difficult to operate inside Japan, Yakuza members will move over to the United States to set up business, a possibility for which the FBI is already preparing.

Young Arab Society (Al Jamiyyah al Arabiyah al Fatat)   Syrian group formed during the first quarter of the twentieth century, dedicated to Syrian independence.

Acronyms

AMORC	Ancient Mystical Order *Rosae Crucic*
ANO	Abu Nidal Organization
ASG	Abu Sayyaf Group
BBC	British Broadcasting Company
CFR	Council on Foreign Relations
CSETI	Center for the Study of Extraterrestrial Intelligence
DHKP	Revolutionary People's Liberation Party
ELA	Revolutionary People's Struggle
ELN	National Liberation Army
ETA	Euzkadi Ta Askatasuna
EU	European Union
FALN	Armed Forces for Puerto Rican National Liberation
FARC	Revolutionary Armed Forces of Colombia
FPMR/D	Manuel Rodriguez Patriotic Front Dissidents
GIA	Armed Islamic Group
GRAPO	First of October Antifascist Resistance Group
GSPC	Salafist Group for Call and Combat
HUA	Harakat ul-Ansar
IAS	Institute for Advanced Study
IRA	Irish Republican Army
JRA	Japanese Red Army
KGC	Knights of the Golden Circle
KKK	Ku Klux Klan
LTTE	Liberation Tigers of Tamil Eelam
MKO	Mujahedin-e Khalq Organization
MRTA	Tupac Amaru Revolutionary Movement
MUFON	Mutual Unidentified Flying Object Network

ODAN	Opus Dei Awareness Network
OTO	Ordo Templi Orientis
PFLP	Popular Front for the Liberation of Palestine
PIJ	Palestine Islamic Jihad
PKK	Kurdistan Workers' Party
PLF	Palestine Liberation Front
RIIA	Royal Institute of International Affairs
SL	Shining Path
SS	Schutzstaffel

Bibliography

Addison, Charles G. *The History of the Knights Templar*. Kempton, Ill.: Adventures Unlimited Press, 1997. With an introduction by David Hatcher Childress.

Alford, Alan F. *Gods of the New Millenium: Scientific Proof of Flesh and Blood Gods*. Walsall, England: Eridu Books, 1996.

Algar, Selim. "200 Mourn Slain Mason." *New York Post*, March 13, 2004, p. 6.

Allen, Gary. *None Dare Call It Conspiracy*. Seal Beach, CA: Concord Press, 1971.

Baigent, Michael, and Richard Leigh. *The Temple and the Lodge*. New York: Arcade Publishing, 1989.

Baigent, Michael, Richard Leigh, and Henry Lincoln. *Holy Blood, Holy Grail*. New York: Dell Publishing, 1986.

Bainbridge, W.S. *Satan's Power: A Deviant Psychotherapy Cult*. Berkeley: University of California Press, 1978.

Barber, Malcolm. *The New Knighthood: A History of the Order of the Temple*. Cambridge, England: Cambridge University Press, 1994.

Beckley, Timothy Green. *MJ-12 and the Riddle of the Hangar*. New Brunswick, NJ: Inner Light Books, 1989.

Begley, Sharon, and Andrew Murr. "The First Americans." *Newsweek*, April 26, 1999, p. 56.

Belgum, E. *Voodoo*. San Diego, CA: Greenhaven Press, 1991.

Benson, Michael. *Encyclopedia of the JFK Assassination*. New York: Checkmark Books, 2001.

Bimba, Anthony. *The Molly Maguires: The True Story of Labor's Martyred Pioneers in the Coalfields*. New York: International Publishers, 1950.

Birmingham, Stephen. *America's Secret Aristocracy*. New York: Berkley Books, 1987.

Bramley, William. *The Gods of Eden*. New York: Avon Books, 1989.

Brandon, Jim. *Rebirth of Pan*. Dunlap, IL: Firebird Press, 1983.

Buchta, Tom, Ed Robinson, and Eric Lenkowitz. "Long Island man shot dead in Masonic initiation accident." *New York Post*, March 9, 2004, p. 3.

Bullock, Steven C. *Revolutionary Brotherhood: Freemasonry and the Transformation of the American Social Order 1730–1840*. Chapel Hill: University of North Carolina Press, 1996.

Bumiller, Elisabeth. "Nude Wrestling? Good Practice for Politics." *New York Times*, February 2, 2004, A19. (Story about John Kerry, like George W. Bush, being a member of Skull & Bones.)

Bunson, Matthew. *The Pope Encyclopedia*. New York: Crown Trade Paperbacks, 1995.

Carter, John. *Sex and Rockets: The Occult World of Jack Parsons*. Venice, CA: Feral House, 1999.

Cavendish, Richard. *The Black Arts*. New York: Perigee Books, 1967.

Cawthorne, Nigel. *Satanic Murder*. Great Britain: True Crime, 1995.

Cayce, Edgar Evans, Gail Cayce Schwartzer, and Douglas Richards. *Mysteries of Atlantis Revisited*. New York: St. Martin's Press, 1997.

Chatelain, Maurice. *Our Ancestors Came from Outer Space*. Garden City, NY: Doubleday, 1978.

Coleman, Dr. John. *Conspirators' Hierarchy: The Story of the Committee of 300*. Carson City, NV: America West Publishers, 1992.

Corrales, Scott. "Bright Lights, Lost Cities." *Fate*, September 1999, p. 23.

Costen, Michael. *The Cathars and the Albigensian Crusade*. Manchester, England: Manchester University Press, 1997.

Cremo, Michael A., and Richard L. Thompson. *Forbidden Archeology*. Los Angeles: Bhaktivedanta Book Publishing, 1998.

Cumings, Bruce. *Origins of the Korean War: Liberation and the Emergence of Separate Regimes*. Princeton: Princeton University Press, 1981.

Dan, Uri. "Blown Away: Israel Kills Hamas Chief in Gaza Raid." *New York Post*, March 22, 2004, p. 1.

Daraul, Arkon. *A History of Secret Societies*. New York: Carol Publishing Group, 1995.

Darnton, John. "Union, but Not Unanimity, as Europe's East Joins West." *New York Times*, March 11, 2004, p. A1. (Story about the expansion of the European Union.)

Davis, John H. *The Kennedy Contract: The Mafia Plot to Assassinate the President*. New York: HarperPaperbacks, 1993.

Davis, Rod. *American Voudou*. Denton, TX: University of North Texas Press, 1999.

Dewees, F.P. *The Molly Maguires: The Origin, Growth, and Character of the Organization*. New York: Burt Franklin, 1877.

Drosnin, Michael. *The Bible Code*. New York: Simon & Schuster, 1997.

Eddy, Patricia G. *Who Tampered With the Bible?* Nashville, TN: Winston-Derek Publishers, 1993.

Epperson, A. Ralph. *Masonry: Conspiracy Against Christianity*. Tuscon, AZ: Publius Press, 1997.

——. *The Unseen Hand: An Introduction to the Conspiratorial View of History*. Tucson, AZ: Publius Press, 1985.

Eringer, Robert, *The Global Manipulators*. Bristol, England: Pentacle Books, 1980.

FitzGerald, Michael. *Storm-Troopers of Satan: An Occult History of the Second World War*. London: Robert Hale, 1990.

Friedman, Stanton T. "MJ-12: The Evidence So Far." *International UFO Reporter*, Vol. XII, No. 5, September/October 1987.

Gardner, Laurence. *Bloodline of the Holy Grail*. Rockport, Mass.: Element Books, 1996.

——. *Genesis of the Grail Kings*. London: Bantam Press, 1999.

Garrison, Jim. *A Heritage of Stone*. New York: G.P. Putnam's Sons, 1970.

——. *On the Trail of the Assassins*. New York: Sheridan Square Press, 1988.

——. "The Murder Talents of the CIA." *Freedom Magazine*, April/May, 1987.

Good, Timothy. *Above Top Secret*. London: Sidgwick & Jackson, 1987; New York: William Morrow, 1988.

Grant, Kenneth. *The Magical Revival*. London: Skoob Books, 1991.

Greider, William. *One World, Ready or Not*. New York: Simon & Schuster, 1997.

——. *Secrets of the Temple: How the Federal Reserve Runs the Country*. New York: Simon & Schuster, 1987.

Groden, Robert J., and Harrison Edward Livingstone. *High Treason*. New York: Berkley Books, 1990.

Grove, Lloyd, and Elisa Lipsky-Karasz. "Lowdown: Yale Bones connect Bush, Kerry." *Daily News*, March 4, 2004, p. 27.

Hall, Manly P. *What the Ancient Wisdom Expects of its Disciples*. Los Angeles: Philosophical Research Society, 1982.

Hall, Richard A. "MJ-12: Still Holding Its Own Through Thickets of Debate." *UFO*, Vol. 6, No. 1, 1991, p. 30–32.

Hammer, Richard. *The Vatican Connection*. New York: Charter Books, 1982.

Hartmann, Franz. *Rosicrucian Symbols*. Edmonds, WA: Holmes Publishing Group, 2000.

Haven, Violet Sweet. *Gentlemen of Japan: A Study in Rapist Diplomacy*. Chicago: Ziff-Davis, 1944.

Healy, Patrick. "A Ritual Gone Fatally Wrong Puts Light on Masonic Secrecy." *New York Times*, March 10, 2004, p. A7.

Hess, Stephen. *America's Political Dynasties*. New York: Doubleday, 1966.

Hoffman, Michael A., II. *Secret Societies and Psychological Warfare*. Coeur d'Alene, ID: Independent History & Research, 2001.

The Holy Bible, King James Version. New York: Meridian, 1974.

Horn, Dr. Arthur David. *Humanity's Extraterrestrial Origins*. Mount Shasta, CA: A&L Horn, 1994.

Howard, Michael. *The Occult Conspiracy: Secret Societies, Their Influence and Power in World History*. Rochester, VT: Destiny Books, 1989.

Hubbell, Webb. *Friends in High Places*. New York: William Morrow & Co., 1997.

"Japanese cult raided." *Daily News*, February 16, 2004, p. 7. (About the Japanese religious sect Aum Shinrikyo.)

Jessup, Philip C. *Elihu Root*. Vol. I, 1845–1909; Vol. II, 1905–1937. New York: Dodd, Mead, 1938.

Johnson, George. *Architects of Fear: Conspiracy Theorists and Paranoia in American Politics*. Los Angeles: Jeremy P. Tarcher, Inc., 1983.

Leopold, Richard W. *Elihu Root and the Conservative Tradition*. Boston: Little, Brown, 1954.

Keith, Jim, ed., *The Gemstone File*. Atlanta: IllumiNet Press, 1992.

Kenyatta, Jomo. *Facing Mount Kenya: The Tribal Life of the Gikuyu*. New York: Vintage Books, 1965.

Knight, Christopher, and Robert Lomas. *The Hiram Key: Pharaohs, Freemasons and the Discovery of the Secret Scrolls of Jesus*. Boston: Element Books, 1997.

Knight, Stephen. *Jack the Ripper: The Final Solution*. Philadelphia: David McKay Company, 1976.

Leigh, Richard, and Henry Lincoln. *The Messianic Legacy*. New York: Dell Publishing, 1986.

Lemire, Jonathan, and Tamer El-Ghobashy. "She dies in ritual: Bronx woman burned at Santeria cleansing." *The Daily News*, February 25, 2004, p. 5.

Levenda, Peter. *Unholy Alliance*. New York: Avon Books, 1995.

Levi, Eliphas. *The Mysteries of Magic*. London: Rider, 1967.

Litchfield, Michael. *It's A Conspiracy*. Berkeley, CA: Earth Works Press, 1992.

Mackey, Albert Gallatin. *Encyclopedia of Freemasonry and Its Kindred Sciences*. Chicago: Masonic History Company, 1925.

———, *The History of Freemasonry*. New York: Gramercy Books, 1996.

Marchetti, Victor, and John Marks. *The CIA and the Cult of Intelligence*. New York: Knopf, 1974.

Marrs, Jim. *Rule by Secrecy*. New York: Perennial, 2000.

Mather, G.A., and L.A. Nichols. *Dictionary of Cults, Sects, Religions and the Occult*. Grand Rapids, MI: Zondervan, 1993.

Meek, James Gordon. "CIA sees wave of Bin Laden wanna-bes," *Daily News*, February 29, 2004, p. 18.

Moore, Alan, and Eddie Campbell. *From Hell*. Paddington, Australia: Eddie Campbell Comics, 1999.

Moore, William L. "The Roswell Investigation: New Evidence, New Conclusions." *Frontiers of Science*, Vol. III, No. 5, July/August 1981.

Moscow, Alvin. *The Rockefeller Inheritance*. Garden City, N.Y.: Doubleday & Company, 1977.

Noble, Christian. *Christian A. Herter*. New York: Cooper Square, 1970.

Noonan, Jr., James-Charles. *The Church Visible: The Ceremonial Life and Protocol of the Roman Catholic Church*. New York: Viking, 1996.

Norwich, John Julius, ed. *The World Atlas of Architecture*. New York: Portland House, 1988.

Ovason, David. *The Secret Architecture of Our Nation's Capitol*. New York: HarperCollins, 1999.

Pagels, Elaine. *The Gnostic Gospels*. New York: Vintage Books, 1981.

Partner, Peter. *The Murdered Magicians: The Templars and Their Myth*. New York: Barnes & Noble, 1987.

Patton, Guy, and Robert Mackness. *Web of Gold: The Secret Power of a Sacred Treasure*. London: Sidgewick & Jackson, 2000.

Pauwel, Louis & Jacques Bergier. *The Morning of the Magicians*. London: Granada Publishing, 1971.

Perloff, James. *The Shadows of Power: The Council on Foreign Relations and the American Decline*. Appleton, WI: Western Islands, 1988.

Prados, John. *Keeper of the Keys: A History of the National Security Council from Truman to Bush*. New York: William Morrow and Company, 1991.

Prouty, L. Fletcher, Colonel, United States Air Force (Retired). *The Secret Team: The CIA and its Allies in Control of the United States and the World*. Englewood Cliffs, NJ: Prentice-Hall, Inc., 1973.

Pulitzer, Lisa, and Bill Sanderson. "Guns and Guillotines Used at Deadly Masonic Ritual." *New York Post*, March 10, 2004, p. 9.

Quigley, Carroll. *Tragedy and Hope: A History of the World in Our Time*. New York: MacMillan, 1966.

———. *The World Since 1939: A History*. New York: Collier Books, 1968.

Ravenscroft, Trevor. *The Spear of Destiny: The Occult Power Behind the Spear Which Pierced the Side of Christ*. York Beach, Maine: Samuel Weiser, 1973.

Read, Piers Paul. *The Templars*. New York: St. Martin's Press, 2000.

Rheingold, Howard. "The Pentacle and the Wand." *Whole Earth Review*, Spring 1992, p. 61.

Richardson, Robert. "The History of Sion Hoax." *Gnosis Magazine*, Spring 1999, p. 54.

Ridley, Jasper. *The Freemasons: A History of the World's Most Powerful Secret Society*. New York: Arcade Publishing, 2001.

Robinson, John J. *Born in Blood: The Lost Secrets of Freemasonry*. New York: M. Evans & Company, 1989.

Rosenbaum, Ron. "The Last Secrets of Skull and Bones." *Esquire*, September 1977, p. 85.

Ross, Robert Gaylon. Sr. *Who's Who of the Elite*. San Marcos, TX: RIE, 1995.

Russell, Dick. *The Man Who Knew Too Much*. New York: Carroll & Graf, 1992.

Sagan, Carl, and Thornton Page, eds. *UFOs: A Scientific Debate*. New York: W.W. Norton & Co., 1974.

Sanders, Ed. *The Family*. New York: E.P. Dutton, 1971.

Scott, Peter Dale. *Deep Politics and the Death of JFK*. Berkeley: University of California Press, 1993.

Segel, Binjamin W., and Richard S. Levy. *A Lie and a Libel: The History of the Protocols of the Elders of Zion*. Lincoln: University of Nebraska Press, 1996.

Sereny, Gitta. *Into That Darkness*. London: Random House UK, 1995.

Seward, Desmond. *The Monks of War: The Military Religious Orders*. London: Penguin, 1972.

Sitchin, Zechariah. *Genesis Revisited*. New York: Avon Books, 1990.

———. *The Wars of Gods and Men*. New York: Avon Books, 1985.

Sora, Steven. *Secret Societies of America's Elite: From the Knights Templar to Skull and Bones*. Rochester, VT: Destiny Books, 2003.

Still, William T. *New World Order: The Ancient Plan of Secret Societies*. Lafayette, LA: Huntington House Publishers, 1990.

Sutton, Anthony C. *America's Secret Establishment: An Introduction to the Order of Skull & Bones*. Billings, MT: Liberty House Press, 1986.

Sutton, Anthony C., and Patrick M. Wood. *Trilaterals Over Washington*. Scottsdale, AZ: The August Corporation, 1979.

Tarpley, Webster Griffin, and Anton Chaitkin. *George Bush: The Unauthorized Biography*. Washington, D.C.: Executive Intelligence Review, 1992.

Terry, Maury. *The Ultimate Evil: An Investigation into a Dangerous Satanic Cult*. New York: HarperCollins, 1988.

Temple, Robert K.G. *The Sirius Mystery*. London: Random House UK, 1999.

Thomas, Landon, Jr. "If Only for a Night, Wall St. Fallen Idol Is One of the Boys." *New York Times*, February 6, 2004, C4.

Thompson, John Westfall, and Edgar Nathanial Johnson. *An Introduction to Medieval Europe*. New York: W.W. Norton Company, 1937.

Vankin, Jonathan. *Conspiracies, Crimes and Cover-ups: Political Manipulation and Mind Control in America*. New York: Paragon House, 1992.

Von Daniken, Erich. *God From Outer Space*. New York: Bantam, 1972.

———. *The Return of the Gods*. Boston: Element Books, 1998.

Waite, Arthur Edward. *A New Encyclopedia of Freemasonry*. New York: Wings Books, 1996.

Ward, J.S.M. *Freemasonry and the Ancient Gods*. Whitefish, MT: Kessinger Publishing Company, 1997.

Weir, Richard. "Mason widow nixes apology." *Daily News,* March 15, 2004, p. 31.

Wes, John Anthony. *Serpent in the Sky*. Wheaton, IL: Quest Books, 1993.

Whaley, William J. *Christianity and American Freemasonry*. Milwaukee: Bruce Publishing Company, 1958.

Wilgus, Neal. *The Illuminoids*. New York: Pocket Books, 1978.

Wilmshurst, W.L. *The Meaning of Masonry*. New York: Bell Publishing Company, 1980.

Wilson, Robert Anton. *Everything is Under Control: Conspiracies, Cults and Cover-ups*. New York: Harper Perennial, 1998.

Websites

www-2.cs.cmu.edu/~dst/Secrets/
"Secrets of Scientology" Accessed January 22, 2004.

www.bbc.co.uk/religion/religions/hinduism/features/thugs/
"BBC—Religion & Ethics—Thugs" Accessed January 15, 2004.

www.BCVC.net
"Barbary Coast Vigilance Committee (BCVC)"
Accessed January 13, 2004.

www.charlesmanson.com
"The Process Church of the Final Judgment"
Accessed March 7, 2004.

www.daywilliams.com/masons_mystery_33rd_parallel.html
"Masons and Mystery at the 33rd Parallel" by Day Williams
Accessed January 15, 2004.

www.mindcontrolforums.com/hambone/oto.html
"The OTO and the CIA" Accessed January 13, 2004.

www.newadvent.org/cathen/11635c.htm
"Catholic Encyclopedia: Los Hermanos Penitentes"
Accessed January 9, 2004.

www.nimatullahi.org/us/WIS/WIS1.html
"What is Sufism?" Accessed March 8, 2004.

www.nireland.com/evangelicaltruth/fmwitch.html
"Freemasonry, the Orange Order, and Wiccan Witchcraft"
Accessed March 10, 2004.

www.oto-usa.org
Ordo Templi Orientis USA website. Accessed January 13, 2004.

www.qss.org/articles/sufism/toc.html
"The Other Side of Sufism" Accessed March 8, 2004.

www.religioustolerance.org/process.htm
"The Process—Church of the Final Judgment"
Accessed March 7, 2004.

www.rosycross.org/Rosicrucians_Philosophy.html
"Rosicrucian Philosophy" Accessed January 9, 2004.

www.scientology-lies.com/whatswrong.html
"What's Wrong with Scientology?" Accessed January 22, 2004.

www.technocracy.ca
"What is Technocracy?" Accessed January 15, 2004.

www.totse.com/en/conspiracy/secret_societies/mason08.html
"A Short History of the Prince Hal Shriners" by Frank J. Miller.
Accessed January 9, 2004.

www.whatisscientology.org/html/foreword/index.html
"What is Scientology?" Accessed January 22, 2004.

www.xeper.org
"Official website of the Temple of Set" Accessed January 20, 2004.

Name Index

Adams, John Quincy, 39, 57–59
Adler, Margot, 242
Ahmed, Sami Said, 144–45
Akhenaton, 169
Aldrich, Nelson W., 77
Aldridge, Nelson, 44
Aldrin, Edwin A. "Buzz," 63
Alexander, John, 11
Alexander III, Pope, 148, 231
Al–Zarqawi, Abu Musab, 209
Andrea, Johann Valentin, 25, 158, 169
Andrew, Abraham Piatt, 77
Ansari, Bayezid, 168
Applewhite, Marshall, 36–37
Aquino, Michael, 205–6
Arthur, King, 73, 184
Ash, Timothy Garton, 42–43
Atef, Muhammad, 207–9
Averell, William, 193

Bacon, Francis, 53–54, 171
Baigent, Michael, vi, 23–24, 148, 162, 171, 182–83
Bainbridge, W. S., 164
Baldwin II, 87, 89
Banister, Guy, 240
Baphomet, 93–95

Barger, Sonny, 72
Baruch, Bernard, 27
Beale, Edward, 66
Becker, Ed, 109
Bey, Hakim, 221–22
Bickley, George W. L., 84–85
Bigou, Antoine, 150
Bin Laden, Osama, 207–9
Bissell, Richard, 30
Blakey, G. Robert, 109
Blanchefort, Bertrand de, 23, 90, 91, 150
Blanton, Thomas, 100–101
Blavatsky, Helena, 218
Blaylock, Ronald E., 80
Bloomberg, Michael, 79, 80
Booth, John Wilkes, 86
Botticelli, Sandro, 155
Boylan, Richard J., 10, 11
Boyle, Robert, 158
Brandenburg, Albrecht von, 217
Brazel, Mac, 120
Brongiel, Jim, 222
Bronk, Detlev Wulf, 123
Brown, Dan, 52, 162, 181, 226
Bruce, George, 219–20
Brzezinski, Zbigniew, 223–24
Bundy, McGeorge, 113, 193
Bunson, Matthew, 228

Burham, James, 204
Bush, George H. W., 127, 193, 195, 196, 225
Bush, George W., 193, 195, 196–97
Bush, Vannevar, 120
Butler, Frank J., 192–93
Butler, Smedley, 82

Cain, Richard, 114
Califano, Joseph, 18
Calvi, Roberto, 165
Calvin, John, 25
Campbell, Eddie, 59
Capone, Al, 107
Carrington, Peter, 15
Carson, Kit, 64
Carter, Jimmy, 127, 224
Casey, William, 82
Cash, Herman, 100–101
Castro, Fidel, 30, 107, 112–14
Cawthorne, Nigel, 25–26
Cayne, James E., 80
Chambliss, Robert, 100–101
Charles, Connétable de Bourbon, 156
Charles V, 156
Cheney, Richard, 18
Cherry, Bobby, 100–101
Civello, Joseph, 111
Clement III, Pope, 216, 231
Clement V, Pope, 93, 96, 231
Clement XII, Pope, 55, 232

Clement XIV, Pope, 74,
    77, 232
Clinton, William "Bill,"
    127
Clovis, 117
Cocteau, Jean, 162
Cody, William F., 64
Coleman, John, 15,
    26–27, 184
Collins, Addie Mae,
    100–101
Collins, Bob, 11
Columbus, Christopher,
    81, 97, 154
Cooper, Leroy Gordon,
    63
Corydon, John Joseph,
    47
Cronkite, Walter, 18
Crook, Annie Elizabeth,
    60–61
Crowley, Aleister, 69, 139,
    141, 188–89
Cruise, Tom, 190
Cumings, Bruce, 199
Cutler, Robert, 118, 126

Dagobert II, 117, 149,
    150, 152
D'Anjou, René, 154–55
Dante Alighieri, 65, 171
Daraul, Arkon, 144
Da Vinci, Leonardo, 155,
    156, 157
Davis, John, 28, 109
Davison, Henry P., 77
De Bar, Edouard, 152–53
De Bar, Iolande, 155
De Bar, Jeanne, 153
Debussy, Claude, 161–62
Dee, John, 140, 157–58
De Gisors, Jean, 149,
    152, 168
D'Evereux, Blanche, 153
De Vries, Gijs, 43
Dimitrijevic, Dragutin
    (Apis), 17
Dixon, Thomas, 99

Donald, Michael, 101
Doolittle, James H., 119
Doty, Richard, 12
Dulles, Allen, 30–31, 198
Dulles, John Foster, 28,
    29, 30, 32
Dye, Thomas R., 197

Eddowes, Catherine, 61
Edward I, 153
Edward II, 153
Eid, Albert, 66–67
Eisenhower, Dwight D.,
    15, 27, 29, 31, 118,
    120, 121–22, 126
Epperson, Ralph A., 31,
    64, 77
Eschenbach, Wolfram
    von, 90
Escrivá de Balaguer,
    Josemaría, 134
Euclid, 51, 166
Evans, Hiram W., 99
Exner, Judith, 113–14

Falk, Hayyim Samuel
    Jacob, 55
Farrakhan, Louis, 129–30
Ferrie, David, 108–9,
    110, 240
Fink, Laurence D., 80
Finney, Dee, 33
Fitje, Carl, 67
Flamel, Nicolas, 153–54,
    159
Fletcher, Richard, 66–67
Florence, William J., 192
Fludd, Robert, 157, 158,
    171
Ford, Gerald, 126–27
Ford, Henry, 170
Ford, Wallace D., 127–28
Forrest, Nathan, 98
Forrestal, James V.,
    119–20
Forsyth, Frederick, 133
Francis, duke of
    Lorraine, 54

Francis I, 156
Franco, Francisco, 199
Franz Ferdinand,
    Archduke, 17

Galt, William (Luigi
    Natoli), 13
Gardner, Laurence, 24,
    56–57
Garrison, Jim, 11, 111,
    239
Gehlen, Reinhard, 199
Gelli, Licio, 82, 165
Genet, Edmond, 39, 76
Germer, Karl, 141
Gheorghieff, Vlada,
    235–36
Giancana, Charles, 114
Giancana, Sam, 113–14
Gill, G. Wray, 108, 110
Gilmore, Peter H., 26
Ginzberg, Asher, 17
Gisors, Guillaume de,
    152
Glenn, John, 63
Godfrey de Bouillon, 52,
    87, 148
Goldwater, Barry, 224–25
Gonzague, Ferdinand de,
    157
Good, Timothy, 118
Gracie, Archibald, 56
Graff, Dale, 12
Grant, Ulysses S., 47,
    98–99
Grasso, Richard A., 79
Gray, Gordon, 121
Green, Christopher, 10
Greenspan, Alan, 15, 31,
    44, 225
Greer, Steven, 123
Griffin, G. Edward, 32
Griffith, D. W., 99
Grimston, Robert de, 163
Grissom, Virgil "Gus," 63
Gruter, Janus, 158
Guler, Muammer, 68
Guzmán, Dominic, 24

Hall, Manly P., 51–52,
88–89
Harding, Warren G., 106
Hartmann, Franz, 171,
172
Hasan bin Sabah, 9–10,
69
Hauser, Joseph, 109, 111
Haushofer, Karl, 70
Haven, Violet Sweet, 16
Hayes, Henry, 101
Hearst, Patty, 215
Hearst, William
Randolph, 18
Henry the Navigator, 81
Henry II, 148–49, 168
Henry III, 92
Henry IV, 157
Henry V, 195
Henry VI, 154
Henry VIII, 52–53, 54
Herter, Christian
Archibald, 28, 29
Herzl, Theodor, 17
Hillenkoetter, Roscoe,
118
Hilton, Charles H., 64
Himmler, Heinrich,
199–201
Hitler, Adolf, 69, 70–71,
97, 117, 137, 170, 199,
200, 202–3, 218, 221
Hoffa, Jimmy, 109–10
Hoffman, Michael A., II,
18–19, 59–60, 61–63,
226
Holland, John Philip, 47
Honorius III, Pope, 217,
231
Hoover, J. Edgar, 107–8,
114, 140
Horn, David, 6, 7
House, Edward Mandell,
27, 185
Howard, Jack, 18
Hubbard, L. Ron, 139,
188–90
Hudal, Alois, 132

Hugo, Victor, 160, 161,
171
Hunt, E. Howard, 240
Hunt, H. L., 198, 199
Huntington, Samuel P.,
224

Ignatius, Saint, 77
Innocent II, Pope, 90,
231
Innocent III, Pope, 24,
231
Irwin, James B., 63

Jackson, Andrew, 59
Jackson, C. D., 15
Jack the Ripper, 48,
59–61
James, Jesse, 86
James, William, 66–67
James II, 76
John Paul II, Pope,
83–84, 166, 232
Johnson, Andrew, 46, 98
Johnson, Lyndon B., 114,
126, 193, 224
Johnson, Tom, 18
John the Baptist, 77–78,
96
Joly, Maurice, 170
Jones, C. B. Scott, 11
Jones, Jim, 33–36
Jones, Melvin, 103

Karageorgevic,
Alexander, 235–36
Karman, Theodore von,
140
Kellner, Carl, 138
Kennedy, John F., 11, 17,
30–31, 44, 45, 77; and
Freemasons, 62–63, 65;
and Mafia, 108–14;
and Vril Society,
238–40
Kennedy, Joseph, Jr., 44
Kennedy, Robert, 108–9,
110, 112

Kerry, John, 196–97
Kettler, Gotthard, 20
King, Martin Luther, Jr.,
240
Kirstein, Gary, 240
Kissinger, Henry, 32, 127
Knight, Christopher, 96,
183
Knight, Stephen, 59, 60
Komansky, David H., 80
Koresh, David, 37–38

Langone, Kenneth G.,
80
LaRouche, Lyndon, 195
LaVey, Anton Szandor,
25–26
Lear, John, 118–19
Lebenthal, Alexandra, 80
Lehman, John, 18
Lehrer, Jim, 32
Leigh, Richard, vi, 23–24,
148, 162, 171, 182–83
Liebenfels, Jorg Lanz
von, 137
Lincoln, Abraham, 45, 86
Lincoln, Henry, vi, 23–24,
148, 162, 171
Lindbergh, Charles, 63
Lipton, Martin, 80
Livingstone, Harrison
Edward, 109
Lomas, Robert, 96, 183
Lorraine, Charles de,
159–60
Lorraine, Maximillian de,
160
Louis VII, 149, 151
Louis IX (Saint Louis),
87, 152
Louis XIV, 159
Louis XVI, 45–46, 76
Lupo, Ignazio, 106
Luther, Martin, 25, 217

MacArthur, Douglas, 4,
32, 198, 199
Maccabee, Bruce, 10–11

McCauley, Maury, 141
McCone, John, 82
McGivney, Michael J., 81
Mackey, Albert Gallatin, 53, 82–83
McKinley, William, 28
McMurty, Grady, 141
McNair, Denise, 100–101
MacNeil, Robert, 32
McPherson, Lisa, 189–90
Malcolm X, 4, 128–30
Manson, Charles, 141, 164–65
Marcello, Carlos, 108–13
Marlowe, Christopher, 157–58
Marrs, Jim, 8–9, 15, 32, 53, 68, 82, 90, 92, 170, 184
Marx, Karl, 102
Mary Magdalene, 23–24, 73, 87, 116–17, 150, 156
Mathers, S. L., 69
Mathison, Dirk, 18
Mayo, Charles H., 63
Mesmer, Franz Anton, 63
Mirabel, Miriam, 144
Molay, Jacques, 96
Monroe, Marilyn, 114
Moore, Alan, 59
Moore, William, 118
Moran, Bugs, 107
Morello, Peter, 106
Morgan, William, 57–59
Moscow, Alvin, 31
Moynihan, Daniel Patrick, 44
Muhammed, Elijah, 127–30
Murat, Gioacchino, 21
Murphy, Franklin, 18
Murret, Charles "Dutz," 111

Natoli, Luigi, 13
Nettles, Bonnie Lu, 36–37
Neuharth, Al, 18
Nevers, Louis de, 157

Newman, Barbara, 141
Newton, Isaac, 21, 54, 147, 158–59
Nixon, Richard, 32, 114, 126–27
Nodier, Charles, 160–61
Noel, Edward Roland, 193
Norton, Charles D., 77
Norwich, John Julius, 91–92
Novel, Gordon, 11

O'Brien, William Smith, 45
Olcott, Henry Steel, 218
O'Mahony, John, 45–46
O'Neill, John, 47
Oppenheimer, J. Robert, 121–22
Oswald, Lee Harvey, 110–11, 238–40

Page, Thornton, 122
Pandolfi, Ron, 10
Paquette, Michael, 67
Parsons, Jack, 188–89
Parsons, John Whiteside, 139–41
Partner, Peter, 94–95
Pataki, George, 196
Payen, Hugues de, 87, 89
Pepe, Guglielmo, 22
Pershing, Richard, 193
Philip II, 148–49
Philip IV, 93, 96
Philip VI, 153
Pieper, Nat J. L., 16
Pius VII, Pope, 77, 232
Pius XI, Pope, 227, 232
Plantard, Pierre, 162–63
Pontius Pilate, 73
Provenzano, Tony, 112
Pullman, George M., 64
Puthoff, Hal, 11

Radclyffe, Charles, 54, 147, 159

Ragano, Frank, 109–10, 113
Raleigh, Walter, 54
Ramsay, Andrew, 54, 147
Raskob, John J., 82
Ratheneau, Walter, 26
Rather, Dan, 32
Ravenscroft, Trevor, 221
Reagan, Ronald, 127, 225
Retinger, Joseph Hieronim, 15
Reuss, Theodor, 138–39
Rhodes, Cecil, 26, 184, 185
Richardson, Elliott, 18
Richard the Lion–Hearted, 86, 92
Rickenbacker, Edward V., 63
Ridgeway, Matthew B., 32
Ridley, Jasper, 236
Roberts, Gary Boyd, 195
Roberts, W. R., 46
Robertson, Carole, 100–101
Robertson, H. P., 122
Robinson, B. A., 163
Robinson, John J., 93–94
Rockefeller, David, 15, 28, 31, 44, 224
Rockwell, George Lincoln, 3–4
Roosevelt, Franklin, 82
Roosevelt, Theodore, 28
Root, Elihu, 28–29
Roselli, Johnny, 112–14, 240
Rosenbaum, Ron, 194–95
Rosenkreuz, Christian, 168–69
Rothschild, Mayer, 77
Ruby, Jack, 111, 113
Ruskin, John, 184
Russell, Dick, 198
Russell, William Huntington, 194
Russert, Tim, 196–97

Saint-Clair, Jean de, 153
Saint-Clair, Marie de, 152
Saint-Clair, William, 182, 183
Saint-Germain, Comte de, 55
Sanchez, Mildred, 188
Sanders, Ed, 164
Sarbacher, Robert I., 120–21
Saunière, François Bérenger, 149–51
Savona, Roberto, 13–14
Schidlof, Leo, 52
Schnoebelen, William J., 242
Schuman, Robert, 42
Scott, Howard, 204
Scott, Peter Dale, 199
Scripps, Charles, 18
Sear, Morey, 109
Sebottendorff, Rudolf Freiherr von, 220
Sereny, Gitta, 132
Sevareid, Eric, 44
Shakespeare, William, 53
Shandera, Jaime, 12, 118
Shaw, George Bernard, 44
Shelton, Robert, 99
Sickert, Walter, 59–61
Sigismund II Augustus, 20
Simmons, William J., 99
Sinclair, Andrew, 181–82
Sindona, Michele, 165
Sitchin, Zecharia, 5
Sleeman, William, 219
Smith, Dan, 11
Smith, Frederick, 193
Smith, W. H., 204
Smith, Walter B., 120–21

Solomon, 23, 51, 87, 88, 159
Souers, Sidney W, 122–23
Steiner, Rudolph, 69
Stephens, James, 45–47
Stephenson, David C., 99
Still, William T., 53, 56
Stone, W. L., 57–59
Stratton, Charles S., 64
Strong, Benjamin, 77
Strong, Kenneth, 31
Summers, Anthony, 113, 114
Sun Myung Moon, 38
Sweeny, T. W., 46

Tabari, A. A., 202
Taft, Alphonso, 194
Tanenbaum, Harold, 111
Taylor, Diana L., 79–80
Taylor, Philip Meadow, 219
Temple, Robert K. G., 62
Terry, Maury, 164
Thornley, Kerry, 238–40
Tojo, Hideki, 16–17
Tompkins, Peter, 93
Touretsky, David S., 190
Trafficante, Santos, 109–10, 112–13
Travolta, John, 190
Truman, Harry S, 32, 118–23, 126, 199, 215
Twain, Mark, 1

Valance, Henry L., 57–59
Valdemar II, 19
Valdemar IV Atterdag, 20
Vallee, Jacques, 11
Vanderlip, Frank A., 77
Van Helsing, John, 221

Verne, Jules, 220
Verona, Jack, 12
Von Moltke, Helmut James Graft, 97
Von Neumann, John, 123
Von Stauffenberg, Claus, 97

Wachter, Kristi, 189–90
Wacks, Mike, 109
Waite, Arthur Edward, 56
Warburg, Paul, 27, 77
Ward, Chester, 31
Ward, J.S.M., 91
Warren, Charles, 59–61
Washington, Booker T., 64
Washington, George, 39
Waters, Frank, 203
Webb, Sidney James, 44
Webster, Nesta, 41
Weill, Sanford I., 80
Weishaupt, Adam, 74–75, 77
Weiss, Philip, 18
Wells, H. G., 44
Wesley, Cynthia, 100–101
Westcott, Wynn, 69
Wildey, Thomas, 133
Williams, Day, 65
Willoughby, Charles, 198–99
Wilson, Ian, 94
Wilson, Woodrow, 27, 77, 185
Witney, William, 16–17
Woods, William P., 103

Yousef, Ramzi, 207

Zeigler, L. Harmon, 197

About the Author

MICHAEL BENSON is the author of thirty-eight books, including *Who's Who in the JFK Assassination* and *Complete Idiot's Guides to NASA*, *National Security*, *The CIA*, *Submarines*, and *Modern China*. He has also written biographies of Ronald Reagan, Bill Clinton, and William Howard Taft. His other biographies include Lance Armstrong, Wayne Gretzky, Hank Aaron, Malcolm X, Muhammad Ali, Dale Earnhardt, and Gloria Estefan. Originally from Rochester, N.Y., he is a graduate of Hofstra University and lives with his wife and two children in Brooklyn, N.Y.